More Praise for *A Politically Incorrect Feminist*

"Highly entertaining . . . never boring, Chesler's memoir will raise more than a few hackles." —*Kirkus Reviews*

"Chesler's honest approach, oscillating between personal narrative and social criticism, illustrates the individual trials and triumps that go into the formation of a nationwide movement." —*Publishers Weekly*

"This is history in the raw. . . . Chesler shines her laser analytic intelligence on the creativity, brilliant insights, heroic actions and sacrifices of the women who led and defined the greatest social movement of the twentieth century. These women are actors on the stage of history and Chesler treats them with the respect and honesty they deserve. Deeply inspiring." —Merle Hoffman, author of *Intimate Wars*

"This work is monumental. It is staggeringly good. Chesler captures us all: the women's movement, the quest for racial equality, nationally and globally." —Barbara Jones, author of *Bike Lust*

"Chesler's memoir is a most important part of the historical record. It discusses our major struggles, but also elucidates issues other feminists haven't touched on, or have glossed over. Chesler names names, and gives us the details."
—Martha Shelley, author of *The Throne in the Heart of the Sea*

"Interspersed with her keen eye is a poignancy reflecting Chesler's loyalty to those who fought the good fight and with whom she clearly has the fondest of memories. Spurred by intellectual honesty and abiding curiosity. . . . This is a book that is sure to educate, irritate, stimulate and illuminate. . . . That is why it is so worthwhile."
—*American Thinker*

Also by Phyllis Chesler

A Politically Incorrect Feminist

Creating a Movement with Bitches, Lunatics, Dykes, Prodigies, Warriors, and WONDER WOMEN

Phyllis Chesler

St. Martin's Press ⋈ New York

This is a work of nonfiction. However, the author has changed the names (and in some cases identifying characteristics) of certain individuals to protect their privacy and has reconstructed dialogue to the best of her recollection.

A POLITICALLY INCORRECT FEMINIST. Copyright © 2018 by Phyllis Chesler. All rights reserved. Printed in the United States of America. For information, address St. Martin's Press, 175 Fifth Avenue, New York, NY 10010.

www.stmartins.com

Designed by Anna Gorovoy

Library of Congress Cataloging in Publication Data is available upon request.

ISBN 978-1-250-09442-1 (hardcover)
ISBN 978-1-250-09443-8 (ebook)

Our books may be purchased in bulk for promotional, educational, or business use. Please contact your local bookseller or the Macmillan Corporate and Premium Sales Department at 1-800-221-7945, extension 5442, or by email at MacmillanSpecialMarkets@macmillan.com.

First Edition: August 2018

10 9 8 7 6 5 4 3 2 1

This book is dedicated to our unknown soldiers whose mighty deeds were either "disappeared" or never documented; those who saved women's lives while risking their own; and those who served the cause of women's freedom with humility and dedication—and, in so doing, braved scorn daily.

This book is dedicated to our women of ideas, our wordsmiths, our artistes of activism, and to every feminist of my generation who fought for women's rights.

This book is also dedicated to the men who helped us.

The author is especially grateful to those who were kind to strong and fiery women.

Contents

16

A Politically Incorrect Feminist

Introduction

I've written many books but never before have I written a book in this way. The chapters tumbled out all at once; I could barely keep up with them. Stories that belonged at the end of the book demanded my attention even as I was writing about something that took place much earlier.

This book happened just like second-wave feminism did: all at once.

The world had never seen anything like us, and we'd never seen anything like each other. We—who only yesterday had been viewed as cunts, whores, dykes, bitches, witches, and madwomen; we who had been second- and third-class citizens—had suddenly become players in history. The world would never be the same, and neither would we.

I was born on October 1, 1940, in Borough Park, Brooklyn, exactly ten months after my parents were married.

Like all firstborn Orthodox Jewish girls, I was supposed to be a boy.

In many ways I behaved like a boy. I refused to help my mother with the dishes, I played punchball and stickball and, soon enough, engaged in other kinds of games with boys. Although I was known as a brain, I was also an early-blooming outlaw. I ran away from home when I was five years old and got a job sweeping the floor in the barbershop across the street. The police found me and brought me home.

Only boys, especially boys who wrote, did things like that. They hit the road, walked across America, drank, took drugs, had sex—lots of sex—led expatriate lives, joined the Navy. Nice Jewish girls—nice *American* girls—were not supposed to do such things. But some of us did.

I'm a quintessential American—the daughter and granddaughter of immigrants.

I'm a Jewish American, heir to a treasured tradition of learning that has survived countless massacres, exiles, and genocides.

I'm a child of the working poor, a "daughter of earth."

America—and the moment in history at which I was born—meant that I received a first-rate education. Such luck—and hard work—may explain how I became a professor of psychology and women's studies, the author of seventeen books, and a feminist leader.

On my father's side, I'm a first-generation American.

I know that my father, Leon, was born in 1912 in Ukraine. He was a child survivor of World War I, the Russian Revolution, a civil war, and pogroms. He never once mentioned any of this. Nothing this important was ever openly discussed. How can I ever piece together his story?

My father named me after the mother he barely knew—my Yiddish name is Perel (Pearl)—a woman hacked to death by Cossacks in her tea shop when my father was only an infant.

My mother was the only member of her family who was born in America—her parents and sisters were born in Poland.

My grandparents never learned to speak English; my mother remained their translator and only caregiver until they died.

————

I wrote the first draft of this book as if it were a mural. Every day you could find me perched on my stool as I checked memory against diaries, correspondence, scrapbooks. I could spend weeks reworking a small detail in one corner of the canvas.

I was everywhere at the same time, all over my feminist life: writing about patriarchy in Kabul in 1961; attending a National Organization for Women meeting in 1967; cofounding the Association for Women in Psychology in 1969; demanding a million dollars in reparations for women from the American Psychological Association and pioneering one of the first women's studies courses in 1970; delivering a keynote speech at the first radical feminist conference on rape in 1971; publishing *Women and Madness* in 1972.

We pioneers emerged between 1963 and 1973 and took ideas seriously. Some of us were geniuses. Many of us were dangerously intelligent, and most of us were radical thinkers. We did not all think alike. We were champion hairsplitters and disagreed with each other with searing passion.

In our midst was the usual assortment of scoundrels, sadists, bullies, con artists, liars, loners, and incompetents, not to mention the high-functioning psychopaths, schizophrenics, manic depressives, and suicide artists.

I loved them all.

I even began to love myself.

Without a feminist movement I would have had a career but not necessarily a calling; I still would have written my books, but they would have had much smaller audiences and far less impact.

We knew nothing—absolutely nothing—about our American and European feminist foremothers, even less about non-Western women, including feminists. In *Women of Ideas and What Men Have Done to Them* (1982), the divine Australian scholar Dale Spender documented how the most remarkable feminist work had been systematically disappeared again and again.

Few of us knew that feminists before us had battled for women's rights in the Western world in the eighteenth, nineteenth, and twentieth centuries. Feminists had opposed sex slavery, wage slavery, marriage, organized religion, and the absence of women's legal, economic, educational, and political rights. Their writings were brilliant and fiery—but unknown to each successive generation.

Each generation of feminists had to reinvent the wheel.

Within ten to fifteen years, books by the best minds of my feminist generation were out of print. Within fifteen to twenty years, university professors and their students were largely unfamiliar with most of our work. They took for granted, or regarded as hopelessly old-fashioned, the grueling lawsuits we had brought and our brave activism—if, indeed, they remembered what we had done at all.

In our own lifetimes we became our suffragist grandmothers and shared their dusty, forgotten fate.

But I remember us as we were, and how we will always be: politically and sexually daring, vivid, vivacious, incredibly vibrant.

Some feminists whose ideas inspired me the most may be unknown to you; this is precisely Dale Spender's point.

I hope that what I've written here will draw you closer to their work, that you'll seek it out and come to know it.

I've been close to most of our feminist visionaries and icons. What I've written may make you laugh, but it may also shock you. Our feminist pioneers were only mortal; they were as flawed as anyone else—save in their work, which was both extraordinary and overinflated.

First, we formed a civil rights organization for women: the National Organization for Women, which brought class-action lawsuits and demonstrated against women's legal, reproductive, political, and economic inequality. For the second time in the twentieth century, women (and some men) crusaded for women's rights, this time by focusing on hundreds of issues, not only one issue, the vote.

Then we picketed, marched, protested, sat in, and famously took over offices and buildings; helped women obtain illegal abortions; joined consciousness-raising groups; learned about orgasms; condemned incest, rape, sexual harassment, and domestic violence; organized speak-outs, crisis hotlines, and shelters for battered women; and came out as lesbians.

Finally, we implemented feminist ideas within our professions and so began a process of transformation that continues to this day.

These were the three mighty tributaries of the second wave. I swam in all three.

Soon, large numbers of women began to integrate previously all-male bastions of power. We became artists, astronauts, business executives, CEOs, clergy, college presidents, composers, construction workers, electricians, firefighters, journalists, judges, lawyers, midlevel managers, physicians, pilots, police officers, politicians, professors, scientists, small-business owners, and soldiers.

Radical feminist ideas and activism were a bit like LSD. So many women became high at the same time that suddenly the world became psychedelically clear, and all the Lost Girls found ourselves and each other.

This was the first time in my life that I experienced female solidarity based on ideas—and it was wondrous.

And yet.

I had such an idealized view of feminism and feminists that when I began to encounter incomprehensibly vicious behavior among feminist leaders, I was stunned, blindsided.

I had expected so much of other feminists, far too much—perhaps we all did—that when we failed to meet our own high standards, many of us felt betrayed.

And then, when we were really betrayed—slandered, shunned by everyone we knew, our ideas stolen, our authorship denied, our history revised—we had no name for what was happening.

Eventually, we called some of this "trashing," and it drove away many a good feminist. It never stopped me—nothing ever did—but it took its toll.

This means that my greatest comfort and strength came from doing the work itself—and from knowing that the work touched, changed, and even saved women's lives.

This memoir isn't a history of second-wave feminism; it's not even a history of my most important feminist ideas and campaigns. This is the story of how a daughter of working-poor immigrants came into her own and helped illuminate the path for others. Here I relate some memories from the war zone, stories that are important to me and that might be of interest to you.

This book isn't about the generations of feminists who succeeded us. Their stories belong to them.

Although I've been blessed in every way, my life has also been hard. Fighting for freedom—and for the right to be heard—is essential to me, but the price I've paid is all that I have. Isn't this always the case?

I was utterly naive and ill-prepared for the life I was destined to lead. Angels must have watched over me; I can offer no better explanation for why I survived and flourished.

For more than a half century I've been a soldier at war. I carry scars; all warriors do. Most of us were felled, daily, both by our opponents and friendly fire.

Despite everything, despite *anything*, I wouldn't have missed this revolution, not for love or money. I remain forever loyal to that moment in time, that collective awakening that set me free from my former life as a girl. Allow me to paraphrase the most memorable speech Shakespeare gave King Henry V:

> *[She] that outlives this day, and comes safe home . . . ,*
> *Then will [she] strip [her] sleeve and show [her] scars.*
> *And say "These wounds I had. . . ."*
> *This story shall the good [woman] teach [her children] . . .*
> *From this day to the ending of the world,*
> *But we in it shall be remember'd;*
> *We few, we happy few, we band of [sisters];*
> *For [she] to-day that sheds [her] blood with me*
> *Shall be my [sister]; be [she] ne'er so vile,*
> *This day shall gentle [her] condition:*
> *And [gentlewomen everywhere] now a-bed*
> *Shall think themselves accursed they were not here,*
> *And hold their [humanity] cheap whiles any speaks*
> *That fought with us. . . .*

1 Growing Up as a Girl in America

A Brooklyn Reverie

My first decade on Earth, the 1940s, was quite different from that of those who were born after 1960. We had no television, no computers, no internet, no video games. Books mattered. We always had homework to do. When it rained, we played Monopoly, checkers, or cards.

I began reading when I was about two-and-a-half years old. In the summer of my third year I attended the Peter Pan Nursery School on Ocean Parkway. When it was time for our afternoon nap, I refused to lie down. I said: "My father is paying good money for me to come here and learn. I don't want to sleep. I can sleep at home." This story became family lore.

My mother took me to the public library on McDonald Avenue; trolleys were still plying their darkened routes under the Brooklyn elevated trains. I loved the hushed nature of the book-filled rooms at the library. I wrote:

> *I haunt the public library. I love to read, I read all the time; the more I read, the more the world beyond my childhood beckons, twinkling. In books, anything is possible. Books save me, but they also exact their price. I jump ship, and leave my family behind when I am very young. I have since come to understand that absolutely no other family can ever become mine. A very American kind of heartbreak/success story.*

Many years later, as a professor, I assigned Richard Rodriguez's *Hunger of Memory: The Education of Richard Rodriguez* to my students. Like him, I understood that when a first-generation American takes to books and receives a formal education, she is doomed to leave her less literate, less fortunate family members behind forever.

My mother never praised me. When I received a 90 or a 95 on a test, she said: "This only proves you can do better." Perhaps she was a genius in terms of preparing a girl child for a life of intellectual achievement.

My mother preferred her sons to her daughter. Becoming the mother of sons had redeemed her, especially because her own mother produced only girls. This preference for sons was just how things were; it was nothing personal. Most girls of my generation would say something similar. Also, a daughter meant trouble—especially if you couldn't break her spirit. If she was rebellious, the rest of the family blamed her mother.

Like the queen of England, my mother kept her feelings to herself; she did not wear her emotions on her sleeve. She never hugged or kissed me—or anyone else, for that matter. Although she never shouted "Off with their heads!" she was really the Queen of Hearts: she criticized me constantly, yelled at me a lot, hit me sometimes, and always threatened to turn me over to my father for more serious discipline.

My mother had wanted to be a ballet dancer, but her parents forbade this as a frivolous and irreverent activity. She had to fight to attend college, and although she won that battle, she was forced to quit after a year to support her invalid, aging parents. "These obligations matter more than anything else," she explained without a trace of self-pity.

Oh, what a disappointment I must have been to her! I couldn't wait to leave home. Or perhaps she just transferred all her thwarted ambition to me and therefore had to disapprove of me.

In 1998, after she died, I found that she had carefully preserved clippings about each of my books. Because she chose to live frugally, she was able to leave *me* some money. I was surprised, grateful, and filled with respect for her.

My father was more of a bon vivant; he kissed me, hugged me, praised me, listened to me. True, he also flew into violent rages and beat me with his belt or his fists. Once he gave me a black eye and I had to lie about how I'd gotten it. My parents believed that physical punishment and harsh words were how to socialize a child.

My father was up and out of the house when it was still dark, but he always came home for an early dinner. He was a seltzer man. Selling seltzer was a family business on my mother's side. He carried heavy cases of seltzer, soda, and Fox's U-Bet chocolate syrup up and down endless flights of stairs so that I could one day attend college.

We never went hungry. On the contrary, we were continually overfed, but I wore hand-me-down clothing and attended a camp for underprivileged youth. I also attended a series of public schools, but it was at a time when these schools were great and anything seemed possible.

In my case, being a first-generation American in the 1940s meant that none of my maternal relatives was a middle-class professional or had access to such exalted circles. We had no lawyers, doctors, professors, or accountants in our family. No one visited museums, attended classical music concerts, or held any political or intellectual opinions.

I'm not suggesting that my older-generation relatives were stupid—that is far from true—only that they could not read English and were not formally educated. No one was cultured in either secular or religious terms. Having crossed the vast, deep sea, they washed ashore exhausted and focused all their energies on surviving. That monumental task took all they had.

In many ways I grew up in a small village in the nineteenth century. My parents were home every night. They sometimes fought fiercely with each other and with their children. They never mentioned divorce. No one we knew was divorced.

My mother, her sisters, and all their friends worked at home, doing the shopping, cooking, cleaning, sewing, laundry, ironing, and holiday preparations; they also took children to and from doctors, dentists, lessons, and school—and still prepared three meals a day.

The only women I ever met who worked outside the home were the dental hygienist, the pediatrician's receptionist (who was also his wife), and saleswomen, in shops usually owned by their husbands. The school nurses and my public-school teachers were women, but I never thought of them as "career women."

Other than actresses, singers, and dancers, these were my only role models.

Adult social life consisted of observing Jewish holidays, attending weddings and funerals, and visiting friends and relatives. My mother rarely smiled; she sometimes did so when her friends came over for coffee and cake on a Saturday night. (They visited too seldom.) I am now far older than they were then, yet I still think of them as forever older than me. Back then, parents looked like grandparents and grandparents looked ancient. People thought they were old at forty.

Seventy-seven years later, I'm revisiting my childhood, perhaps for the last time. I have always focused on the humiliations and prohibitions, the injustices routinely visited upon a girl child. Now I'm trying to see things more evenhandedly.

My parents sacrificed themselves completely in order to give their children every necessity. We were all they had; we were everything to them. My mother always knew exactly where I was—and I always knew where she was, too, either by my side or in the next room. I felt I was always under hostile surveillance. But now, when I compare my childhood with the lives of children without parents, I'm ashamed of my ingratitude. My parents made sure I was fed, housed, clothed, medically attended to, and educated, and that my life was safe and secure.

I saw no future for myself there. My departure was inevitable, but I lost so much in my headlong flight toward freedom. As one always does.

An American Teenager

There is no way to convey what being a teenager in 1950s America was like.

I may have grown up in America, but I was veiled—physically, psychologically, sexually, politically, and intellectually. For a teenage girl in those years, living in the United States was like living in a fundamentalist country.

Women wore hats, gloves, and girdles, and they expected their daughters to one day do likewise. At night I slept on pink plastic rollers to give my hair body. Becoming proper meant embracing discomfort at an early age. I remember cinching my waist with a wide belt and wearing two crinolines beneath a gray felt skirt that featured a poodle with rhinestone eyes.

The rules in my house were strictly Old Country. I was not allowed to wear pants, shave my legs, or pierce my ears. I had early curfews. Even so, my parents always interrogated me about where I'd been and what I'd done. I was treated like a criminal. I seethed. I burned with resentment.

My parents may have prized education, even for girls, but they valued obedience and chastity even more. However, they never discussed sex with me. Human anatomy remained a complete mystery.

I was boy crazy. In school and on the block I was known as a brain but also as a tramp—simply because I'd developed breasts and was just as curious about them as the boys were. Oh, I wanted it all, just like the guys—that is, the human beings—did.

My generation of white girls came into our sexuality as we danced to the music of predominantly black male groups—the Penguins' "Earth Angel," the Diamonds' "Little Darlin'." In 1956, I sang along with Elvis ("the Pelvis"), who sounded black, to "Heartbreak Hotel," "Love me Tender," "I Want You, I Need You, I Love You," and "Don't Be Cruel."

My parents did not understand me at all. Although I was boy crazy, I was still studying the prophets Isaiah and Jeremiah, writing poetry, reading Freud and Shakespeare, and delivering monologues from plays by George Bernard Shaw and Thornton Wilder at the Henry Street Playhouse.

I discovered Birdland, the jazz club on Broadway near West Fifty-second Street. No man ever harassed me there. They were either high, already with a lady friend, engrossed in the spellbinding music, or not looking for trouble; as a result, they didn't bother underage chicks. Birdland boasted an area for teenagers where no alcohol was served.

I always had a job after school; my family needed the money. I worked from the time I was about thirteen, doing whatever paid: clerical work at my Hebrew school, receptionist/assistant for a dentist and a plumber, selling toys at Macy's. During college I waited tables as part of my financial aid package. On winter and summer breaks I worked as a waitress and as a camp counselor.

I have traumatic memories of being sexually harassed by one male employer after another when I was a teenager and when I worked as a waitress in Greenwich Village.

Imagine the effect upon me, upon all of us, when the issue of sexual harassment in the workplace became one that feminists collectively and emphatically exposed and condemned. It was a breathtaking moment—we could literally breathe for the first time since early childhood.

We also had our Harvey Weinstein moments—as well as our Bill Clinton, Bill Cosby, Bill O'Reilly, and Tariq Ramadan moments—and we were on fire about it for the first time in our lives. We each had many sexual harassers and rapists in our lives. They were not necessarily men who were celebrities or whose names were known. However, all our analyses, published works, and lawsuits against sexual harassers and rapists never abolished the behavior that women still continue to suffer.

If one woman bears false witness, it will be over for the rest of us. When a man commits a crime, we do not usually judge all men for his crime, but when a woman commits a crime, all women are judged collectively and harshly.

I did not know who I was or who I might become; I knew only that I was not like most other girls. How I wanted to be! But that was impossible. I was too much of an outlaw, an individualist, a loner. Girls snitched and obeyed orders. Girls didn't stick together. Except for two female high school teachers, all my discussions about ideas were with men, not women.

No older woman (or man) ever told me anything about what it might take to survive on my own. No one ever—not even once—mentioned that women were oppressed or discriminated against, or that women had a history of fighting for freedom. I had no plans for my future. I knew only that I had to keep reading and leave home as soon as possible.

My parents were good nineteenth-century parents. I wanted for nothing—except affection, understanding, the most minimal kindness, and privacy. I left home because my mother was cruel and hostile toward me and my father never intervened.

My parents wanted me to go to Brooklyn College and live at home. I refused to do this. I applied to only one college because it had no required courses. In 1958, I left home to attend Bard College in Dutchess County, New York, on a full scholarship.

Steve was my official boyfriend at New Utrecht High School in Brooklyn. He was tall, kind, and a good kisser. His parents owned a candy store. He recently came to visit me. He said, "You know, you threw me under the bus when you left Brooklyn to go to an out-of-town college." He paused and then said, in all seriousness, "But I knew you had a destiny to follow." He is the sweetest man.

Steve reminded me that I used to literally dance down the street.

He said that I was always singing. I don't remember this. He told me something I hadn't known. My father took him aside and said: "If you really care for my daughter, you will not ruin her. Will you promise me that?" Steve said he made that promise—and he kept it.

My first dormitory was a Beaux-Arts mansion, Blithewood, which had a magnificent view of the Hudson River and the most amazing Italianate gardens. It was a setting for any one of Henry James's or Edith Wharton's heroines.

In the 1940s, Bard had welcomed glittering European refugees to its faculty: Hannah Arendt's husband Heinrich Blücher, Stefan Hirsch, Justus Rosenberg, Werner Wolff and his wife Kate. Bard was known as a bohemian paradise for rich kids who vacationed in Europe. It was also known as "the little red whorehouse on the Hudson."

And so there I was, a wild child out of Borough Park, finally away from my mother's critical eye for the first time in my life. I had no idea how vulnerable and naive I was. I was flying solo with no instructor or even a manual.

On our first winter break I wore beatnik black and waited tables at the Rienzi coffeehouse in Greenwich Village. I shared a rental apartment on Prince Street, in what is now SoHo. I wrote poetry at cafes and imagined I was living as an expatriate in Paris, which I was, at least in my head.

By the time my second semester at Bard rolled around, I'd met the man who would become my first husband. We met in the college coffee shop. He was from Afghanistan. I thought he was terribly sophisticated.

I found him so interesting that I brought him home for Shabbos. He had attended elite private schools in America for more than a decade. I wanted to impress my parents with how many interesting people I was meeting—people who were finding *me* interesting, too.

The visit was a complete disaster. We left early and drove back to

Bard. This fiasco drove me right into his arms. Had my family accepted him as my friend, the entire episode might have passed. Instead, sotto voce, they hissed: "He's not Jewish. He's not even white!" And he said, "I had no idea your family was so provincial, such peasants." His statement was quite ironic given who his family was.

Two and a half years later I was on my way to Kabul to meet his (far more provincial) relatives.

My Awful, Pretty Bad, Prefeminist 1960s

What do people think about the 1960s?

Some think of the Fab Four (the Beatles), Janis Joplin, free love, Woodstock, and sex, drugs, and rock 'n' roll. Others think about the American civil rights and antiwar movements; the murders of civil rights workers in Mississippi and Alabama; the assassinations of JFK, Malcolm X, Martin Luther King, and Robert Kennedy; the student sit-ins, protests, marches, and riots; the rise of the Black Panthers, the Young Lords, and Students for a Democratic Society.

I think about all this—I lived it all—but first I think about Kabul, where I was held captive for five months in 1961. "Only five months," you might say, but each day felt like a month. I felt as if I'd been held hostage for ten years and felt deceived by the man I'd married.

When we landed in Kabul, an airport official smoothly removed my American passport, which I would never see again. Suddenly I was the citizen of no country and the property of a large, wealthy, polygamous—news to me—Afghan family.

I witnessed a pre-Taliban level of gender apartheid: polygamy, purdah, women in burqas who were forced to sit at the back of the bus, arranged first-cousin marriages, child brides, honor killings. Forever after I understood that Western foreign powers did not cause such indigenous and barbaric customs. Few American feminists of my generation ever grasped this.

I also experienced some good old-fashioned Islamic religious apartheid. My Afghan mother-in-law, with whom I had to live, tried hard to convert me to Islam, and my sophisticated, Westernized husband did nothing to stop her.

I encountered a geographically isolated, fanatically religious tribal society in a country that endured extreme weather conditions. My diaries remind me that I described Afghanistan as a police state, one that crushes all those who have ideals. I found the "monitoring of thought unbelievable." I was writing about the absence of free thought and free speech in Afghanistan long before Khomeini's revolution and the rise of the Taliban, al-Qaeda, and ISIS, and I was writing about it as if my heart were breaking.

Yes, Kabul was where I learned how to see gender injustice with shattering clarity.

I also was shocked by the child beggars and child servants, and by the poverty, lack of hygiene, illiteracy, cruelty, and slave-like working conditions of the servants. They had no days off, slept on the floor, and rarely saw their families.

On one of my rare supervised visits to the bazaar, I bought a brown plastic-covered notebook and started keeping a diary. I have that tattered journal still, with its interior map of England and the British Isles. I faithfully continued this diary in a series of notebooks throughout the 1960s, '70s, and '80s.

Meeting my younger self on its pages is exhilarating, like time travel, but it's also embarrassing. My diaries from the 1960s are a mixture of dreadful, often incomprehensible writing, historic details, literary gossip, and incredible insights.

I had a feminist point of view before there was a movement. I think that, early on, my captivity in Afghanistan—followed by my experiences as a young woman back in America—clarified for me how things were for women.

I contracted dysentery, followed by a strain of hepatitis from which every other similarly afflicted foreigner had already died during that cursed winter. At the end of December 1961, my dapper father-in-law, who had three wives and twenty-one children, obtained an Afghan passport with a six-month visa for me and a plane ticket home.

I was saved. I was free. I got out. I weighed ninety pounds—and I was pregnant. Had I not left then, I would have been trapped there forever. I might have died of dysentery or hepatitis or in childbirth at the substandard maternity hospital that we once visited.

When my plane landed, I literally kissed the ground at Idlewild Airport, I was so happy to be back in America, the land of libraries and liberty.

And so I once lived in the Muslim world and was unexpectedly held captive in Kabul. I wrote about it in *An American Bride in Kabul*. Perhaps my American feminist consciousness was forged in the fires of tribal captivity and purdah.

I now understand how much more dangerous life is for non-Western, tribal women. I have witnessed Eastern shame and honor practices, vigilante lawlessness, pandemic corruption, and a contempt for women that few Americans are willing to comprehend.

Although I remain a critic of America's failings, I understand in my bones that America is nevertheless an exceptional country.

I used the word *patriarchy* for the first time in 1961, in Kabul. I have no idea where I found that word. I wrote that the "family is a vicious institution." Am I thinking about tribal polygamous families or about Western nuclear monogamous families?

Nevertheless, despite my own feminist vision—which was evolving *without other feminists*—I continued to endure and to minimize routine, normalized sexual harassment and marital rape, and subsequently rape by a series of boyfriends who could not make commitments, lied to me about being unmarried, were overly possessive, or were sadistic woman haters.

I was a lost soul, a rolling stone, a young woman who had failed herself, someone who fit in nowhere. I returned to find an America in the early throes of a nonfeminist sexual revolution and about to dedicate itself to a civil rights struggle for African Americans.

I returned to Bard to complete my final semester. No one understood what I was trying to say. My friends asked: "Did you meet the king?" "Are you now some kind of princess?" "How many servants did you have?" Even my professor Heinrich Blücher told me to have an affair to help me forget it all. Then, from out of nowhere, I wrote:

> *I'm wrestling with the nature of female friendships and with the limited roles women seem to have. In Eastern communities, women are not valued. Their only refuge and salvation is in the propagation of tradition, in marriage, domesticity. Tradition, the very thing that renders them worthless, is the only bulwark that may save them from the logical consequences of their worthlessness. So women guard the traditions more than men do. We might say that, in all societies, women's insistence on the keeping of the 'laws' is the strongest proof of their powerlessness.*

The spring semester over, everyone left—rolled up their posters and madras wall hangings, packed away their half-finished sculptures, books, and Joan Baez records like so many childhood toys. I had only my college thesis on Stendhal to complete. I had nowhere to go but home.

What can a young woman do if her home is intolerable, a madhouse? Why did my mother resent my going out? Should I have chained myself to the wall to avoid fights about curfews and men? Her bizarre demands and nightly scenes were bound to drive me out.

Was I in Brooklyn or Kabul?

I walked out of my mother's house carrying my typewriter, my papers, and some clothes. I was terrified about having no place to go and no money. Did they know what could happen to a young woman who broke with her family and was completely on her own?

I needed a job if I wanted to eat. I'd have liked a job in publishing. I asked one of my Bard College literature professors for help.

Diego was a wiry South American with black eyes and flared nostrils like those of a Renaissance satyr. We had lunch together—once, twice. He said he was in a position to get me a job in publishing. But why so many lunches? Why so much alcohol? I was *so* purposefully blind.

He invited me to his apartment to "get to the heart of things." Did I want a fellowship to Harvard? Or did I want to travel with him, helping him to write an article? Did I want to meet the Russian poet Yevtushenko? I *could*, because Diego was hosting a party for him the next day.

Then he began to chase me—literally, he chased me—around his apartment. "Diego," I panted, "I want a job, not a love affair." How could he do this? I had been his student for years. He knew my intellectual worth. He threatened to withdraw his letters of recommendation, vowed never to write another. I fled his apartment. We never spoke again.

The only gentleman-professor, through and through, was the great Ralph Ellison, with whom I had studied American literature. He dressed formally, always wore a fedora, a jacket, and a tie. He gave me an A on my paper about racism in *Moby Dick*. I treasured that paper; I have it still. I was rather bold for so young a student, and he was very kind.

I learned to live on the edge, not always sure that I would be able to meet my bills. Through a college friend I found work as a secretary for two weeks on a Sid Caesar special, *As Caesar Sees It*. That man was a comic genius. I also worked on Dave Garroway's program for public television, *Exploring the Universe*.

I worked at the Gaslight Club as a singing waitress; I wore fishnet stockings, a French-cut corset-like costume, and high heels. It was decorated in Gay Nineties style and the atmosphere was slightly naughty. Burton Brown founded the Gaslight Clubs in 1953, seven years before Hugh Hefner opened the Playboy Club.

———

I found work farther uptown, as a waitress at Tom's Restaurant—the diner that Jerry Seinfeld would one day make famous.

I had decided to become a college professor and a "Viennese witch doctor"—a psychoanalyst—someone who could both work and write at home. I applied to five universities and requested scholarships and other financial aid. I chose the New School for Social Research in New York City for a doctoral degree in psychology because I could enroll in a full-time night program and work full time during the day.

I worked at the *New York Post* as a "copy boy" and met the journalists Nora Ephron, Sid Zion, and Jack Newfield; I wrote for Jack at the *West Side News*.

When JFK was assassinated, I bought my first television set. Jack was shocked by the purchase. I said, "I want to see the next assassinations on my own set rather than having to run over to the corner bar." I was convinced that the decade would have many more political assassinations.

I interviewed the journalist Lisa Howard in 1964, and the teen magazine *Ingenue* published my piece. A former actress, Howard became the first female anchor of any news program in America, at ABC. She interviewed Khrushchev, Kennedy, Adlai Stevenson, the Shah of Iran, Fidel Castro, and Che Guevara. She covered the riots in Oxford, Mississippi. I asked her how she was able to do it all—be an actress, write a novel, lecture women's groups, research the subjects of her interviews. She was also a wife and the mother of two children. Howard told me: "The quality you have to develop, most of all, is discipline. If you want something, go for the target and don't be deterred. [The mark of a professional] is homework, tenacity and perseverance. You have to be better than the men. [You need] hard work and courage."

When the interview appeared, Howard sent me a lovely thank-you note.

In 1965, ten months after ABC fired her and after a miscarriage, Howard committed suicide. She was only thirty-nine years old. Marilyn Monroe had killed herself as well; she died in 1962 when she was thirty-six years old. They were young, good-looking, talented, and uniquely successful women who came of age in the 1940s and 1950s. And yet, this was what could happen to a woman in the prefeminist 1960s.

I then worked as a welfare investigator on the Lower East Side. I had believed that my job was to help people. How wrong I was. My job was to frustrate, punish, humiliate, and drive away welfare recipients.

I was stunned and saddened by the hopeless misery of my clients and even more so by the bureaucracy and personnel that callously humiliated them. Welfare officials saw all welfare recipients as frauds and liars and treated them accordingly: the eighty-five-year-old disabled woman; the young single mother of an infant; the middle-aged, formerly middle-class but now unemployed female graphic artist. If my supervisor could find any loophole that justified denying people the smallest sum of money, he would find it and use it with great, determined relish.

I attended meetings of the Congress of Racial Equality and joined the Northern Student Movement, an outgrowth of student groups that were raising money for the Student Nonviolent Coordinating Committee. I also worked with the Harlem Education Project (HEP), which was part of the Northern Student Movement.

Jack Newfield and I went up to 147th Street and met "Chickie," aka Matthew, who was the liaison between the street gangs and junkies and HEP. At first he was suspicious and played a two-way game, spying for the block's power elite to find out what HEP really wanted. HEP sent him down South. Chickie saw white kids getting beaten up for participating in the civil rights movement—"putting their life where their mouth was," as he put it.

My boyfriend, David, opposed my working in Harlem. He said: "I don't want you going up there—it's one of the most dangerous areas in the country. Goddamn it, I don't want my flank exposed."

We fought. David told me, "You can't commit yourself to a revolutionary path and still have a private love life."

I responded, "When there's a revolutionary choice and you refuse to make it, your love life is not worth a damn."

Betty Friedan had published *The Feminine Mystique* in 1963, but I had not yet read it. I was not a married housewife or a mother, and I didn't live in the suburbs; my priorities were getting my doctoral degree, earning a living, and the civil rights movement. However, I was still writing in my diary about women in a feminist voice:

Have great artists portrayed male nudes for women as aesthetic or erotic? Or only for gay men? We are surrounded by the erotic aggrandizement of the young female body. A woman has almost never seen the male body presented as an object of beauty, as a magnet of raw desire for women. Women are doomed to an unnatural dependence on marriage. Most men are seduced into having erotic associations with only young, nubile girls—not with middle-aged women. What is needed is:

1. Human emancipation for both sexes.

2. A new method of socializing the next generation.

3. A new community arrangement.

I do not want a husband. I want myself.

Sylvia Plath, why did you have to die?

David and I moved from East Seventh Street to East Thirteenth Street. About once a month I found some excuse to knock on the apartment door right across the hall. I needed sugar. Or coffee. What drew me was a group of women who gathered there on a regular basis. They included a playwright (Lorraine Hansberry, the author of *A Raisin in the Sun*); an opera librettist and poet (Ilsa Gilbert, who would come to be known as "the Poet of Bleecker Street" and who wrote the lyrics for "Songs of Revelations and Secrets" and "The Bundle Man"); Sandra Scoppettone and Louise Fitzhugh (Sandra wrote and Louise illustrated *Suzuki Beane*, about a downtown Eloise, and Louise wrote *Harriet the Spy*; Sandra wrote *Happy Endings Are All Alike*, among the earliest young-adult books about lesbianism, and also wrote hard-boiled detective fiction like *Everything You Have Is Mine*); and a sculptor and poet (France Burke). These were intense and interesting women. No one said so, but all the women were lesbians; however, they were, first and foremost, artists.

France fell in love with me when I was still straight. I loved our friendship, I loved the attention, but above all I loved the conversations we had and the worlds in which she moved.

I enjoyed meeting her father, Kenneth, America's preeminent literary critic (the man with whom I watched the first landing on the moon, both of us in a rare and drunken state), who introduced the great Djuna Barnes to America; her sister Eleanor "Happy" Leacock, the socialist-feminist anthropologist, who was then married to the filmmaker Richard "Ricky" Leacock; and her sister Jeanne Elspeth "Duchy" Chapin, a musician and the mother of singer Harry Chapin.

In other words, I was impressed by such cultural royalty and by the Burkes' longtime compound in New Jersey, where each sister had her own cabin.

Having an extended family all of whom were artists and intellectuals felt like home to me, except it was not really my home. Having access to it depended upon my falling in love with France. Although we traveled through Europe together (that's another tale entirely), this romance was not to be. I was still far too much of a man junkie.

By 1965 I was working as a researcher for the Institute for Developmental Studies at New York Medical College on a project that led to and monitored the Head Start program. In 1967, I left to conduct research at what would become E. Roy John's prestigious Brain Research Laboratories, based at Flower-Fifth Avenue Hospital, on upper Fifth Avenue.

We were studying the electrophysiological correlates of brain activity. In graduate school I had enjoyed my course in physiological psychology so much that I worked with one of my professors, Ausma Rabe, at her lab in Princeton. I was having a delayed romance with science, quickly took some pre-med courses, and applied for the job at the Brain Research Labs.

I eventually published two studies in *Science Magazine* and obtained a fellowship to medical school. However, my background in chemistry and physics was far too shaky; I did not like the cadavers; and I was already close to completing my doctoral degree in psychology— all this, plus the ingrained sexism of medical school culture, made it easy for me to back away.

Here I was, an educated and ambitious woman, but I knew nothing about women's or feminist history. I was still unaware of contemporary feminist stirrings. I was only dimly aware that Gene Boyer, Kathryn Clarenbach, Mary Eastwood, Betty Friedan, Dr. Pauli Murray, and Dr. Caroline Ware (among others) were in the midst of founding the National Organization for Women (NOW).

I had a great love affair with Jim, one of the male geniuses in the Brain Research Labs. We made love at work, in hotels, on his sailboat, in my apartment, and we attended math and science conferences. I was falling, falling—and then he told me he was married but that it "didn't count," that he stayed only because they had a young child. I was devastated, outraged.

I left him for one of the medical school professors, someone I thought was more appropriate. Now it was Jim's turn to weep. He told me that married life was nothing like what we had.

I had made another bad choice. The professor, whom I had considered the right man (husband material), a Jewish doctor, turned out to be a monster, a man who made me suffer terribly. I don't understand why I didn't walk out right away. He was unfaithful. I learned that he had a longtime mistress who was ten years older than he and twenty years older than I was. She typed all his research papers. She had a married lover who took her to the country once a week. I was trapped in a novel by the Marquis de Sade; I was a bit player in *Les Liaisons dangereuses*.

I was writing more and more in my diary in a feminist voice. However, my insights alone could not free me. "Because of women's economic and consequent psychological enslavement and dependence, they find escape in 'romance,' and 'passion,'" I wrote. "Once women free themselves—economically, socially, psychologically, they may be less 'romantic' and less monogamous." I was suggesting that romantic love is a forced, not free, choice. In three years, feminist activist and author Shulamith "Shulie" Firestone would publish *The Dialectic of Sex*, a radical analysis of how falling in love is like having an illness. I already was writing that marriage might become less important to an economically independent woman. I had yet to read Virginia Woolf's *A Room of One's Own*. I wrote:

> A woman dresses "to kill," to arouse jealousy, devastate other women, to "star" in the room, to make an economic/romantic "killing" with a man. Some women take the beauty of other women as a personal affront: their first cool, side-glance appraisal dissolves into a little girl's pout.
>
> This fear of aging in women, so often criticized as proof of her narcissism, is not that. She is desperately trying to outlive her approved shelf life.
>
> Women will stop being dependent and masochistic when they are free. For now, women are just as bad as men in the matter of their slavery, to which they cling.

I could have been describing myself. Then I added: "I love the Story of Ruth in the Bible more than any other—love between women would be redemptive and might lead to messianic times."

———

Why was I still with the Monster? Why did I stay? Why didn't I just walk out?

We lived together. I had nowhere else to go. I had no time to apartment-hunt and no savings. I had a full-time job, a full-time doctoral dissertation, and graduate school papers to complete. I was comfortable in our apartment on the Hudson: the view, Riverside Park, my own bed.

He was an unmarried Jewish doctor. I was genetically programmed to stay. The Monster was like my mother, which was probably why I could not leave him. I once wrote about him in this way:

> *I found my mother in this sternly beautiful physician astride a ballet-horse: Lucifer, in search of me, fleeing. In the wilderness of sexual deceit, a Jewish Prince is searching for his Father. He looks for him in women, but never finds him there. Always he is disappointed, haunted, by these Fathers who turn into Mothers: like me, they are all dumbly eager to please. Like his own mother, abandoned by her husband, who died when H. was six years old.*

I was waiting for something big to happen. I needed something big to happen. I needed to do something big. This misery with men could not continue. This problem, which had no name, was really a thousand problems, and they were all pretty big. To counter it would require—what? Something else, something new, maybe a miracle.

2 Am I Dreaming or Am I Awake? Feminist Paradise Rising

It's impossible to convey how excited I was—how excited we *all* were. While at work at the Brain Research Labs, I somehow heard about a women's meeting. I rushed out, still wearing my white lab coat. I was on the streets searching for "the women," as if a group of aliens had suddenly landed on Earth.

We were all lost in a dream—but we had never been so awake. Women who were once invisible to each other were now the only visible creatures. Women—who used to see one another as wicked stepsisters—had magically transformed into fairy godmothers.

Some of us smoked and drank, wore motorcycle boots, tough leather jackets, and no makeup; we were rather butch, whether we were straight or not. Suddenly we were the ones who made things happen, not those to whom things happened.

Some of us wore feathers, jewelry, soft suede vests, bell bottoms, and lots of makeup. We looked like gypsies or glamorous pirates, and we too made stuff happen. You didn't mess with us anymore.

I was as foolish as only a young dreamer could be. I—but I was no longer alone; now there was a *we*—and *we* wanted to end the subjugation of women—now! We, who had put up with it from the moment we were born, wanted it to end immediately—or definitely within the decade. None of us understood that this work would occupy us for the rest of our lives and that all we would be able to claim was the struggle, not the victory.

Looking over my early feminist correspondence reminded me of how much affection we had for each other. We, to whom men had not listened, now found that our ideas mattered a great deal: to ourselves, to each other, to countless other women.

Oh, the number of feminists who signed their letters to me "With love"! As did I. We hugged and kissed each other as if we were relatives or longtime friends. But we were really strangers, bound only by the moment and our shared vision.

I am writing about heroic historical figures. What defines them is the work they did, not their fearful, mortal failings. Most women have internalized sexist values—but they don't lead movements that change the world. However, from a psychological point of view, women—and feminists are mainly women—are as great a challenge to our liberation as men are.

For example, we proclaimed that "sisterhood is powerful"—it's such a lovely idea—but such a sisterhood did not normally exist; it had to be created day by day. Women did not always treat each other kindly. Somehow we expected feminists, who are also women, to behave in radically different ways. We were shocked as we learned, one by one, that feminists didn't even always treat each other with respect or compassion.

I know this now. I did not know it in 1967.

We said that women were more compassionate and less aggressive than men, but this isn't true.

We second-wavers took our battles seriously and fought with strength and conviction. We fought about essentialism versus social construction; reform versus revolution; Marxism versus capitalism; pornography versus censorship; prostitution versus a woman's right to "choose to be a sex worker"; focusing only on abortion versus motherhood; viewing women as innocent victims versus viewing women as having agency and responsibility for what happens to them; and about whether a woman can be a real feminist if she sleeps with the enemy—men.

Like most women, feminists engaged in smear and ostracism campaigns against any woman with whom they disagreed, whom they envied, or who was different in some way. Unlike men, most women were not psychologically prepared for such intense and overt battles and experienced them personally, not politically—and sometimes as near-death experiences.

This didn't drive most of us away; failing to acknowledge this phenomenon often did.

We now understand that all women, both white and of color, have internalized racial prejudice, but we fail to comprehend that women are also sexists and that, like racism or homophobia, we have to consciously resist this on a daily basis in order to hold our own against it; and that we will never be able to overcome it completely.

Once upon a time, long ago, I believed that all women were kind, caring, maternal, valiant, and noble under siege, and that all men were their oppressors. As everyone but a handful of idealistic feminists knew, this was not true. Living my life has helped me to understand that, like men, women are human beings, as close to the apes as to the angels, capable of both cruelty and compassion, envy and generosity, competition and cooperation.

Seemingly contradictory things can be true psychologically. Women mainly compete against and envy and sabotage other women, and women mainly rely upon other women for intimate relationships.

In 1980, when I began researching what would become my tenth book, *Woman's Inhumanity to Woman*, many feminist leaders told me that I should cease and desist, that "the men" would use it against us. Years later I was talking to Shulie Firestone, and she said, "Phyllis, if only you had written *Woman's Inhumanity to Woman* long ago, it might have saved our movement."

"Shulie, I doubt that any book could have done that—but how kind of you to say so," I replied. "Do you know how strongly feminist leaders and their followers opposed my writing this book? Their disapproval probably stayed my hand for years."

"But why did you listen to them?" She was a bit agitated. I hugged her.

Psychologically, we second-wavers had no feminist foremothers and no biological mothers. We had only sisters.

If only we had known something—anything—about women's history, specifically about our feminist foremothers, we might have been better prepared for the unholy feminist civil wars in which we often took no prisoners and never spoke to each other again.

If only we had known that suffragists had also fought hard and dirty and that politicians and ideologues behave this way, we might not have taken it all so personally.

If only we had understood more about the dark side of female psychology, we might have been able to find ways to resist our own mean-girl treachery.

If only.

Only now, a half century later, do I understand that women in groups tend to demand uniformity, conformity, shoulder-to-shoulder nonhierarchical sisterhood—one in which no one is more rewarded than anyone else. Marxism and female psychology are a natural fit psychologically, but not for me.

People say, "Women are their own worst enemies." I cringe when I hear this. It's not always true. Sometimes we save each other; most women could not live for more than a day without intimate female relationships.

In the beginning we delighted in each other; we wrote about our friends in published works of poetry and self-published mimeo handouts as if these women were already historic or mythic figures. Marge Piercy, by 1969 already the author of one novel and two books of poetry, and Martha Shelley, a poet with a growing reputation who was also an amazing lesbian feminist activist, both wrote poems to me. To be admired by women of ideas, by serious and talented women, is indeed wondrous.

Betty Friedan and others had founded the National Organization for Women (NOW) in 1966. As soon as I learned that a chapter had opened in New York City, I joined and signed up for the first committee I was offered: childcare. Heading it, most improbably, was radical feminist Ti-Grace Atkinson. Ti-Grace was close to Flo Kennedy, an African American lawyer and Mistress of the Quick Quip. Flo-of-the-snappy-comeback affectionately called me various nicknames. Later, Flo and Gloria Steinem delivered lectures together.

Ti-Grace was a tall, willowy blonde who lived on East Seventy-ninth Street. A large photo dominated the wall behind her living room couch: Ti-Grace as a bride, which she had slashed diagonally. Right there, in her apartment, I stood up and delivered a full-blown, fiery feminist speech; I said things I didn't know I knew. We were no longer ordinary; we were all superheroes.

I attended meetings of the National Organization for Women. That's where I first met Kate Millett. Kate wore her hair in a sleek bun, sported large dark-framed intellectual glasses, and spoke with a slight British accent—just to make sure you knew that she'd been to Oxford. She was a bit timid, pseudo-humble, and rather charming. She was married—her husband was a soft-spoken Japanese artist named Fumio Yoshimura.

Valerie Solanas's self-published 1967 *SCUM Manifesto* is an angry, frightening, kick-ass feminist work. It's daring and brilliant, a clarion call to arms, perhaps satiric, probably literal; she urges women to "overthrow the government, eliminate the money system, and eliminate the male sex." Her manifesto is crazy.

Solanas was a physically abused child and incest victim who became homeless at fifteen; she was a lesbian, a panhandler, and a prostitute. Solanas gave birth to a child when she was seventeen; the child was taken from her.

Solanas's life history resembles that of Aileen Wuornos, the woman who became known as the "first female serial killer" and the "hitch-hiking prostitute."

Both Solanas and Wuornos (in whose case I eventually became involved) became cult figures à la Jesse James. They were outlaws, but they were female outlaws, far beyond the cinematic *Thelma and Louise*. They attracted many straight and lesbian feminist supporters whose creative works—films, plays, books, songs, an opera—portrayed them. Solanas's book was translated into more than a dozen languages. Academics wrote about both of them.

Solanas became known as the woman who tried to kill Andy Warhol. In her mind Warhol had promised to film her play, *Up Your Ass*, which is about a prostitute who kills a man. Warhol never made the film; in Solanas's mind he had ruined her career. When Maurice Girodias of Olympia Press offered to publish her future work and gave her money, Solanas decided that Girodias had tricked her, bought her off cheaply, now owned everything she might ever write, and was probably conspiring against her with Andy Warhol.

On June 3, 1968, Valerie intended to shoot Girodias, but when she could not find him, she shot Warhol instead. This was the act of a mentally ill woman.

Flo Kennedy and Ti-Grace Atkinson embraced Solanas as a symbol of feminist militancy and rushed to her side. They claimed Solanas as one of ours. They visited her in jail. Both Flo and Ti-Grace were identified with NOW. Their attempt to present a mentally ill criminal as a feminist hero made Betty Friedan crazy. Betty viewed Solanas as a man-hating lunatic, not as a feminist hero. Betty feared that NOW would be seen as supporting the murder of men.

Yes, Solanas's act could be interpreted in feminist terms and, as such, exploited by feminists, but Solanas herself was not a feminist. She had acted irrationally, without a goal; she represented no one but herself.

Solanas hotly denied any association with feminism, which she described as a "civil disobedience luncheon club."

Touché, Valerie Solanas, *touché*.

Solanas accused Ti-Grace and Flo of using her to gain fame. Predictably, many years later Wuornos accused me and all those who tried to help her of the same thing.

Ti-Grace resigned from NOW and Flo quit in solidarity with her; Flo formed the Feminist Party, Ti-Grace formed the October 17th Movement. Solanas was diagnosed as a paranoid schizophrenic and hospitalized for three years in an asylum for the criminally insane. In 1988 she died of pneumonia in a San Francisco single-occupancy hotel in the Tenderloin district.

Initially I supported Solanas, just as I supported the issues of self-defense raised by the Aileen Wuornos case. However, once Solanas turned on Ti-Grace and Flo, I respected Betty's point of view a bit more.

Betty Friedan wanted women with status and power, preferably married to upstanding and powerful men, to represent the feminist movement. She wanted no wild-eyed riffraff, no one unpredictable or too radical, to become associated in the public eye with what she viewed as her respectable and rational movement.

When I was in college I discovered Simone de Beauvoir's *The Second Sex*. I read it privately and passionately. In college and graduate school I had been assigned Jane Austen, the Brontës, Colette, George Eliot, Virginia Woolf, and the psychoanalytic theorist Karen Horney, but their work—even Woolf's—was never presented as feminist. I knew nothing of the writings of women of color. I read the work of Frederick Douglass—but not that of Harriet Ann Jacobs or Sojourner Truth; I read the work of Langston Hughes, Richard Wright, and Ralph Ellison—but not that of Zora Neale Hurston, who had yet to be rediscovered.

I had chosen to live with the Monster and I blamed only myself for having done so. I didn't think of myself as a member of a group whose history and destiny I shared.

I knew nothing about a major feminist hero, Bill Baird, the man who brought lawsuits that led to the recognition of women's right to access to birth control.

In the 1960s Baird was jailed eight times in five states for fighting for women's right to abortion and birth control. In 1972 his work led to a landmark Supreme Court decision that legalized birth control for unmarried couples and single women, *Eisenstadt v. Baird*. This lawsuit established a right to privacy that became the foundation for a series of other lawsuits, beginning with *Roe v. Wade* in 1973.

A left-wing feminist is someone who views reality through the prism of class warfare and who is either far to the left of Lenin or Marx or slightly to his right. This means that she fiercely opposes capitalism and private enterprise; believes that the ends justify the means; only regretfully blames Stalin, Mao, or Fidel for their totalitarian regimes and vast gulags of torture because she believes in Big Government; and acknowledges that changing the status quo can be messy. A left-wing feminist believes that no woman will be free until all women are free, and that without a massive redistribution of both wealth and opportunity, only a minority of women will be able to join the corrupt system. Left-wing feminists have a point—but they are usually ideologues, and ideologues are often blinded by what should be and fail to see what is merely possible.

From 1967 to 1975, left-wing feminists were the most creative activists and theorists. For example, in 1968, during the Jeannette Rankin Brigade's antiwar march in Washington, D.C., radical feminists opposed to the Vietnam War staged a funeral procession to Arlington National Cemetery for a blond dummy of "traditional womanhood" surrounded by garters, curlers, and hair spray.

Left-wing feminists, especially Shulie Firestone, the activist author of *The Dialectics of Sex*, and members of the legendary groups Redstockings and New York Radical Women, such as Kathie Sarachild, Ann Forer, and Carol Hanisch, were meeting and publishing guidelines about what they called consciousness raising.

Carol Hanisch was a founder of Redstockings, a passionate activist group bent on feminist revolution. She had quite an inspiring idea: enlist hundreds of feminists to help organize or participate in a carnival-like, visually creative protest in Atlantic City at the Miss America Pageant in September 1968. I was not there, but women I know—including Jacqui Ceballos, Cindy Cisler, Flo Kennedy, Kate Millett, Robin Morgan, Kathie Sarachild, and Alix Kates Shulman—were, and told me about it.

I am naming names you should know because this event really happened and it was important. Over the years some of these names have disappeared or simply been forgotten. At the time, these women lit up my imagination.

Four hundred feminists carried signs that read: WELCOME TO THE MISS AMERICA CATTLE AUCTION; WOMEN ARE PEOPLE, NOT LIVESTOCK; CAN MAKEUP COVER THE WOUNDS OF OUR OPPRESSION? and ALL WOMEN ARE BEAUTIFUL. They refused to talk to male reporters—which jump-started the careers of several female journalists. These feminists did not burn bras (the authorities would not give them a permit to burn anything; the boardwalk was made of wood). Instead, they tossed items like lipsticks, bras, girdles, and hair curlers into a "freedom trash can." They crowned a live sheep. Peggy Dobbins and some others had tickets to the balcony, where they unfurled a banner reading WOMEN'S LIBERATION.

Men on the boardwalk jeered, jostled, stared, paced, and generally reacted negatively. The police presence was enormous. So was the media coverage.

Most demonstrators had emerged from the civil rights, antiwar, and other left-wing movements. A month later, the Women's International Terrorist Conspiracy from Hell (WITCH) put a hex on Wall Street. I've seen photos of Ros Baxandall at that demonstration; like me, she was an activist as well as an aspiring academic. Years later I wrote a letter to help her obtain a distinguished professorship at the State University of New York at Old Westbury.

In 1969 a group of feminist psychologists who had been meeting for a year cofounded the Association for Women in Psychology (AWP). I was among them. I was sharing a hotel room with Naomi Weisstein. Back then, I was five feet, four-and-a-half inches, and she was even shorter. In 1968 she published the essay "Kinder, Küche, Kirche as Scientific Law: Psychology Constructs the Female." Naomi was also a cofounder of the Chicago Women's Liberation Union, a group that introduced women to their bodies and to Marxism. Naomi and I discussed feminism. But late at night we started looking at each other somewhat shyly.

I asked her: "Are you Weisstein of . . . ?" and cited one of her studies published in *Science*. And she replied: "Are you Chesler of . . . ?" and cited one of my studies, also published in *Science*.

We were both studying the brain but in different ways. We were alone in our hotel room, yet we looked around, afraid that Big Sister might be listening. Almost in unison we asked: "Are we allowed to talk about brain research?"

Then we laughed—and discussed our studies.

Naomi was a world-class scientist; I was only a dabbler, dazzled by physiological psychology, working in a cutting-edge research lab, attending medical school on a fellowship. Still, I had been documenting the electrophysiological correlates of learning by observation—the sudden "aha moment" of consciousness.

Naomi was also more than just a psychologist. She was a tough little comedian and a cofounder of the Chicago Women's Liberation Rock Band (1970–73). She wanted an outlaw, badass, agit-rock, all-girl band that sang and "took shit from no one." She regarded lyrics sung by male rockers to be a "cultural carpet-bombing of girls, based on the amplified idea that male abuse was all that we girls wanted to live for." Soon enough, some women who loved to dance to rock music but found the lyrics that denigrated them distasteful formed their own politically oriented rock bands.

Yes, we had the great Janis Joplin, who too soon went up in flames. But her lyrics were not feminist; she rocked the blues and did not stop loving the men who rejected her in both song and life. We had tough, sassy, proud black women blues singers—we had Aretha! We had Nina Simone!—but we had no tough white girl singers.

The Chicago and the New Haven Women's Liberation Rock Band appeared all over the country; wherever they went, they induced "massive euphoria" (Naomi's words) in their audiences. Women would start singing along, clapping, crying, laughing, and demanding that the band repeat songs over and over. Sometimes women stripped to the waist and danced in circles.

All through high school I had taken private singing lessons and sung with bands. I jammed with Neil Sedaka in Brooklyn and studied opera in college. I loved music: blues, jazz, doo-wop, gospel, folk, Broadway, opera—and I still do. Once I was privileged to jam with the Chicago Women's Liberation Rock Band. What a high! What excitement!

I am talking about the early 1970s, when such music and such bands were absolutely unheard of. Song titles included "Secretary," "Abortion Song," "Sister Witch," "Ain't Gonna Marry," "Papa," and "Mountain Moving Day." The lyrics were sensational: "Papa don't lay that shit on me, the fun and games are gone / It wasn't my game / it wasn't my fun / All that trashing is over and done." Naomi and Jennifer Abod set a 1904 poem by the Japanese feminist Yosano Akiko to music: "The mountain moving day is coming / All sleeping women / Now will awake and move."

These women's music was mostly lesbian music, and therefore, at the time, it was feminist and political. Alix Dobkin (*Lavender Jane*

Loves Women), Margie Adam ("We Shall Go Forth," a song she performed at the 1977 National Women's Conference in Houston), Holly Near (*Imagine My Surprise*), and Cris Williamson (*The Changer and the Changed*) rocked our hearts. We sang along, danced, made love, and engaged in revolutionary politics to their woman-friendly, sassy, and increasingly spiritual soundtracks. Women fully owned their experiences and shared them as artists, actresses, comedians, directors, and playwrights. I remember lesbian theater troupes such as Split Britches and Medusa's Revenge. I did a benefit for Split Britches, founded by Lois Weaver, Peggy Shaw, and Deb Margolin. They were hilarious, daring, outrageous, and good at what they did. Lois played ultrafemme, Peggy played ultrabutch, and Deb was the funniest comedian and playwright in the universe. They made us laugh about serious matters (*Women Who Kill*) and cry about a colonial-era lesbian love story (*Patience and Sarah*, based on Isabel Miller's 1969 novel).

It's hard for people who didn't live through it to understand how important these musicians and actors were to us, how their music and theatre expressed our dreams and served as our most faithful and encouraging companions on the road to freedom. These composers, singers, and actors were women fighting back. Their comic routines were not based on self-degradation or denigration of how they looked. Their ideas were daring, loving, and inspiring. They mirrored and inspired our evolving selves.

I met the journalist Vivian Gornick when she interviewed me for her important November 1969 piece in the *Village Voice* "The Next Great Moment in History Is Theirs." We hit it off and become instant friends without knowing anything about each other; it was enough that we delighted in each other's love of literature and words. Excited feminists, busy women, initiated such feminist-based friendships all the time.

Vivian and I hosted the first feminist literary salon in Manhattan at her apartment on First Avenue and then held a second meeting in my West Village apartment. She credits me with teaching her some of the feminist essentials for her own, soon-to-be-celebrated work.

I was drunk on the writing that continued to explode daily. Extraordinary writing appeared in 1968 and 1969: *Bread and Roses*; *The New Woman: A Motive Anthology on Women's Liberation*; *Problems of Women's Lib*; *Redstockings Manifesto*; *Women: A Bibliography*; *Toward a Female Liberation Movement*; *Notes from the First Year*; *Notes from the Second Year: Women's Liberation*.

Shulie Firestone analyzed falling in love and declared it akin to an illness. This made me laugh out loud. I tended to fall into lust, and it passed soon enough. Her analysis was bold and oddly comforting. It undid years of fairy tales and animated films in which the female protagonist must marry a prince or die.

Anne Koedt exploded the myth of the vaginal orgasm. Feminists stopped blaming themselves for failing to have them, stopped trying to have them, and started concentrating on their clitorises as their primary source of orgasmic pleasure. Early on, I suggested to my students that they go home and practice doing this.

Pat Mainardi spoke for us all when she documented that women were doing nearly all the housework, pointing out that we were not supposed to complain or nag husbands about this but were expected to "carry on," even if we brought in a larger percentage of our household's income than our husbands did.

Frances Beale and Beverly Jones described the "double jeopardy" involved in being both black and female.

The anthology *Sisterhood Is Powerful*, edited by Robin Morgan, was published in 1970; it is a heady compilation of early feminist writings from 1968, 1969, and 1970 that first appeared as articles, pamphlets, mimeographed handouts, an anthology, and an annotated bibliography.

Ms. magazine appeared two years later, in 1972.

Perhaps I'm a case study of what one woman needs in order to free herself. I didn't leave my sadistic boyfriend (the Monster) until I was surrounded by feminist ideas and amazing feminist activists and until I'd completed my education, had a decent job, and could afford the rent for a place of my own.

I left the Monster literally the day after I received my Ph.D. I found an apartment on West Thirteenth Street in the Village. In the fall I was to begin work as an assistant professor. To my surprise, the Monster found me. He was trembling with rage; he accused me of stealing a particular spoon, one that was special to him—he could not find it anywhere. I invited him to look for it and then told him he had to leave. I closed the door on him and on that chapter of my life.

Something was going on every day and every night in every major city across the nation. I knew in my bones that one particular event—a speak-out about abortion—would resonate.

Every woman I knew had had an abortion. It was something we didn't discuss.

I had my first abortion when I was about nineteen years old and still a student at Bard. I was terrified about dying but relieved that I had an appointment with the famed Dr. Robert Douglas Spencer in Ashland, Pennsylvania. When I arrived, I learned that he had left— he was a hunted humanitarian, always one step ahead of the authorities, who constantly stalked him. I remember sitting disconsolately on a swing in a nearby park as I considered my fate.

I found another man, on the Upper East Side, right near the Metropolitan Museum of Art. I was not even sure he was a doctor. He used no anesthesia and the procedure was unbearable. I was being punished for having sex and refusing to carry a child against my will. Enormously relieved, I rushed back to school to take an exam.

I had my second abortion when I returned from Kabul. My mother's doctor assured me that, given how sick I was, I could not safely carry a child to term. My abortion was an induced miscarriage. It was quite painful.

Both abortions were the result of my relationship with the same Afghan man.

In March 1969, Redstockings held a feminist speak-out on abortion at the Washington Square United Methodist Church. This speak-out changed lives and laws, and inspired a number of journalists, including Gloria Steinem. New York Radical Feminists Noreen Connell and Cassandra Wilson described the event this way:

> *Using the consciousness-raising technique, twelve women 'testified' about abortion, from their own personal experience, before an audience of 300 men and women. The political message of the emotion-charged evening was that women were the only true experts on unwanted pregnancy and abortion, and that every woman has an inalienable right to decide whether or not she wishes to bear a child.*

My earliest feminist activism consisted of helping women obtain abortions. My oldest friend in the women's movement, Barbara Joans, and I passed the women along an underground railroad of doctors' names and locations. Wealthy women flew to the Caribbean or to Europe. Poor women scrambled, scrimped, and "made do" with back-alley abortions.

A feminist abortion underground in Chicago was known as Jane. Women there raised money for abortions, and eventually their overworked doctors taught these feminists how to perform abortions themselves. It was a real cloak-and-dagger operation, with women being moved from house to house to avoid being found and arrested.

Religious fundamentalists have fought hard against legalized abortion from the moment the Supreme Court handed down its ruling in *Roe v. Wade* in 1973. At first the fundamentalists used Orwellian language to shame pro-choice women and to gain allies. They presented their antiabortion views as "pro-life," not as anti-woman. Then they and their supporters began to harass, stalk, threaten, and even murder doctors who performed abortions. They also fire-bombed clinics. Because violence by pro-lifers did not serve their image, fundamentalists turned to other means. They began to chip away at legislation on a state-by-state basis, making it impossible for millions of poor women to obtain high-quality, low-cost abortions, especially in rural areas and in small towns.

Today some churches still regularly send protesters to clinics to harass incoming patients with chants of "baby murderer" and "You'll regret this for the rest of your life." A woman who requires a medical abortion; a woman who chooses not to carry a seriously ill fetus to term; a mother of five who cannot afford another child; a woman who needs radiation for cancer and whose physician has advised her to have an abortion; a rape-impregnated victim; a young woman who cannot afford to raise a child and also work a full-time job so she can attend college—it doesn't matter what the reason is: these protesters still force these women to experience physically menacing and verbal assaults as they walk toward the clinic. Antiabortion activists use false advertising to trick women into appointments with church-based adoption services where they try to persuade the women to carry to term and give their babies up. The fundamentalists do not tell the women that birth mothers rarely make peace with having done this or that adopted children have a significantly higher risk than other children of serious psychiatric problems.

My dear friend Merle Hoffman, who owns the largest abortion clinic in the country (Choices Women's Medical Center), reminds me that "abortion has been called, and in reality is, a second Civil War."

———

Coast to coast, women were in a rare state of ecstasy. Many insisted that it took only one speak-out, one march, one consciousness-raising group to experience a state of "sublime sisterhood."

The concept that "the personal is political" allowed women to share our supposedly minor miseries; this led to our understanding that we were all similarly oppressed and that it was not our fault. Having to do the housework after working the same eight- to ten-hour day as our husbands was unjust, and our weariness—often bitterness—was understandable, not proof that we were deficient or deranged.

Many feminists have claimed credit for the phrase "the personal is political." I can assure everyone: it wasn't me. It was Carol Hanisch, perhaps in discussions with Shulie Firestone and Kathie Sarachild, who first uttered these immortal words.

I also knew that groups were forming and splintering, that Women of Ideas took Ideas very seriously, and that if there were serious differences they put the Idea before the individual woman. Lesbians were meeting only with other lesbians. But they, too, swiftly shattered, for reasons that weren't yet clear to me.

As I noted earlier, feminists had substantive battles about Marxism versus capitalism, revolution versus reform, violent overthrow versus the evolutionary transformation of patriarchy, racism, and lesbians as the only true feminists versus lesbians as man-haters who will destroy the work of heterosexual reformers.

Feminists experienced all these battles not only as political differences but as personal attacks, from which many failed to recover.

I worked full time. I had a part-time therapy practice at a psychoanalytic institute. I had begun to deliver feminist lectures and, most important, to research female psychology.

In 1969 I began as an assistant professor of psychology at Richmond College, a junior-senior–year college on Staten Island that was part of the City University of New York (CUNY). My beginning salary was $11,000 a year. I thought it was a bloody fortune. The campus was known as CUNY's "radical playpen." I prepared for and taught three classes, graded and counseled students, attended faculty meetings, and spent an hour each way on the commute from Manhattan. I didn't mind. I liked the ferry. I read. I pretended I was on a boat plying the waters of Scandinavia or Greece.

I was the first and only woman in the psychology department at the time.

In the 1960s and 1970s, men dominated CUNY at every level. The chancellor was a man and his staff of sixteen were all men. Of the eighteen CUNY college presidents, seventeen were men. CUNY had ninety-four male deans and five female deans. Thirteen of the fifteen chief librarians were men. The university had few female full or associate professors. All the secretaries were women. However, most women accepted their inferior status as a given and didn't protest. They felt grateful to even have a job. Many didn't believe they were being discriminated against.

I've made it a point to forget this. I've banished all memories about how painful, frustrating, and anxiety provoking each and every day at CUNY really was. Writing this memoir meant that I had to remember and relive it.

I did whatever I had to do to get through it, past it, over it—in short, like every other woman, I learned to live with job insecurity, constant challenges to my right to hold a formerly male-only job; daily doses of sexism; slights, scorn, utter indifference, or even hostility toward my professional accomplishments; witch hunts; routine sexual harassment; and, eventually, economic and social punishment for getting pregnant.

I had no choice. I got used to working in a hostile environment.

Back then (which was not so long ago), the patriarchal academic order viewed women who were not working as secretaries as dangerous threats. We were hazed. We ran gauntlets of disapproval. We were judged on our looks and on whether we were "women's libbers."

I was a feminist at a time when to be a feminist was actually threatening to the academic establishment; this is no longer true.

My male colleagues were in charge of deciding whether I'd ever be promoted or get tenure. They told me my research on women was not as important as my brain research. At a department meeting three-and-a-half months after I was hired, the chair turned to me and said, quite genially: "We'll count on you to choose the Christmas gifts for the secretaries. Right?"

I turned halfway around to see to whom he was speaking. Oh, it was me. I said, also genially, apologetically: "Oh, I'm not one of those happy little human shoppers. I never shop. Sorry, guys."

This did not bode well for me.

As the saying goes, the reason academics fight so viciously is that the rewards are so small. And these fights target men as well as women.

I once got into the elevator with a male colleague who had just won a national literary prize. I congratulated him heartily. He started weeping.

"Have I said something to upset you?" I asked.

"No," he responded. "But you're the first and only one on campus who has recognized my achievement."

How to understand this? Here's how: most academics are an envious lot who despise true talent and outside recognition because it makes them look bad.

But not all of them are like that. My dearest ally at this time was Barbara Joans. She was once married to a man to whom she refers as the Monster. Barbara was a resourceful woman. As stated earlier, we helped women obtain illegal abortions. We also taught at a free school near West Fourteenth Street and plotted revolution. She was much more of a hippie and a street person than I was. She dropped acid, had two young sons, and lived in a commune on Bedford Street. She was also in graduate school. After she got her doctoral degree in anthropology, she ran a university department and a museum in California. I would call on her to work with me at the United Nations. We remain close to this day.

Barbara and I delivered our first grown-up, drop-dead-gorgeous, take-no-prisoners lecture on feminism in 1970 for the Long Island Forum in Great Neck. The joint was packed to the rafters. We received wild applause. It was covered in the local newspaper. This lecture turned the Sarah Lawrence professor Amy Swerdlow into a feminist, or so she said.

My mother attended. Afterward she said to me, "You don't look so good. You should see a doctor."

I replied, "I *am* a doctor."

She said, "Phyllis, we may not see eye to eye on a lot of things, but who's going to marry you if you say such things out loud?"

Every time someone accused me of hating men, I had to laugh. If only that were true! I may have been a firebrand feminist, but I was still very much a man junkie. Well, what was wrong with that?

"You sleep with men because you're too afraid to sleep with women," a lesbian-feminist friend announced.

I responded: "I'm attracted to men. It's chemistry."

I may have thought I wanted love, but I chose men who were incapable of making a commitment. Men like that were so easy to find, and I had no time to squander on a personal life anyway. Not then. Maybe not ever. I was committed to books and ideas and a struggle for liberation.

When I was not teaching, writing, lecturing, or attending a feminist meeting, I was with Mark or Thomas or Liam or Nick or someone else, one after the other.

Mark, who was also a psychologist, taught me how to climb mountains and how to camp. He even got me up on skis.

Thomas was a genius composer whose first opera was performed when he was twenty years old. I watched him compose a piece for a small (or large) orchestra entirely in his head; every so often, he'd amble over to the piano, play a note or two, and then return to his composition paper. I found this magical, the way he "heard" each note and composed harmonies while sitting in his armchair. Thomas cooked midnight suppers, as if we lived in an opera in Paris in 1905, and he indulged me by playing the blues on his expensive piano so that I could sing my little heart out.

Liam lived in a house near the Hudson River and wrote poetry. We sat in different rooms, each writing poems. He had thick, inky black hair and I liked him a lot. He was a mournful kind of guy and we were a brief interlude.

I was and am politically incorrect in every way.

3 Raising My Consciousness and Pioneering Women's Studies

Consciousness-raising (CR) groups were composed of seven to ten women who might not have known each other beforehand or who might have met briefly on the barricades. These were not therapy groups. No one paid to be a member. We were not there to solve personal problems. The group's purpose was to help women recognize that we were oppressed so that we would engage in political activism of one kind or another.

Because some women talk nervously nonstop and other women rarely speak at all, each of us was expected to speak only once until everyone had taken her turn. We went around a circle, never interrupted one another, spoke only about our own experience, never criticized what someone else said, and refrained from giving advice. The groups were not supposed to have leaders.

Topics included our gendered training in childhood; the kinds of mothers and fathers we had; whether education was important for girls in our family; our adult sexual experiences; whether we knew how to masturbate (most of the women did not); whether we had orgasms (again, most of the women did not); whether we had ever been raped, had an abortion, married, or lived with a man; whether we had children and, if so, whether anyone helped us with child care, housework, and shopping; whether we had ever been attracted to another woman; and whether we were employed and, if so, had careers or merely jobs.

New groups kept forming. Groups splintered. Socialists chose other socialists; women in publishing preferred other women in publishing; lesbians were more comfortable in all-lesbian groups.

These CR groups introduced a large number of women to reality. Before CR, most of us did not understand that we were oppressed and discriminated against economically, politically, legally, sexually, and socially.

But some members of CR groups viewed accomplished women, or merely women who spoke well, suspiciously. At the time I did not know this, so I enthusiastically joined a CR group. I knew no one in my group. We were about six or seven women with radically different backgrounds and skill sets.

Once, I arrived seven minutes late. This was a major crime. It meant that I didn't respect women's time and space.

"You think you're special. But you're not."

"You're the same as we are. Lateness will not be tolerated. You know that's one of our rules."

Suddenly Marge Piercy, with whom I'd never had a private conversation, interrupted the punishment session in progress.

"Phyllis is writing a book that will change the world for women forever. And she teaches full time. Why not cut her some slack?"

I loved this woman.

Thereafter Marge and I met secretly, not sure that we were allowed to do this, as if CR followed nunnery or Maoist rules; maybe it forbade "private affiliations" because they did not enhance group solidarity. Marge wrote a poem about our friendship, "The Bumpity Road to Mutual Devotion." I proposed that our CR group rent a house in the country for the summer. I went ahead and rented a house in Hillsdale, New York (not far from Great Barrington, Massachusetts). The women waited to see if better plans with boyfriends materialized.

One by one the Prince Charmings failed to propose summer plans, and the women took a share in the house. I told them: "Please don't cook for me, don't include me in your plans. I'll take care of myself." I went into the study, closed the door, and wrote.

At some point in the evening someone invariably brought in a plate of food and slammed it down on the desk. Sometimes someone knocked on the door and in a harsh voice said: "Dinner's ready. Do you want to eat in your room or out here with us?"

Since Marge wasn't there, I was on my own.

I was focused entirely on my writing. I did not join my sisters in summertime and bonding activities like shopping, cooking, gardening, or flower picking. They resented it, thought me an elitist, and treated me as if I were a man.

Many members of this group went on to become feminist therapists. I didn't stay in touch with anyone but Marge and Barbara Chasen. Years later I asked Barbara, a psychotherapist, what she remembered about our CR group. She wrote: "I worried about what the hell you wear to a CR group. Then, you got famous with *Women and Madness* and people treated you like a rock star. People—women, feminists— were jealous of your success, which I found shocking/sad. I thought we were supposed to hail each other's success."

I just Googled "Feminism in Greenwich Village, circa 1960s and 1970s" and was surprised by how quickly we have all been disappeared. I found a lot about early bohemians, African American artists, jazz clubs, Beat-era poets and artists, the sexual revolution, the folk music scene, and antiwar movements, but practically nothing about the feminists and lesbian feminists of my generation. A single paragraph mentions Betty Friedan and Gloria Steinem, neither of whom lived in the Village or were part of the downtown feminist and lesbian-feminist scene.

Then I Googled "gay and lesbian bars in Greenwich Village" and mainly found information about gay *male* bars and clubs. In my time lesbian bars were as much about politics as they were about sexual hookups; those bars were where I got important information about radical goings-on.

If we don't remember and share what we once knew, it will be lost forever.

By the early 1970s, radical feminists and lesbian feminists *owned* the Village. It was our town. We all lived within a mile or two of each other.

I attended feminist meetings at all the venerable coffeehouses on MacDougal and Bleecker Streets and on Greenwich Avenue, where my agent, Elaine Markson, had her offices. I also met feminist friends for a drink or for dinner at bohemian/literary joints like the Cedar Tavern, Chumley's, the Pink Teacup, and the White Horse Tavern, and at lesbian joints such as Bonnie & Clyde, the Cubbyhole, the Duchess, and Henrietta Hudson.

Alix Kates Shulman (*Memoirs of an Ex-Prom Queen*) lived right across the street from Washington Square Park. We held the meeting that led to the founding of the feminist academic journal *Signs* in her book-lined study; we were all so excited that when someone had to use the bathroom she kept the door slightly ajar so she could keep listening to the conversation.

Alix was an expert on Emma Goldman and a staunch socialist. She was also beautiful, with the chiseled cheekbones of a high-fashion model.

Barbara Joans (*Bike Lust: Harleys, Women, and American Society*) lived on Bedford Street. Barbara was the boldest, baddest straight woman I've ever known.

Vivian Gornick (*Woman in Sexist Society, Fierce Attachments: A Memoir*) lived on First Avenue near East Twelfth Street but moved to West Twelfth Street near Seventh Avenue.

Vivian had an embattled relationship with her mother; who among us did not? Vivian was in Egypt during the Yom Kippur War, when many Arab countries, including Egypt, attacked Israel. Her mother called me at least every other day.

"Will they kill my Vivian? Do they know she's Jewish?"

"Mrs. Gornick," I'd tell her, "I'm sure Vivian is okay. She's moving in very educated circles. Most writers and intellectuals don't kill people."

Vivian was actually doing quite well. In fact, she was having the time of her life. When she came home, she wrote a beautiful book about her time in Egypt.

Susan Brownmiller (*Against Our Will: Men, Women, and Rape*) and the social worker Florence Rush (*The Best Kept Secret: The Sexual Abuse of Children*) both lived on Jane Street.

Jill Johnston, a *Village Voice* columnist and the author of *Lesbian Nation*, lived on Charles Street.

Johnston and I had an unexpectedly enduring but stormy relationship. We butted heads on many issues, beginning with my being an unacceptably straight woman and "one of them"—a shrink—the likes of which may have offended her because of her various stays in psychiatric facilities. She was not pleased that I was writing about madness, which she viewed as strictly her territory, or that I was a Jew at a time when Jill believed that "the Jews" seemed to have taken over the feminist movement. Through it all our genuine enjoyment of each other's company and our love of mythology and poetry saw us through our differences.

The poet, novelist, and lesbian feminist activist Martha Shelley (*Crossing the DMZ, The Throne in the Heart of the Sea*), one of the few women who participated in the Stonewall uprising, lived in the East Village, as did Kate Millett (*Sexual Politics, Flying*) and Catharine Stimpson (*Class Notes*), who both lived on the Bowery.

Ellen Frankfort (*Vaginal Politics*) also lived in the hood. Ellen and I became close friends. She wrote a woman's health column for the *Village Voice*. She was a tireless journalist and champion of women in distress.

The ever-cheery novelist Lila Karp (*The Queen Is in the Garbage*) had sailed back to the United States from England as soon as she read about our feminist uprising. I loved Lila's breezy continental charm. She was married to Renos, an agreeable man from Greece, but her heart was with us. I remember one Thanksgiving at Lila's loft in SoHo as especially warm. There we were—Ti-Grace Atkinson, Kate Millett, Kate Stimpson, and me, all trying to be family to each other, though hardly capable of doing much more than our own work.

Merlin Stone, the author of *When God Was a Woman*, was a shy but seductive recluse who lived on Sixth Avenue just below Charlton Street. Her apartment was unexpectedly filled with slot and gumball machines.

My good friend Nancy Azara, the founder of the New York Feminist Art Institute, lived in what would become SoHo.

The Women's Coffeehouse was on Seventh Avenue South below Christopher Street. The building was owned by June Arnold and Patty Bowman, who would publish Rita Mae Brown's *Rubyfruit Jungle*. At some point Bertha Harris (*Lover*, *The Joy of Lesbian Sex*) also lived above the coffeehouse.

In 1972, Dolores Alexander and Jill Ward opened the first feminist restaurant in New York City. They called it Mother Courage; it stood at the corner of West Eleventh and Washington Streets, down by the Hudson River. I went there for dinner as often as possible. Alix Kates Shulman, Susan Brownmiller, Lucy Komisar, Kate Millett, and I attended the celebration of its third anniversary. *People* magazine published a photo of Kate and I engaged in spirited conversation in front of the restaurant. Unfortunately, too little capital, no bank loans, and too much dependence on volunteer labor meant that this little piece of heaven closed in 1978.

When Bonnie & Clyde first opened on West Third Street, it was not a gay bar; it was a feminist and lesbian-feminist bar and restaurant. No one was role playing gender; we were all feminists together. The atmosphere was not erotically charged, but it was still exciting. After two weeks, customers split according to their roles, butch and femme, just as in other lesbian bars. White women gravitated to the upstairs restaurant. Women of color preferred to remain downstairs at the bar, where the inevitable pool table had appeared.

I had begun talking about a feminist government to every feminist I knew. I conceived of this as an international entity. Obviously, we needed governments to become more feminist, that is, more responsive to women's issues. Equally clearly, this was not happening. Thus this government was in formation (at least in my mind) and in exile at the same time.

The poet and civil rights activist Barbara Deming (*Prison Notes*) met me for dinner at Bonnie & Clyde. Barbara gave me a winsome bird feather to commemorate our meeting; she respected my idea of a feminist government in exile. This mattered to me because Barbara was a venerated civil rights veteran of southern jails.

Years later, for my fiftieth birthday, my close friend Merle Hoffman designed a T-shirt and gave one to each guest; the shirts proclaimed FEMINIST GOVERNMENT IN EXILE with an Amazon astride her trusty mount, spear in hand, hair flying.

Multiply my single meeting with Barbara at Bonnie & Clyde by thousands more, and you can begin to imagine this era of feminists in the Village.

I have hardly named or properly identified everyone who lived within this blessed radius, whose work mattered, and who mattered to me personally. They include Sidney Abbott (lesbian activist and author), Ros Baxandall (author and activist), Phyllis Birkby (architect), Alice Denham (novelist and memoirist), Claudia Dreifus (journalist), Betty Fischer (publisher and author), Shulie Firestone (author and activist), Buffie Johnson (artist), Lucy Komisar (journalist), Barbara Love (lesbian activist and author), Robin Morgan (poet and activist), and Alida Walsh (sculptor).

Some of us (more than half) were straight, some were gay, some were bi, and all were Caucasian. Decry this if you will, interpret it as you must, but one cannot deny these demographic realities.

These women made up an immediate geographical universe—my universe. Of those I have mentioned, as of this writing twenty have already died. Two killed themselves, one died in an accidental fire of her own making, and one died probably of a lifetime of alcoholism. Sweet women, try to rest—or play—in peace.

At a recent memorial service for Sidney Abbott, Alix Kates Shulman walked over to me and said, sadly, wisely, "I guess we'll be seeing a lot more of each other at all the memorial services."

Ah, my Girls of Summer, our days of wine and roses, our political youth . . .

In 1990, the *New York Times Magazine* photographed five feminists for the cover to accompany a piece by Vivian Gornick titled "Who Says We Haven't Made a Revolution?" I joined Kate Millett, Alix Kates Shulman, Ann Snitow, and Ellen Willis for the photo shoot.

Vivian was not in the photo. I asked the photographer to take a picture of all of us including Vivian just for my personal collection, and I framed this shot. In this photo we are all aswirl in conversation; this photo captures our vivacity and conversational intensity. The photo that ran with the article has us posed looking front and center like Supreme Court justices—so not us. We are nonstop talkers. We gesture, laugh hysterically, and express ourselves like kids. At other times we converse with great gravity and self-importance.

And there we were, twenty-three years after our feminist beginnings, the downtown girls, on the cover of our hometown magazine, still standing, still at it. This I liked.

Much of what we take for granted today was not even whispered about fifty or sixty years ago. During the 1950s and 1960s clinicians were still being taught that women suffer from penis envy, are morally inferior to men, and are innately masochistic, dependent, passive, heterosexual, and monogamous. We also learned that only mothers—never fathers—caused neurosis and psychosis.

None of my professors ever said that women (or men) were oppressed or that oppression is traumatizing—especially when those who suffer are blamed for their own misery and diagnostically pathologized.

No one ever taught me how to administer a test for mental health—only for mental illness.

I still think of this as psychiatric imperialism.

In graduate school, during my clinical internship, and at the psychoanalytic institute where I trained in the late 1960s and early 1970s, I was taught that it was necessary to diagnostically pathologize a totally normal human response to trauma. For example, we were taught to view the normal female (and human) response to sexual violence, including incest, as a psychiatric illness. We were taught to blame the woman as seductive or sick. We learned to believe that women cried incest or rape to get sympathetic attention or revenge.

In my time we were taught to view women as somehow *naturally* mentally ill. Women were hysterics, malingerers, childlike, manipulative, either cold or smothering as mothers, and driven to excess by their hormones.

We assumed that men were mentally healthy. We were not taught to diagnostically pathologize or criminalize male drug addicts or alcoholics, men who battered, raped, or even murdered women or other men. We did not have diagnostic categories for male sexual predators or pedophiles. The psychiatric literature actually blamed the mothers, not the fathers, of such men for having sent them over the edge.

In other words, our so-called professional training merely repeated and falsely professionalized our previous cultural education. I knew that what I was being taught was not true. At this point I'd been attending feminist meetings almost nonstop for nearly three years, surrounded by other women who were equally passionate, confident, vocal, and educated.

In 1969 I cofounded the Association for Women in Psychology (AWP). In those days women founded new organizations every month—sometimes every day. Emboldened by feminism, we created our own organizations where we and our ideas would be welcome and where we could teach ourselves and each other what we needed to know. We hadn't learned it elsewhere.

I was secretly studying what women really wanted from psychotherapy. I planned to present my findings at the annual convention of the American Psychological Association (APA) in the fall of 1970. Mental health professions had never helped most women and had in fact further abused them by punitively labeling them, overtranquilizing them, sexually seducing them while they were in treatment, hospitalizing them involuntarily, administering shock therapy to them, lobotomizing them, and, above all, unnecessarily describing women as too aggressive, promiscuous, depressed, ugly, old, angry, or fat or as incurable.

I no longer remember exactly how many cofounders there were of the AWP—something like eight or ten—and we all attended the annual convention of the American Psychological Association. We decided that Dorothy Riddle and I would speak for us. I threw away my prepared speech, which was based on my research into whether patients wanted a male or female therapist.

I knew this was the moment, the absolutely right time, to expose the practitioners of mental illness as the unenlightened sexists that they were, not the liberators they imagined themselves to be. I was in something of an altered state when I demanded reparations for the mistreatment of female mental patients and, in so doing, positioned women's struggle for freedom in relation to the struggles of other oppressed groups.

Two thousand—mostly male—psychologists had gathered in Miami. Dorothy and I mounted the stage. The faces in the audience were dutifully attentive, a bit bored, perhaps uneasy. Our group was new, and they had no idea what we were about to say. I spoke first. I detailed the ways in which the mental health professions had psychiatrically stigmatized women, poorly serving them and totally misunderstanding them. I spoke without hesitation because I had been steeped in feminist and psychoanalytic ideas for many years. Maybe I'd been preparing for that moment all my life.

"Have you ever tested a woman for mental health and declared her mentally healthy?" I asked them. "Have you ever treated a rape victim, an incest victim, a battered wife with both understanding and respect?"

I then demanded $1 million—little enough—in reparations for the harm done to women and for the purpose of establishing an alternative to a psychiatric asylum. "Let's think of it as a halfway house for women on the run or as a station on a new kind of underground railway."

The crowd went crazy. At first, there were ripples of nervous laughter. Then Dr. Kenneth Clark, whose work had been central to the decision in *Brown v. Board of Education*, leaped up, screaming, "Whenever a black man has been lynched, a white woman was behind it."

I have no idea what my demand had to do with the horrors of racism. I think he was trying to say that white women were not oppressed because they belonged to the oppressor class, and how dare white oppressors claim victim status, thereby stealing attention away from the suffering of black men?

And then—most delicious of all—I began to hear psychologists muttering, "These women have penis envy."

I laughed and vowed never to return to the APA until or unless we got the reparations. All my feminist colleagues returned. Their papers were accepted; they formed new divisions; they did good work. I returned only once, to conduct a workshop with Dr. Lenore Walker (*The Battered Woman*) about mothers and custody battles. I respect Lenore's work enormously, and the opportunity to work with her was simply irresistible.

I started writing *Women and Madness* on the plane from Miami to New York. The next day I learned that my fiery little speech had made international headlines. My words were in South America, Europe, Australia, the Middle East, and all over the United States. My phone was ringing, publishers were calling. They wanted me to write a book.

That's how it was, back in the day, in the beginning—for some of us, for a blessed little while.

AWP never got a penny of reparations.

I benefited from the publicity. I had seven publishers bidding on my book, but I would have written it anyway. I would have handed it out for free on street corners.

Emboldened, empowered, I filled out all the necessary paperwork to offer a women's studies course for credit. I was a pioneer in doing so. At the last minute, the department chair turned me down. "Why not try again next semester?" he said. He seemed to be relishing my disappointment.

I had been meeting students to discuss feminist ideas for no credit. They became my staunch supporters. At my signal, five of these students joined me. I had filled out all the forms required to teach a new course. At the last minute, I had been told that there wasn't a budget to hire an adjunct to replace me for my Introductory Psychology course. And so we walked into the department head's office and locked him in with us. We sat down. We talked about how little it would cost the university to replace me—about $850 for one semester to teach one such course. Looking around, I said, "If we hock that new black leather chair and this desk, we can raise the money for a one-course adjunct."

We made it clear that we wouldn't leave without the department head's authorization to offer the course. And within the hour we had it.

Thinking back, I'm slightly ashamed of what I did. But at the time it was the kind of thing that students at Berkeley, Columbia, and the Sorbonne were doing. I hope that the chair wasn't really scared, though I think he must have been.

It was the season for that kind of thing.

At that moment in history, Women's Studies was like the Wild West. There was no set curriculum, no uniform standards, no easy way of encouraging female students to speak about certain subjects if male students were present. In fact, the women deferred to the men, and the men felt that the classroom discussion should privilege them. They were used to being called on first and often. The women were used to hiding in plain sight. I tried everything: asking the men to wait until enough women had had a chance to speak, but also asking the men to *consider* studying with me separately when we came to sensitive subjects such as sex. Likewise, I told the women that they would have to learn how to hold their own in integrated settings and that doing so in a classroom was a safe training ground.

Each Women's Studies professor drew upon her own strengths. Women's Studies was not yet part of the academy; teaching women's history and the history of feminist ideas (if we could find them), as well as writing by women, was viewed as radical and threatening. I went a step further and founded a childcare center for both staff and students, a rape crisis and gynecological referral service, and self-defense courses for women for gym credit.

This was long before Women's Studies morphed into Gender Studies, which in turn morphed into LGBTQI studies and became a postcolonial and postmodern enterprise. This was also many years before the Ivy League colleges allowed their professoriate to develop Women's Studies as a minor or a major.

I did not envision Women's Studies as a department. I feared it would become a ghetto, set apart from the other disciplines. What I envisioned was an integration of our developing curriculum into other departments.

My founding of this Women's Studies course led to a minor in the area and became the basis for the City University of New York to accredit other university-wide courses in Women's Studies.

At the same time, other professors were launching their own programs across the country, most often at state and junior colleges.

The year 1970 was something of a radical-feminist high point in New York City.

That was the year that women journalists at *Newsweek* brought a class action lawsuit against the magazine. One of my college mates was part of it, as was another woman with whom I would work in the future. On the very day that *Newsweek* published a cover story about the growing feminist movement, forty-six women on its staff held a press conference to announce they were suing *Newsweek* for gender discrimination. Bright, educated, ambitious women were not allowed to write stories or have bylines; they could work only as researchers, clippers, and mail sorters.

Feminists took over the underground left-wing newspaper *RAT Subterranean News*, turning it into *Women's LibeRATion*.

Feminists sat in at the *Ladies' Home Journal*, where they held the editor in chief, John Mack Carter, hostage for eleven hours. At least one hundred women, including my friend Barbara Joans, presented a mock-up of a "Women's Liberated Journal" and presented demands, including hiring a female editor in chief, hiring women of color, providing childcare on the premises, writing serious articles without male bias, and rejecting ads that denigrated women.

Grove Press employees tried to form a union and were fired for doing so. They then broke into the offices, barricaded themselves inside, and staged a sit-in to protest Grove's union busting and, while they were at it, Grove's sexual exploitation of women in their "erotic" and other sexually explicit books. Grove published Henry Miller, D.H. Lawrence, and Jean Genet, and their film division distributed *I Am Curious (Yellow)*. The protestors wanted the proceeds to benefit the women who had been harmed by such pornography. As long as they were there, the protestors also demanded that the black community profit from the writing of Malcolm X, who Grove Press also published.

The protesters, including Martha Shelley, Ti-Grace Atkinson, and Robin Morgan, were arrested and shunted from jail to jail so that their lawyers, Flo Kennedy and Emily Jane Goodman, could not find them. Some were strip-searched.

Friends of mine were present at each of these events, making me privy to conflicting and overlapping stories about feminists who threatened physical violence at the *Journal* sit-in and others who were traumatized by being strip-searched.

Back in the day, most women knew almost nothing about their bodies; few were educated about menstruation, sexual intercourse, sexual pleasure, birth control, sexually transmitted diseases, breast and uterine cancer, pregnancy, childbirth, breastfeeding, and menopause. When we complained of headaches, dizziness, and stomach pains, our physicians often gave us tranquilizers; they did not order neurological or gastrointestinal tests because they attributed most female suffering to "nerves."

Taking back our bodies—getting to know them—was both personally and politically thrilling. Feminists viewed their own cervixes for the first time; were trained to perform menstrual extractions and abortions; and began writing and talking about "our bodies, ourselves," which became the title of a 1973 book published by a Boston-based women's health collective.

Barbara Seaman, my darling friend and a women's health journalist, almost single-handedly started a feminist health movement. She warned women about the dangers of the Pill. Her 1969 book *The Doctor's Case Against the Pill* argued that the large amounts of estrogen then contained in birth control pills could cause heart attacks, strokes, cancer, and blood clots, among other dangers. Her book led to the 1970 Nelson Pill Hearings in the Senate, which in turn led to a warning label on the drug and the mandatory inclusion of patient information inserts in each package. She saved millions of women's lives. Drug companies punished her. The women's magazines she had been writing for fired and blacklisted her, since they relied upon pharmaceutical advertising.

In 1975, she founded the National Women's Health Network (I'm a cofounder). This organization is still going strong.

On the West Coast, a different awakening was brewing. The Daughters of Bilitis was the first lesbian civil and political rights organization in America. It was founded in 1955 in San Francisco and was conceived of as a way for lesbians to socialize away from the mafia-owned bars. Bilitis was the name attributed to one of the female lovers of the Greek poet Sappho. In early 1967, I attended a meeting of this organization but encountered an atmosphere that was not politically radical, feminist, or bohemian.

So I was pleased to see the arrival of the uppity and flaming "Lavender Menace," which made its debut in 1970. I was sitting at the Second Congress to Unite Women when suddenly we were plunged into darkness and silence. Then the lights came up and badass lesbians in lavender T-shirts that read LAVENDER MENACE streamed down the aisles, asking audience members to join them. They then led an impromptu speak-out on lesbianism. Some of these delightful, Yippie-like mischief makers would soon become my friends: Rita Mae Brown, Karla Jay, Barbara Love, and Martha Shelley.

The dykes wore lavender because Betty Friedan feared that NOW would lose middle America if her own worst nightmare came true, namely, that feminists were man-hating lesbians, that is, a lavender menace.

I must have been in the bathroom when the journalists Susan Brownmiller and Lucy Komisar were accused by conference attendees for using the movement to become famous. The killjoys at the congress believed that a central committee should assess all written work about the movement and that this work should never be signed.

Attacks on talented women would haunt our movement. Accomplished and eloquent women—those with high profiles, bylines, publishing contracts, really any skill at all—suffered attacks as traitors to the revolution. This happened to me and to Kate Millett and to Naomi Weisstein.

4   This First-Generation American Keynotes a Historic Speak-Out on Rape and Joins a Class-Action Lawsuit

In prefeminist times society always considered rape the woman's fault. The victim of sexual violence was viewed as having provoked it, "asked for it," wanted it, enjoyed it—and if a woman reported rape to the police, it meant that she was seeking revenge against a lover who had jilted her or against a married man who had refused to give her money to keep quiet.

Mental health professionals, family members, and law enforcement officers believed that rape was rare and usually committed by strangers. The concepts of employer rape, intimate-partner rape, neighbor rape, uncle rape, father rape, classmate rape, acquaintance rape, and marital rape were unknown. The police were routinely indifferent to rape victims, or else they questioned the women with prurient interest. Sometimes police sexually propositioned them.

The rape victim herself felt dirty, soiled, guilty. She blamed herself. Authorities rarely believed a woman who reported rape. Her own lawyer instinctively viewed her as impermissibly sexual, as if she were a prostituted woman. If a rape victim became depressed and could not shake the blues, she was invariably told to get over it.

If a victim of rape lodged a formal complaint that came to trial, she, not her accused rapist, was the one on trial. Prosecutors and defense attorneys routinely asked rape victims about their previous sex lives: whether they were virgins, had ever had an abortion, used birth control, sold sex for money, had previously had sex with the alleged rapist, were under psychiatric care, and on and on.

Jurors, especially female jurors, tended to feel sorry for the accused rapist, whose whole life could now be ruined. They did not automatically sympathize with his victim because, obviously, she was alive, was not facing a jail sentence, and did not seem to have been permanently damaged. Also, she was probably lying or exaggerating.

Women who'd been raped did not often talk about it, not to their families and not to other women.

You can imagine our excitement when a heroic group of feminists advertised the first-ever speak-out on rape in 1971.

It was held at St. Clement's, a gay- and woman-friendly Episcopal church in the theatre district. New York Radical Feminists organized this event, describing it as an "open act of rebellion."

For the first time in history, feminists were speaking out publicly and collectively about the sexual sadism for which women have been blamed, shamed, and silenced all over the world. By exposing and condemning this violence—which can result in our being murdered, impregnated, infected with disease, psychologically traumatized, and psychiatrically pathologized—we had taken the first step toward having rapists prosecuted and women treated with compassion, not voyeuristic disgust. The testimonies were sobering, shocking, and sadly similar. Come hear some of their voices:

One winter night, coming home [to a group home], six boy inmates surrounded me, holding knives. I was forced to have intercourse with all of them. The next day I found a boyfriend who became my protector. Once I got a boyfriend, I was never molested or raped again.

The police were white. I would be guilty in turning in another Third World person who had raped me. If I went to the police, they weren't going to do anything and the man would just come back and get me if I turned him in. I was [too] terrified to go anywhere on my own. I felt defenseless and afraid.

I was told to be quiet or I'd be buried here and no one would know. They told me that they do this regularly, usually with more guys. One attempted to rape me again. I played "passed out" and he gave up. I ran out. When I reported the rape, I was coherent and the police said, "You're so clear? How come you can tell us everything?" The police treated me like I was a criminal.

About five years ago, I awoke one night gagged, my hands pinned down by someone wearing leather gloves and holding a razor to my throat. I realized that I'd better hold still and let the man have intercourse with me. [The police] started coming about three in the morning, and they continually came out of curiosity, just to see what the victim looked like. I managed to find a doctor, who said I had to take all my clothes off in order to fill out a report, and this man tried to attack me. The last policeman that I saw came with photographs of men whom I could not identify, and asked me for a date.

Professor Lilia Melani, my good friend, and an organizer of the speak-out, remembered driving home in a rage.

New York Radical Feminists next convened a conference on rape at Washington Irving High School. The auditorium was packed, the excitement palpable. This single all-day event was more therapeutic than a year of the best private therapy.

A member of the keynote panel, Florence Rush, spoke about the sexual abuse of children. I spoke about the biased psychiatric view of women in terms of sexual violence and how psychotherapists abuse their female patients, both psychologically and sexually. We listened to a consciousness-raising group discussing rape in a workshop:

Helen: Would you report a rape?

Rita: Not really. If there's one conviction in a thousand, why go through all that torment?

Connie: My boyfriend is a policeman. He told me there's no such thing [as rape] and that a woman is asking for it subconsciously.

Pam: When I went to the hospital after being raped, a man was knocked out and brought into emergency at the same time. The nurses were very upset with me because I was hysterical and taking their attention away from this man.

Pam: I'm not ready to hate all men.

Marge: It's not that you hate all men, you can hate what they do to you.

Both Susan Brownmiller and Germaine Greer attended this conference. Four years later, in 1975, Brownmiller published *Against Our Will: Men, Women, and Rape*. Greer was already known for her book *The Female Eunuch*, which had been published in 1970.

Toward the end of the day we were treated to a women's martial arts demonstration. I told the *New York Daily News* reporter who interviewed me that we "must take the weapon away from the offender." Too late, I reconsidered my words. Men also rape with brooms and broken bottles; the weapon is located in the rapist's mind. I received my first-ever death threats after the story appeared.

This day transformed many lives. *Brava* New York Radical Feminists. *Brava!*

And tremendous kudos to Noreen Connell, who went on to become the New York State president of NOW and a longtime national NOW board member, and Cassandra Wilson, who coedited and published the proceedings of this conference in 1974, titling it *Rape: The First Sourcebook for Women*.

When did I first meet Gloria Steinem? That's lost in the mists of time. I was impressed by her 1964 exposé in *Show* magazine of a bunny's life at the Playboy Club. However, that excellent piece sparked no movement, nor did it free Gloria from what I perceived as the tyranny of having to maintain a perfected female appearance.

Gloria has a "little girl lost" appeal about her that gets people to want to help and take care of her. It affected me that way too. She would sometimes look up at me with a trusting, even slightly helpless look, and it worked like a charm. The effect is somewhat unnerving as well as flattering. Neither of us was a lesbian, although it was a subject we sometimes discussed. We were both told, over and over again, that lesbianism was either a more perfect form of feminism or a form of excessive man-hating.

The first time I was attracted to a woman (not that it led anywhere) I told Gloria about it immediately, as if it were some kind of breakthrough.

She sighed and asked, "Do you think it will ever happen to me?"

Gloria wasn't part of the downtown Manhattan feminist scene. Her activism was preceded by the revolutionary speak-outs on abortion and on rape; the consciousness-raising groups; the sit-ins, marches, and demonstrations; the founding of NOW; and the enormous proliferation of feminist articles, books, and ideas. Also by the publication of Betty Friedan's *The Feminine Mystique* and hundreds of amazing feminist articles and books, including Simone de Beauvoir's *The Sec-*

ond Sex, Kate Millett's *Sexual Politics*, Shulie Firestone's *The Dialectic of Sex*, Germaine Greer's *The Female Eunuch*, and Juliet Mitchell's *Woman's Estate*.

Gloria came to the party a bit late, but when she did she desperately wanted to be part of it.

Bella Abzug pulled Gloria into the National Women's Political Caucus. Bella was a civil rights lawyer and an antiwar-antinuclear activist in Women Strike for Peace. She didn't start out as a feminist, but she was a quick learner. The woman, the politician—the champion—in her saw an opening in women's fight for equal rights. In 1970 she won a seat in the U.S. House of Representatives.

Bella was teaching Gloria everything; she took Gloria everywhere, introduced her to everyone—a canny move because Gloria drew the cameras and the laughter. Bella was a heavyweight; Gloria was her arm candy. Bella bellowed; Gloria charmed.

Bella was a colorful New York character, a little bit Damon Runyon, a little bit Mollie Goldberg, maybe even a little bit Mae West. Bella had a pretty face, Jewish lungs, and New York chutzpah. Despite her bulk, she always cut a fashionable and colorful figure in her signature hats.

Gloria began speaking publicly, usually with African American women. Dorothy Pitman Hughes, Flo Kennedy, and Margaret Sloan-Hunter were among her speaking partners.

Gloria's partnering with African American women was a principled act, even if it was only a symbolic one, a way to minimize the fact the too few African American and minority women joined CR groups, marched, and made common cause with white women—at least, at that time. In my view, psychologically, I'm guessing that perhaps Gloria felt she wasn't as tough, savvy, or street-smart as African American women have to be to survive. I think that she felt she needed that kind of backup.

Gloria invited me to a meeting at Brenda Feigen's Tudor City apartment. Years later, Feigen wrote that she had been treated badly as a student at Harvard Law School in the mid-1960s, an experience that turned her into a "feminist by default." At Harvard at that time, sports facilities and eating clubs were off-limits to women. After she graduated, law firms refused to interview her because "they were not hiring women." Brenda went on to direct the Women's Rights Project of the American Civil Liberties Union with Ruth Bader Ginsburg and advised NOW about abortion rights and the Equal Rights Amendment. Brenda was also a founding member of the National Women's Political Caucus.

Brenda married a businessman, gave birth to a daughter, got divorced, took up with women, moved to Los Angeles, became an entertainment lawyer, and produced a movie (*Navy Seals*). In 2000 she published a good book, *Not One of the Boys: Living Life as a Feminist*.

The meeting at Brenda's home was about whether we should all found a new feminist magazine. The room was filled with the wives and daughters of wealthy and influential men; the women themselves were lawyers, writers, and editors at women's magazines. Clay Felker, the editor of *New York* magazine, was interested in helping, and in fact he published the pilot issue of *Ms.* magazine as an insert in *New York* at the end of 1971.

This was a time when feminists everywhere were founding groups, organizations, academic journals, economic networks and credit unions (which did not last), and a women's bank (which also did not last). *Ms.* was another such heady venture. I favored it. I did not foresee how successful the first issue would be; how hard Gloria would have to work to keep it afloat; how demanding the feminist writers would be; and how so many writers would feel mistreated (because their words were changed without permission and their fees were late). Most of all, I did not foresee how Gloria's very being would become consumed by the magazine, which increasingly became her baby, her identity, and her brand.

At the time I thought, *Yes!* But I also thought, *What they're after is a front-page* New York Times *photo featuring a long line of women, civil rights style, all holding hands. At the far left is a smiling Angela Davis. At the other end of this unlikely Rockettes line is Happy Rockefeller. The point: sisterhood trumps class, race, and ideology. Sounds great, but is it possible?*

The journalist Jill Johnston was a lesbian Pied Piper. Dykes followed her everywhere. She was also something of a Kerouac figure, always on the road: now she's here, now she's gone.

Jill and I talked about Greek myths and psychoanalytic thinking. We were not attracted to each other sexually; at least, I wasn't attracted to her. But I was attracted to her mind. In later years we gossiped up a storm about editors and book advances and the foibles of other writers.

Jill had come out in the pages of the *Village Voice* ("Lois Lane Is a Lesbian"). She kept asking me, the straight girl, why she had felt compelled to do so. She also confided in me.

"Don't you think the Jews are taking over our movement?" she asked me.

"Why do you say that?" Answering her question with one of my own was a typically Jewish response.

"There are so many loud and pushy Jewish feminists in New York City."

"Do you have any idea what you're saying?"

Jill insisted she was not anti-Semitic. "My very best friend, Shainde, is Jewish," she explained.

"You're digging a deeper hole for yourself, my friend," I replied.

I took her comments as racist and anti-Semitic. I resolved to visit Israel for the first time.

Jill decided to atone for this conversation by giving a party and inviting some glamorous guests to her place in New Paltz, New York. She was nervous about the party, so she got drunk and couldn't drive. She also couldn't buy party food, so I did it for her on my way down.

When I got there Jill said: "Phyllis, I want you to meet Martha Shelley, a Jewish lesbian. I invited her just for you."

Martha was a poet and also a member of Radical Lesbians and the Gay Liberation Front. She had participated in the feminist takeover of *RAT Subterranean News*, the Grove Press sit-in, and the Lavender Menace action. Martha was lesbian feminist royalty. At Jill's party, Martha and I stood in a corner and talked revolutionary politics for an hour. Every so often we looked over at the other women, noted that they were getting drunk and not talking feminism, and laughed.

"Are we the only two Jews here? Is that it? The non-Jews get drunk and get into bed with each other, and the Jews analyze and organize?"

No; Susan Sontag was there too.

Susan was known as the Dark Lady of Letters and often was the only woman whose name was listed among the otherwise all-male Manhattan glitterati. Susan sported a sophisticated streak of white hair atop her long black mane. In 1964, *Partisan Review* published her "Notes on 'Camp'." Years later, the coeditor of the magazine, Edith Kurzweil, told me that the piece had had to be heavily edited and that no one had expected it to become a literary sensation.

When Susan and I first met I was shocked that she knew so little about feminism, given her reputation. I may have been the only person who didn't treat her as formidable. I told her, "You know, I read your book *Against Interpretation*. I loved it. And now here you are, not looking that much older than me, and you're so naive." She responded immediately by saying, "Listen, why don't we get together and, you know, just talk or go to a movie or play records or whatever you'd like."

It took me a year to take her up on her invitation.

Once, Susan was speaking on a panel about female power. She asked me whether I thought that Margaret Thatcher could represent positive power for women. I told her that, psychologically speaking, even when a nonfeminist woman becomes a prime minister, her achievement may exert an unconscious, positive influence in terms of women feeling empowered and men's understanding that woman can be powerful. Susan said that she'd have to think about that.

She introduced me to her lover, María Irene Fornés, a Cuban-born playwright. In 1977, I attended one of María's plays, *Fefu and Her Friends*, which required the audience to move from one small stage to another while the actors repeated the same act three times. Who could ever forget that? It was enchanting.

Years later, Susan and I met by accident at a screening of Carl Dreyer's 1928 masterpiece *The Passion of Joan of Arc*. We stopped, smiled, and acknowledged each other's presence. Susan said, "Of course, *you'd* be here."

"Well," I responded, "you're here too."

Maybe she was there as a filmmaker or as a film critic, but maybe, like me, she was also riveted by a warrior in female form, a woman in drag, a doomed visionary betrayed by the king she saved.

I was already fielding a lot of invitations to speak. In the early 1970s I was invited to address a meeting of psychiatrists in Washington, D.C. I'd rapidly become known as *the* expert on gender bias in mental health and on the mistreatment of female psychiatric and psycho-therapeutic patients.

At one lecture I discussed psychotherapists who misdiagnosed women and who abused them sexually. (This subject was hotly denied until it was finally acknowledged, and many researchers began studying it.)

At the time, women were psychiatrically incarcerated against their will and could not leave until their doctors discharged them. Thus I also spoke about what women had to do to "earn" discharges from state asylums.

They had to start taking care of their appearance, thanking the staff, and generally behaving in an obedient, girlish way. Sometimes they had to work as unpaid servants for their psychiatrists. I'd been interviewing institutionalized women who told me that they had been expected to vacuum, dust, and do laundry for their doctors, who had cottages on the grounds of the psychiatric hospital. They told me that doing so proved that they were "adjusting properly" and might be eligible for what they called "parole."

Afterward, a woman who was not a psychiatrist came up to me and whispered: "What you're saying is true. My husband is a psychiatrist, and we've always had inmate-servants." I asked her name and why she was whispering. She told me that her name was Barbara Seaman and that she was an author and feminist health activist. From that moment until the day she died in 2008 we remained fast friends. We began to socialize and work together.

Barbara grew up with, was related to, and partied with A-listers in Manhattan: literary agents, politicians, journalists, authors, filmmakers, editors, painters, musicians, philanthropists, film stars—all manner of celebrities. She turned out to be the most generous and least envious feminist I knew. Attending one of her soirees made me feel very "in" and gave me the illusion of having access to some of the masters and mistresses of the immediate universe.

I was a bridge between women like Barbara and the downtown dykes and radical-feminist activists, as well as to other women in the professions. Barbara was leery of all professionals, and she was my bridge to feminist health activists, who also mistrusted professionals—especially doctors—including women with doctoral degrees like me.

The National Women's Health Network (NWHN) was Barbara's idea. It was her baby, and she dragged me right into it. Together with Belita Cowan, Dr. Mary Howell, and Alice Wolfson, we founded this organization in 1975, and it continues more than forty years later. The NWHN reflected Barbara's passion about women's health, both reproductive and otherwise, and the dangerous nature of unrestricted, profit-driven drug companies that advertise drugs like the birth control pill, which can increase a woman's chance of getting cancer. The Network views health as a human right and develops and promotes a critical analysis of health issues for both consumers and policy makers.

Barbara always said that the women's health movement was the "healthiest" part of the feminist movement. This was her mantra and she clung to it.

Most American feminists believe that women's rights are universal; however, most feminists have never lived in a non-Western, tribal, or Muslim culture—and I have.

Therefore I was outraged when I read that Pakistani Muslim soldiers and fundamentalist paramilitary gangs were gang-raping the Muslim women of what in 1971 became Bangladesh. They were engaging in what I had come to call "gender cleansing" because such public and repeated gang rapes were meant to drive the women to suicide or to their being honor-killed by their families. It was becoming clear that thousands of girls and women were meeting this fate.

Soon, I was sharing my thoughts with other feminist leaders. "Their families will kill them or they'll kill themselves," I said. "If they're pregnant, they're as good as dead."

"What can we do to help?"

"We would have to rescue them militarily—do we have a feminist air force?—and then apply for political asylum on their behalf. Assuming they would want to come."

Silence and some nervous laughter ensued.

"You're speaking metaphorically, aren't you?" one woman asked.

"No, I'm speaking realistically, practically."

In the mid-1990s I was at a Feminist Majority conference in Washington, D.C., representing the feminist magazine *On the Issues Magazine* and said something similar about Afghan women to a behind-closed-doors meeting of feminist leaders.

"If we don't rescue each endangered woman, one by one, physically, militarily, and then sponsor each woman, one by one, for political asylum and citizenship, they will die, one by one."

This time, I was met with a frustrated silence.

Because I was a feminist who'd made international headlines and was working on a book under contract to a major publishing house, I was accepted for a fellowship at the MacDowell Colony in Peterborough, New Hampshire.

I was there for two summers in a row, working first on *Women and Madness* and then on an essay about Amazons for a book on Wonder Woman comics with Gloria Steinem. My essay was based on Greek myths, plays, art, and history. Scholars have documented the historical existence of Amazons, but I think this has been overshadowed by the psychological effect on the human imagination of the vision of armed female warriors.

I had a wonderful time at the colony. Each artist had her or his own cottage deep in the woods. Someone silently left lunch in a picnic basket on the porch. The place had no phones, there were no spontaneous visitors—absolutely no excuse for not getting the work done. Some artists couldn't bear it; suddenly they were gone. Me? I loved the silence. Everyone met at night for dinner in the dining room at tables that seated two, four, or six people.

The poet Bill Knott was an eccentric loner. He had already written *The Naomi Poems*, which he'd published under the pseudonym Saint Geraud. He usually sat alone at dinner. Sometimes I did too. It allowed me to read and spared me from having to make small talk.

One evening Bill defended my feminist honor. Someone told him: "Look, Phyllis thinks she's Bill Knott." Bill yelled: "That's an outrageous sexist comment. Phyllis is doing this in her own right. She's not copying me."

I was moved and, as a gallant gesture, invited him to join me at my table at any time and promised not to engage in conversation.

The playwright Romulus Linney (Laura Linney's father) kept chasing after me. Leonard Bernstein cut a dashing figure with his white scarf thrown back diva style and his all-male entourage.

I befriended some of the women, including the novelist Alice Denham and the artist Eunice Golden, who painted male nudes as a feminist statement. I sometimes accompanied the landscape painter Marjorie Portnow on one of her long afternoons when she carefully, almost magically, transferred a magnificent field onto canvas, memorializing the time and place forever.

I climbed Mount Monadnock and Pack Monadnock Mountain about twice a week. I loved my Fabiano hiking boots.

The blessed summer drew to a close and it was back to teaching. Some of my closest feminist students and the left-wing, gay, and feminist faculty to whom I was close—as well as some antifeminist faculty men—ganged up on me because of the book I was writing, *Women and Madness*.

"Phyllis, if you mean what you say, you'll publish this book of yours anonymously," one of them informed me. Refusing to do so would mean that I was a counterrevolutionary egotist and not serious about sacrificing myself for the revolution. Their concept of revolution meant destroying ego and identity and smashing everything and everyone to create a new and perfect utopia in which everyone was equal and exactly the same.

One professor asked, "Phyllis, you *are* going to donate all your earnings to the larger revolution, aren't you?" Another: "Do you honestly mean to publish your book under your own name? Won't that be counterrevolutionary?"

I was confronted by one of my students, Alice, who would go on to work with another of the students at my college, Susie Orbach, who, in 1978, would publish *Fat Is a Feminist Issue* and who became Princess Diana's eating disorder therapist. Alice was in a rage. "You're using your own name? That goes against everything you've ever taught us. I loved you, but now you've betrayed me, and I'll never be able to trust you again if you take all the credit for your book." She seemed genuinely in anguish. Another student, Claudia, was my research assistant on my book and was being paid for her work. I acknowledged her contribution in the book.

I had learned early on that no one—neither the misogynists nor the allegedly revolutionary feminists—wanted women to be known for accomplishing something. For different reasons both groups wanted women—or at least women of ideas—to be obliterated. This odd yearning for a time when anonymous was a woman was bizarre, but I was grateful that it happened; it allowed me to see the extent to which the Chinese Cultural Revolution had infiltrated feminist America.

The radicals believed I had deserted the barricades; the establishment believed I was too much of a political activist.

Nearly fifty years later, what was once painful and enraging now seems pathetic and slightly funny.

I've been reading since I was two-and-a-half years old. I began writing when I was eight. I won a citywide high school poetry contest when I was sixteen. I was the editor of both my high school yearbook and the literary magazine. I assumed that a university represented integrity and a devotion to the highest standards of scholarship. I did not imagine that I would ever be mistreated—*targeted* might be a more accurate word—in the fabled groves of academe. I had no idea that being a woman would be an impediment to my career.

I didn't know it but, like every other female professor at the City University of New York (CUNY), I was being grossly underpaid compared with our male colleagues. In 1973, the labor lawyer Judith Vladeck filed a class action suit on our behalf. A decade later, the judge ruled in our favor. At some point Judy wanted to open a separate cause of action just for me on the basis of the discrimination because of my political beliefs, that is, feminism. I chose not to do this.

As I noted previously, when I started out, the university despised and feared feminism. A formerly all-male and rather patriarchal faculty opposed feminist ideas. I researched women, not men. I helped my department hire more women than men—and all the new hires were feminists.

And I had created international headlines by demanding reparations for women psychiatric and psychotherapeutic patients. My male colleagues probably hated me. And they punished me in every way possible.

Every year—every year!—the male faculty in my department found students to accuse me of high crimes and misdemeanors. I faced a witch hunt every damn year. One year, two students were prompted to write a letter that accused me of being "obsessed with Women's Liberation" (true enough), not preparing lectures, not attending classes, always arriving late, hating men, and using vulgar language (not true at all).

For each witch hunt I had to organize a petition on my behalf that many of my students signed, along with every major feminist I knew. It was nerve-wracking and tedious work.

But I had to respond. The administrator in charge of the witch hunt that year was a man; two other feminists, a professor and a dean, told me that they had witnessed him being so verbally abusive to his girlfriend that they both left the gathering. He was my interrogator.

He was temporarily living with one of my colleagues, George Fischer, a professor of social science, who once wanted to sleep with me and got quite angry when I refused to do so. He had taken part in the student uprising at Columbia in 1968; George was a Jewish man who had already run through two WASP wives—with rapiers, I'm sure. I called George and asked for his help.

I told George that he *knew* I didn't use vulgar language or discriminate against my male students. I simply did not privilege male students by always calling on them first or allowing them to interrupt a female student, and the male students may have experienced this as unfair or even abusive. I asked him whether my refusing to sleep with him meant that he would not have my back.

He said in a rather indifferent tone: "Take it any way you'd like. We're all imperfect."

I then reminded George that I knew which male professors were sleeping with their female students and I might ask these students to write to the administration to demand an investigation.

That threat worked. He agreed to help me and the latest volley of charges disappeared.

I did not want to quit my job. I wanted to become tenured. I wanted a steady job and a steady income. Unlike so many feminist activists, I did not think I could live abstractly on feminist ideals, nor did I think I'd want to travel constantly to deliver paid lectures. When it came to work, I did not relish one-night stands, which is how I saw the paid lecture business.

Yet like so many women, I was forced to fight hard first to obtain and then to keep tenure—and this at a time when academic jobs were plentiful. Faculty and administration perpetually challenged my job security. I had to fight for each and every salary increase. I tried but failed to obtain CUNY grant money for my research projects.

This was how most female faculty were treated. My lectures at other universities and at professional conferences, as well as my early appearances on television and radio, were used against me: "How can you do all that and still teach?"

But I could and I did. I also loved my students, and they loved me. That, too, was problematic. "You're too close to your students—it can't be good for them." This from professors who taught by reading aloud from textbooks for the entire class, who seduced and abandoned their female students, who made no substantive contribution to their disciplines.

Many years later, the chair of a nonacademic department helped block my tenure and promotion yet again. Looking puzzled, he stated: "But she only researches women. What the hell is that?"

I was also never allowed to teach at the CUNY Graduate Center.

I never became a Distinguished Professor, which meant that my salary and pension remained relatively paltry. Far more important, I was never allowed to serve on dissertation committees or have access to the most ambitious students.

I really loved my students, especially the older women who were returning to college, the immigrant and minority students, and the young Catholic students from Staten Island who were so receptive to my teaching. The secretaries were friendly, and I developed wonderful relationships with the students who assisted me in my research, whether for credit, money, or the sheer love of ideas.

One of my students had an affair with one of my male colleagues. She became pregnant and nearly died of an ectopic pregnancy. She had no one to turn to and I took pity on her, so I visited her in the hospital and invited her to stay with me afterward. I took care of her.

One day she was up and about, cheery, bustling about in the kitchen. She was cooking dinner for the impregnator–abuser of power. She explained: "He's afraid of hospitals—his mother died in one. That's why he never visited me there. I'm so excited that he's coming tonight."

I was stunned, furious, heartbroken. I was also saddened that such a person could win the foolish heart of this young woman. She was happy to cook for the man who got her in trouble and then deserted her, but she hadn't a clue about how to express her appreciation to the female mentor who took her in. Perhaps a bouquet of flowers would have gone a long way to express thanks to me. This behavior is like taking for granted whatever our mothers do for us, day in, day out, without ever feeling we have to thank them. (I'm a great sinner in this regard.)

I decided that the battle against patriarchy was too hard: women were just as afflicted by sexist double standards as men were. I suggested she move in with him.

My student was not coerced. She treasured this affair with her professor that I viewed as abusive.

Men routinely used their power to elicit sexual favors. Women were trained to accept this as the way things were and had always been. It was something you were not supposed to talk about. Women had to keep their shame and self-blame to themselves. Most of us had no choice. Whistle-blowers were fired and their careers were usually ruined. Sometimes their lives were ruined.

One woman I interviewed exposed her boss for providing girls, booze, and pot for the political party regulars. Her job was to recruit the girls and manipulate report findings. She went to her immediate superior in tears. When a reporter discovered these facts and exposed them, not only did this brave woman lose her job, but her former boss took revenge and arranged for her to lose custody of her children.

I was not yet famous, but I was increasingly known in certain circles. I was receiving invitations to more events than I could attend. Sometimes, I made a mistake and chose to attend the wrong party.

One such example involved Margaret Sloan-Hunter, who founded the National Black Feminist Organization. Flo Kennedy had recommended her as Gloria's speaking partner. Margaret traveled out to Staten Island several times to audit my classes and gushed about my lectures.

So when she invited me to a party, I had no cause for alarm.

I brought some friends with me to the Upper West Side: the feminist lawyer and future judge Emily Jane Goodman, and Martha

Shelley and her lover. Shortly after we arrived, women were talking, talking, and then—suddenly, a white woman jumped out of the crowd, stripped naked, took out a large vibrator, placed a towel over her vulva, and began masturbating.

Conversation stopped. Margaret watched, caressed, and cooed over the exhibitionist's breasts. Emily was shell-shocked. I was embarrassed, so I said, "This might be a significant political statement. Women like her once jumped out of cakes for men. Now, here she is, trying to turn on women."

Talk about the tyranny of the orgasm. No one dared leave until the exhibitionist had had one.

No one seemed particularly turned on. I was grossed out and left as soon as I could.

In 1971 and 1972, I was living alone in Lomontville, New York, on my winter and spring breaks and working on the final chapters of *Women and Madness*. Jill Johnston often stopped by. She sometimes called first and asked to sleep over, telling me that she was Joan of Arc and the king's men were coming to get her so she had to hide. I thought this affectation was charming and I always said yes—but I also locked my bedroom door.

I was hopelessly straight—well, maybe not hopelessly, since, like so many straight women, I was persuaded that the most revolutionary feminists were lesbians. If only this were true! (It's not.)

I thought of Jill, with her long, lean dancer's legs, as Gentleman Jill; she was a bit of a British beanpole and, as she'd learn, the illegitimate daughter of a British man who, if not royal, was close to royalty. So it was "Down with patriarchy" but also "I want Daddy to acknowledge me."

I had no idea that Jill had been married and had two children she had stashed with a gay male collective. I didn't yet know that, as she put it, she sometimes "stepped out." By that she meant she had to go to a loony bin because she had stepped out of her mind.

Jill wrote weekly columns about her coterie; she once described how it felt to dance with me. Apparently, I was squishy. I didn't know whether to be embarrassed or pleased.

Jill was so good at being helpless that she turned all her friends and allies into her unpaid staff. She asked everyone to make calls for her, get her out of trouble, and give her urgently needed advice about lovers, publishers, editors, movement heavies, movie and restaurant choices, and anything else she could think of.

Soon enough I introduced her to someone and they became a pair. This was an act of self-defense on my part. But in general I was quite the movement matchmaker and made many long-lasting pairings.

5 A Psychiatrist Sues Me for $10 Million, I Publish *Women and Madness*, and I Flee the Country

Winter break.

I was in Antigua: wind-swept beaches, emerald-green low-lying mountains, Nelson's Dockyard, carefree tourists—and the most grueling, hopeless poverty imaginable.

Hotel meals were served outdoors, where we dined on the freshest fruit, the sweetest pastries, the darkest coffee. I was the sugar momma, paying for Nick, my young lover from New Hampshire. We were celebrating: I had almost finished *Women and Madness* and was taking a brief holiday. We swam, we sunned, we danced, we made love, we toured the island.

Trouble soon found me. A young British lad, high on LSD, had tried to attack his girlfriend with a harpoon gun on the beach. Somehow this girlfriend, wet and weeping, appeared at my door; perhaps someone had told her that I was a psychologist.

"Please don't let them take Chris. He's a good boy. The drugs just overcame him. I don't want to press charges. The police are hunting for him."

I threw a dress on over my bikini and made for the British Consulate.

"Sir," I said to the consul, "this island is known for restraining psychiatric patients, overmedicating them, and administering shock therapy—lots of it."

These practices were all European inspired, but mental illness was heavily stigmatized on Antigua. The first department of psychiatry at the medical school in Antigua had opened only five or six years earlier.

"Once they get hold of this boy, they'll shock the hell out of him, and he'll never be the same. Can you help?"

The British consul refused to get involved.

The girlfriend, frightened, brought Chris to me. He was completely out of it: didn't know where he was or what he had done. I gave him every conceivable tranquilizer I could lay my hands on and hid him in the shower stall in my hotel room.

Given what I knew about institutional psychiatry and shock therapy—people often lose both their short- and long-term memories—I had a choice: to act on what I knew or look the other way. In my view, if you have an opportunity to save one soul, why not take it, consequences be damned?

Soon the police arrived to ask me if I had seen Chris. Wide-eyed, I denied it.

And then I went to the airport and found a British pilot to whom I pleaded Chris's case. The pilot agreed to take him if I accompanied him to Heathrow.

"I cannot do that, but his girlfriend will. I've called his mother in London, who'll be waiting with an ambulance at the airport," I told the pilot. "He's completely sedated. I doubt he'll even be able to leave his seat."

Nick was angry that I had spent so much time on what he called "your work." He was my own petulant *Chéri*.

Gloria and I were both being interviewed everywhere. We often met on a television or radio program. In 1972 she invited me to appear with her on *The David Frost Show*. She had asked others to join her as well: Jeannette Rankin, the first woman elected to Congress and therefore the only woman who was able to vote for women's suffrage; Eleanor Holmes Norton, then the head of the New York City

Human Rights Commission; the British feminist Juliet Mitchell, author of *Woman's Estate*; Jane O'Reilly, a journalist at *Ms.*; and the singer Judy Collins.

Gloria was most comfortable with a pleasant but zany mix of people. She was very nervous about speaking. I am among the blessed who do not suffer from stage fright.

The Montana-born Rankin owned a farm in Athens, Georgia. She was so moved by my feminist critique of the psychiatric profession that she offered me her Athens property to use as a place for an alternative to a psychiatric hospital for women.

"That's so generous of you," I said. "Thank you so much. But I'm not really an administrator or a fund raiser, which such an undertaking requires."

I had chosen to work with Betty Prashker, who was Kate Millett's editor at Doubleday.

After Kate read *Women and Madness*, she immediately endorsed it, which made me very happy. This was new—women being able to blurb each other's books in a way that impressed publishers. I called Kate to thank her. We made plans to get together.

I visited Kate at her farm near Poughkeepsie, New York. She viewed the land she had bought in a nineteenth-century kind of way, as the only thing that one can count on. Kate planned to grow Christmas trees and sell them to pay the taxes and for renovations. The property had three big buildings that needed upgrading and perpetual care. Kate also envisioned the place as a summer retreat for women artists, who would work on the farm half the day (mowing, planting, building) and on their own work the rest of the time.

Kate and I had a wonderful evening. She grilled thick steaks and opened bottle after bottle of wine, and we laughed about "our movement." It was a bit like being in a college dormitory or like having a sister, something I knew nothing about.

We were up quite late. Kate said: "They may think they've seen everything, but wait until they see you. You're something else."

Our dear friend Linda Clarke tells me that Kate told her: "Phyllis is going straight to the top."

How much pleasure I took in being able to pledge the sorority of our first feminist icon. Icons are mesmerizing. Kate was there first, right on the cover of *Time* magazine. Kate had died for our sins, so to speak. Kate knew how to boss women around, but all the bullying she'd done could not compare with how prominent antifeminists mocked her and how lesbian feminists had bullied her into coming out as bisexual and/or as a lesbian. Kate also suffered resentment, envy, even hatred because she was famous. She wrote about this in her next book, *Flying*.

A year later, our editor, Betty, followed me into the bathroom and urged me to persuade Kate to remove "all the lesbian material" from *Flying*, because with it the book was not going to fly at Doubleday. I told her I couldn't do that. Betty probably feared that the lesbian content would doom the book. How could she have known that a gay and lesbian movement would soon become a major and visible force fighting for equality?

Perhaps Betty also did not like the self-indulgent and demanding voice of the book, which I found Joycean and was the very thing that I admired about it.

In 1973, my friend Erica Jong's comic novel *Fear of Flying* was published. It garnered John Updike's effusive praise and began its path to best-sellerdom. Kate lost Doubleday and moved to Bob Gottlieb at Knopf, where the book was published in 1974 and bombed. I love both books.

Before the 1970s, most women who worked in publishing were secretaries and editorial assistants, were grossly underpaid, and watched as young man after young man was promoted to editor. Reviews of women's books were not as frequent or as positive as reviews of books by men; more men reviewed books in mainstream and intellectual media than women did. Eventually feminists protested this and made some headway, but all too soon editors began to tap feminists who were at loggerheads ideologically to review each other's works, which they were only too happy to do.

In the 1960s, women did not write feminist books. Women wrote some best sellers, but mainly they were cookbooks or about sex, not liberation. Helen Gurley Brown's *Sex and the Single Girl* (1962) and William Masters and Virginia Johnson's *Human Sexual Response* (1966) were sensations. Betty Friedan's landmark book *The Feminine Mystique* (1963) was not an immediate best seller.

However, from 1970 to 1975, "dancing dog" feminists (the phrase is Cynthia Ozick's) turned out book after book. We were sought after, written up, interviewed, and could do no wrong. Suddenly our work was celebrated, and publishers or other writers gave us book parties.

At a book party for Alix Kates Shulman's 1972 novel *Memoirs of an Ex-Prom Queen*, Vivian Gornick rushed up to me, breathless and panicked.

"What does she want from me?" Vivian pleaded. "What am I supposed to do?"

"She" was the lesbian activist Rita Mae Brown.

Rita Mae casually strolled by and said: "Just look at her beautiful green cat eyes. I can't stop looking at them."

She was completely and defiantly oblivious to the panic she was causing.

Rita Mae, a daughter of poverty, went on to publish *Rubyfruit Jungle*, live briefly with the tennis star Martina Navratilova, settle down, fox-hunt in the southern countryside, and write best-selling detective novels with her cat, Sneaky Pie Brown.

I organized a CR group for Gloria so she could finally have the experience, but it didn't work. We had some meetings in my apartment and in hers. But she had invited celebrity friends (Marlo Thomas and Judy Collins), who could not make long commitments. Both, by the way, were smart, warm, and open to the most radical feminist ideas. Marlo had embarked upon a first-of-its-kind venture. Together with the Ms. Foundation, she created and produced a book and record album that featured nonsexist stories and songs for children sung or told by celebrities, including Alan Alda, Cicely Tyson, Carol Channing, Michael Jackson, and Diana Ross. Their goal was to teach children not to feel limited by gender stereotypes. The football hero Rosy Grier sang "It's All Right to Cry"; *Free to Be You and Me* encouraged boys to play with dolls if they wanted to. The album also became an award-winning television special and remains in circulation.

Jill Johnston attended this CR group once; she cried and made a scene—she actually threw potato chips at us—then left and refused to return. Jill could not bear it when she was not the center of attention.

Gloria also invited women from *Ms.* They were essentially her employees and groupies. These women wouldn't tell Gloria the truth. They kissed up to her and lied. And Gloria would not risk yelling at any of them. Imagine the consequences!

As a result, Gloria never had the CR experience she said she craved—one that would teach her how to express her anger directly—which was something she kept telling me she needed to learn.

Ms. magazine excerpted two chapters from *Women and Madness*. In June 1972 *New York* magazine published a cover story about sex between patients and their therapists that excerpted my chapter on this subject in *Women and Madness*. The headline was "The Sensuous Psychiatrists" and the subtitle was "Lie Down and Tell Me Where It Hurts." The cover showed an older man and a young female patient embracing on the psychoanalytic couch. I did not like this but had no control over how this was presented.

I may have been the first to expose such relationships from a feminist perspective. Feminists cheered me on, and many "therapeutically raped" female patients began writing and calling to thank me. Some wanted me to testify on their behalf and others wanted me to be their therapist.

Initially I was savaged by antifeminist shrinks who claimed that such women were lying, exaggerating, or crazy, or that all these patients had seduced their therapists and when their therapists would not marry them they cried foul.

This was precisely what clinicians once said when their patients tried to talk about having been sexually abused in childhood.

Within ten to fifteen years after I published *Women and Madness*, male therapists' taking unethical sexual advantage of female patients became a cottage industry. Distinguished researchers such as Dr. Judith Herman, Dr. Kenneth Pope, Dr. Nanette Gartrell, and Dr. Annette Brodsky confirmed my findings and studied the matter further.

I view sex between patient and therapist (or, rather, the sexual violation of vulnerable patients) as an incest-like abuse of male power. At the time I had no idea that this specific abuse of power has a long and sordid history, that many "great men" once indulged themselves to their patients' detriment, and that one great man covered for another. Carl Jung, Otto Gross, Wilhelm Stekel, and Otto Rank were all guilty of this crime.

A psychiatrist sued me and *New York* for $10 million because of a missing middle initial. Here's the story.

In 1966, the psychiatrist James *L.* McCartney published an article titled "Overt Transference" in *The Journal of Sex Research*. McCartney described sexual intercourse with his patients as overt transference. He claimed to have enjoyed hundreds of such overt transferences with female patients. He was ousted from the American Psychiatric Association.

But it was not the elder McCartney who sued me. McCartney had a son of the same name but with a different middle initial. This son was also a psychiatrist and had broken with his father over this issue. The son believed that the excerpt in *New York* endangered him because he might be mistaken for his father and his patients and colleagues might think that he practiced "overt transference." In the editorial process, the father's middle initial had somehow been dropped, and this was the basis for the son's lawsuit.

If we lost, would he take my books and records? I had no other property. I wanted to call up the son, take him to lunch, work it out. *New York* magazine's well-tailored Suits told me, "You can't have anything to do with him."

They would be representing both me and the magazine. I had no choice but to follow their advice.

The lawyers took depositions, time passed, and by 1975 a trial was at hand. It suddenly occurred to me that the last thing this son-psychiatrist would want was more painful publicity. I asked some journalist friends to start calling him to say they'd be covering the trial and hoped to interview him. The move was both canny and compassionate.

The day before the trial was supposed to begin, the plaintiff settled for one dollar.

As I mentioned earlier, I worked with Gloria Steinem on a compilation of Wonder Woman comic strips from the 1940s for a volume to be published by Holt, Rinehart & Winston. The editor Marion Wood had approached Gloria after *Ms.* featured Wonder Woman on the cover of its first stand-alone issue. In turn, Gloria approached me. She knew that I'd written about Amazons in *Women and Madness*. I agreed to help choose the strips and to assist Gloria with an introduction. I would also write an interpretive essay with a bibliography.

Amazons—a quintessential patriarchal nightmare—are a young

feminist's dream fantasy. In the late 1960s, these women warriors, champion horse trainers and riders, actually came to me in a dream, after which I ran to the library and found a wonderful book about them written in 1930 by Helen Diner under the pseudonym Sir Galahad. She titled her book *Mothers and Amazons: The First Feminine History of Culture*.

I believe that knowing about Amazons, as both historical and mythological figures, strengthens women psychologically. Wonder Woman's creator, William Moulton Marston, seems to have been a "free love" polygamist who nevertheless saw that women lacked role models. In 1943, when I was three years old, Marston wrote: "Not even girls want to be girls so long as our feminine archetype lacks force, strength, and power."

Wonder Woman debuted in the early 1940s. I remember avidly reading these strips in the late 1940s. As a child, I didn't notice that Wonder Woman was white, nor did I realize that she was involved in a great many bondage scenes.

Gloria and I posed wearing Greek-style helmets, but we never used the photos. Perhaps we didn't think we looked credible as Amazon warriors in Greek headgear, or perhaps the photos were not flattering.

Years later, the History Channel interviewed me about Amazons. I was disappointed when the program aired. Its Amazons were clunky, their fighting skills amateur. I'm such a romantic.

I probably would have written my first book no matter what century I'd lived in. That I did so as second wave feminism was gathering power nationally ensured that the book had an audience, one that instantly embraced its ideas.

Why this subject and not another one? Did I have mentally ill relatives? Of course—who doesn't? But most people don't get up one day and write *Women and Madness* in order to understand their relatives.

I'm not exactly sure what I did the summer before *Women and Madness* arrived in bookstores. I believe I was at the MacDowell Colony for a few weeks, completing my interpretive essay about the psychohistory of Amazon warriors.

I do remember renting a house in Lomontville, New York, not far from the Ashokan Dam, later that same summer. I loved living alone. It was a sacred time. I finished the introduction to *Women and Madness* there and I clearly remember stepping out late one night, looking at the moon, and knowing that I might change the world—and my own world too.

October 1, 1972. Publication day. My editor Betty sent me a red leather-bound copy of my book. I have it still. (I've always wanted to bind one copy of each of my books in leather, but it's too expensive.)

Judy Kuppersmith, my Bard College and New School buddy who had joined me at Richmond College, gave me a surprise birthday party. When I look at the photos today, I grow misty-eyed.

Here's Alix Kates Shulman, holding her fork aloft, tossing her head back, vivacious. Here's Gloria, sitting on the floor, wearing jeans, our heads touching. Here's Tina Mandel, one of the founders of Identity House, which pioneered peer counseling for gay people.

Gloria gave me a ring fashioned from a Greek coin depicting the goddess Athena; women were responding to my reintroduction of divinity in female form in *Women and Madness*. Psychologically, this seemed empowering. Wouldn't learning that people once worshipped goddesses, that the divine is female as well as male, and that God has a female or feminine side transform women's self-esteem and how women are seen and experienced?

Catharine Stimpson was a professor of literature and a fiercely ambitious feminist academic. Stimpson taught at Barnard and lived on the Bowery near Kate Millett. Stimpson was also the founding editor of the academic journal *Signs: Journal of Women in Culture and Society*. She went on to serve as the president of the Modern Language Association, an adviser for the MacArthur "Genius" Awards, and dean of the Graduate School at New York University. Stimpson generously insisted on giving me a book party for *Women and Madness* because, like Kate, I was becoming hot.

The party passed by in a blur—an author is hardly present at her own book party. She is in an altered state but is expected to greet everyone like a politician running for office.

Stimpson's loft was dark but large. My editor Betty was there, as were several potential reviewers of the book. Two former lovers and my family also attended. My relatives sat stiffly together, the women clutching their handbags. The party was filled with feminists. My best buds Barbara Joans, Barbara Chasen, and Judy Kuppersmith were there, as were the actress and film and theater buff Anselma Dell'Olio, the lawyer Emily Jane Goodman (with whom I later coauthored a book), the psychologists Leigh Marlowe and Elaine Stocker, and all my feminist psychology colleagues from Richmond College.

Jill Johnston was outside, picketing. She was wearing a sandwich board that said CERTIFIED INSANE. I couldn't argue with that, but I kept inviting her to come in. Remember: Jill had a thing against doctors writing about mental illness.

The southern writer and lesbian lush Bertha Harris (whose 1976 novel *Lover* is very Djuna Barnes–like) was drunk and punched Dr. Sal Maddi, who was reviewing my book for *Saturday Review*.

Nice going, sisters.

This Brooklyn girl, who once wore hand-me-down clothes and allowed herself to be so badly treated by men, had arrived. Nothing compares to celebrating the publication of your first book.

————

I was asked to speak at a Radcliffe Conference on Women and Mental Health and at Harvard's Graduate Program in Community Psychiatry. At the time, I thought that if I had been a man, this might have meant I was being considered for a teaching appointment.

Within a week of my lecture, four women physicians quit their residencies in psychiatry. They wrote me to say that my lecture had changed their lives. I attended a party in Cambridge at the apartment of Dr. Paul Rosenkrantz and his wife, Barbara, which overlooked the Charles River. (Paul was not associated with Harvard, but Barbara was an associate professor of History of Science and in 1974 became the first woman to hold the position of house master at Harvard, with Paul as co-master.) Together with Dr. Inge Broverman, Paul had published an important study documenting sex-role stereotyping in mental illness diagnoses, and I had cited it in *Women and Madness*.

Suddenly Adrienne Rich, the poet, someone I had never met, was standing before me.

"You have just revolutionized mental health for women," she said. "I have come to pay my respects."

I was floored. We talked briefly, and then I said, "The *New York Times* has not and probably will not review it. At least, that's what my editor thinks."

"Oh, really," she said. "Well, we'll see about that."

At the end of November, her scathing review of Midge Decter's *The New Chastity and Other Arguments Against Women's Liberation* in the *New York Review of Books* mentioned my work.

Phil Donahue (who would marry Marlo Thomas) was the Oprah of his day. He featured feminists like me for a respectful hour of conversation. He was a wonderful interviewer.

Women began writing to me.

The book had been out for a month, with reviews in *Kirkus Review*, *Publisher's Weekly*, *Library Journal*—all industry publications—and in *Saturday Review*, *Psychology Today*, the *Village Voice*, and the *New Republic*. The *New York Times* had still not reviewed it.

To the glitterati, receiving a positive review in the *Times* is the equivalent of being knighted or kissed by the gods. Books by women—*feminist* books by women—were still viewed as strident, man-hating, hysterical, dancing-dog sensations, not the stuff of which classics were made.

In a season when some other feminist books had received six-figure sums for paperback rights, *Women and Madness* did not. Doubleday had decided that without a major review and incredible sales, it would be smart to hold the paperback auction before people lost interest.

Doubleday was right. It sold my paperback rights for a song—and it might have been the best or only offer in town. Still, I was so distraught that I called Betty, my editor, late at night, weeping. I had no perspective. I had been planning to donate money to various feminist causes and now I couldn't.

Well, maybe it was for the best. At that point I realized, more than ever, that I'd better hold on to my job. Otherwise I would not be able to afford my writing and my activism.

About a month later, Adrienne Rich's long and glowing review of *Women and Madness* appeared on the cover of the *New York Times Book Review*. This may have been the first feminist work of my generation to be so garlanded.

Sales soared and my editor smelled a winner. Yes, a single newspaper had that much gatekeeping power. It still does.

Adrienne: Wherever you are, I am in your debt, as are the millions of women whose lives were changed because your review meant they would now read my book.

I paid it forward when, twenty years later, I reviewed Judith Lewis Herman's important book *Trauma and Recovery* in the pages of the *New York Times Book Review*.

Within a month, reviews of *Women and Madness* appeared in newspapers in Boston; Charlotte, North Carolina; Chicago; Cincinnati;

Cleveland; Long Beach, California; New York City; Philadelphia; Phoenix; Pittsburgh; San Francisco; Seattle; and Vancouver—and in *Time*, the *Guardian*, and in dozens of other places.

Lecture agents clamored to represent me. University student groups asked me to speak. Despite these one-night stands, I would never receive an offer to join the faculty of any of the universities where thousands of students—mainly *female* students, and only a handful of male students or male faculty—crowded to hear me preach the word.

I was becoming famous—I *was* famous. Yet I didn't like the loneliness, the demands, and the envy, or that mere fame was not the same as power. Although fame glowed, it was problematic. Being famous certainly helped my writing and lecture career. Sometimes it also meant being recognized on the street, and it always meant being recognized in feminist circles. Strangers related to me as if we were intimates. People who knew me pulled away. Perhaps they felt that I had—or would soon—abandon them for other famous people, that my fleeting success made them see themselves as lesser beings, as if I had somehow "shown them up." Perhaps they could not forgive me for having been recognized when they had not been. Kate Millett writes about this phenomenon in *Flying*, a book that had not yet been published.

A life on the road made me feel harassed, not flattered, especially when young women tried to jump into my bed. It drove me to drink. For a few years I drank to fall asleep in motel and hotel rooms. I was so far from home—this *was* my home, but I was so alone, so set apart, by my admirers: I was not one of them; I was the sacrifice. My reaction to fame was, to paraphrase one of Martha Shelley's poems, it's too late to take it back but I'm not sure it's an improvement.

My job security at Richmond College was shaky—this public prominence had put me at risk. I did not yet have tenure. Women's studies had not yet merged with the patriarchal academy. We were not yet considered a proper academic area of knowledge; we were activist outsiders and pretenders to the throne.

Ultimately, however, I was one of the few radical feminists who actually got—and got to keep—a tenured professorship. Most of us who had such prized positions endured similar ordeals. Sister sufferers included the psychologist Paula Caplan (Ontario Institute for Studies in Education), the physician Mary Howell (Harvard Medical School), and the theologian Mary Daly (Boston College). Paula subsequently wrote an excellent book on this subject, *Lifting a Ton of Feathers: A Woman's Guide to Surviving in the Academic World*.

We—whose primary job description was that of constantly having to justify having the job in the first place—were ever so much luckier than all the radical feminists who spent their salad years organizing, marching, sitting in, and writing articles and books that quite literally changed our world. Too late, they realized that they needed a day job after all.

I suppose I could have gone on the road to make money for as long as I was still a hot commodity. But what kind of life is that? An actor's life, a circus life, a hobo's life? Given my working-class origins, I needed stability—a civil servant's salary. I wanted to read and write. I couldn't do that if I was always on the road. Lifelong writers need a steady schedule. I need to be in the same spot, working at my craft day after day, so that inspiration, should she seek me out, will know exactly where to find me.

I made the right decision: to stay put and keep the job I had. I never received a single (tenured, long-term) job offer from another university.

During my 1972–73 winter break I took off to Greece and Israel for the first time. Greece is the birthplace of the dramas, poetry, and myths that I draw upon in *Women and Madness*. I went to thank my intellectual ancestors. I loved the goddesses in the National Museum in Athens. There they stand, almost ten feet tall, in all their bronze or marble glory. One of my Amazons wears a Phrygian cap on horseback; she's from Epidaurus.

I visited Sounion, where ancient Greek sailors offered libations before sea voyages. The rocky promontory, the high wind, and the open sea were exhilarating. I saw that Byron, lord of poetry and philandering, was here before me; he carved his name into one of the surviving columns.

I loved Delphi the most. I lingered by the Rock of the Sibyl because it's so perfectly poised between mountain and sea.

From Athens I flew to Israel. This was a long overdue visit. I traveled to Haifa, Jerusalem, the Negev, Tel Aviv, Rehovot, and Eilat.

Arab men with languorous lashes smiled sideways at me in Eilat, which was exquisitely coral pink yet far too neon-noisy with its strobe-lit discotheques. It was Miami Beach on the Gulf of Aqaba.

I picked up a copy of *Time* in my Tel Aviv hotel and was shocked by the review of *Women and Madness*—not by the negative review but by the accompanying cartoon, which I experienced as blatantly anti-Semitic. It depicts Freud as a big-nosed pygmy and his client as a beautiful blonde, long-legged, apparently non-Jewish woman.

My book had sold two thousand copies in a single week and was going into a second printing. It would go on to sell 3.5 million copies.

I didn't want to leave Israel, but leave I had to. I had classes to teach.

6 Fame Hits Hard, Thousands of Letters Arrive, and I Marry Again

I was back in the States and busy. I was teaching a full load of classes, doing media interviews, lecturing at other universities and at conferences, and attending meetings and book parties.

I was on the radio and television all the time: *AM Chicago*, *AM New York*, Canadian Broadcasting, Phil Donahue, Mike Douglas, Barry Farber, Sonia Hamlin, Stephanie Shelton, Howard Smith. Interviews and reviews appeared in countless print media—and this was only the beginning.

My plate was full; my cup ranneth over.

I had stepped onto a madcap merry-go-round, and I was whirling. I *was* the whirlwind.

As soon as I began appearing on television, the letters arrived. Could I save this woman's sanity, that woman's marriage? Could I rescue someone from an asylum, assist her in suing her abusive therapist, help publish her tale of woe? Would I consult on a lawsuit, testify in court?

Oh, the letters! Day after day, month after month they arrived, written by girls and women from all over North America. Many were from housewives with stories of being clapped into asylums by husbands who wanted to get rid of them. Some were typed. Others were handwritten on hopelessly girlish stationery adorned with flowers, leaves, and cute animals. They were like missives from the nineteenth century, letters in a bottle, begging to be rescued, or at least remembered. Marge Piercy's poem "Women of Letters" tried to capture this moment:

> *After Phyllis wrote* Women and Madness
> *they brought the mail in boxes . . .*
> *each full of bloody hanks of hair. . . .*

The voices of the letter writers are still fresh after all these years. From Massachusetts:

> *I need your help. I'm 45 years old. I'm the mother of ten and my husband is trying to put me into the state mental hospital. I know he has another woman, but he says I'm paranoid and need shock therapy. I got some. It didn't change his fooling around on me or his wanting a divorce. I would die if I was taken away from my little ones.*

From New Mexico:

> *I write to you in desperation, in hope. I spent years in psycho-analysis. I am dreadfully unhappy. I'm married to a tender man, a nurturing man. I love my husband. How, Dr. Chesler, to keep from destroying the marriage on which I am totally and utterly dependent? I'd rather not become a lesbian. I could not live with the imagined disgust of others. An answer, a question, an insight?*

From Idaho:

> *My husband is a philanderer. He keeps talking about the insurance policy he has when I die. Even though I'm more*

educated than he is, he handles all the money. Will he kill me?
What can I do?

Once the husbands installed new girlfriends, they claimed that their wives were crazy and got psychiatrists to evaluate them. At that point, if not sooner, the wives began to fall apart. They drank, they took pills, they overate, they slept late—and soon enough they *did* qualify for some kind of punitive psychiatric diagnosis.

These were 1950s-style housewives and mothers. They didn't know what their rights were. In fact, they had few rights. They were forced to fight for custody while living out of a suitcase and sleeping on a relative's couch—if they were lucky enough to have a supportive relative.

There were letters about sadistic, incompetent board-certified psychiatrists, psychotherapists, and fraudsters.

From Wisconsin:

You are giving me some startling new insight into my sister's twenty-year mental illness—an illness ostensibly perpetrated by her rebellion against marriage and male domination. Her psychiatrist convinced her that all her physical symptoms were "only in her head" and then she died of cancer that had gone undiagnosed and untreated.

From North Carolina:

My roommate "Ellen" (a pseudonym) was in therapy with a fully accredited MD whom she saw five times a week. When she began displaying alarming symptoms, I wanted to call her doctor but waited. Then, that very day, "Ellen" jumped in front of a train. It turned out that another friend had called her doctor, who reassured her, "Ellen is very well able to handle her own problems, thank you." When "Ellen's" brother spoke to the doctor after the tragedy, the doctor reassured him. "Don't feel guilty, there was nothing anyone could have done about it anyway."

Other letters were about seductive therapists who slept with their female patients, abandoned them, and sometimes impregnated them. From California:

I was in "therapy" with Dr. Hartogs in NYC in 1967. [Renatus Hartogs was one of the therapists whom I named as a serial seducer of his most vulnerable female patients.] I would be very happy to write a more detailed letter if it would help build a legal case against him.

Letters poured in from the young and the lovelorn. They accepted being abused by a husband because "this is how a man acts when he loves you." They were living a more extreme version of the life I had led in the 1960s—and from which I'd escaped.
From Maine:

He won't even let me go to the library. We never go out together. He locks me in during the day when he's at work. If I ever complain, he has a tantrum. If he sees me looking at one of the attractive actors when we watch a TV program he hits me. Now I'm smoking, and have terrible headaches. Please tell me what to do. I need guidance.

I was inundated, engulfed by the thousands of letters I received that confirmed all that I'd written. I was outraged by my correspondents' needless suffering and humbled by their trust and praise. Many letters were beautifully written.
From Indiana:

Thank you for your book. It is a life raft for me as I swim in a violent sea to reach a shore I sometimes believe is only an illusion. Your book helps me see the shore again as I deal with sorrow and unemployment. Your work renews my power for the swim. I sometimes feel as though I've gone down twice already. I would like to be the regional director of your Feminist Institute of Mental Health.

I routinely received and dealt with fifty calls and letters a week from women in crisis and at least fifty requests a week to sign petitions; attend meetings, demonstrations, and press conferences; read and comment on manuscripts; appear on television and radio; talk to newspaper reporters; meet with visiting feminists; lobby legislatures; and coordinate fund-raisers.

I had suddenly become the minister of women's suffering, a feminist Dear Abby. I didn't think I could save everyone—I didn't think I could save *anyone*—but clearly my work was a liberating lightning rod. The responsibility I felt was overwhelming.

My publishing advances were not enough to live on. I now had four jobs: teaching at CUNY, delivering paid lectures across the country, working as a part-time psychotherapist, and writing my next book. There was always a next book. Together these jobs allowed me to hire an assistant to help me meet my obligations.

Feminists read all kinds of meaning into *Women and Madness* that weren't there.

For the record: I believe that mental illness exists. I warn against romanticizing it.

I did not write that mentally ill women are by definition feminist rebels. I argued that women had been diagnostically punished when they rebelled against their assigned sex roles: punished for expressing extreme femininity (passivity, dependence) or extreme masculinity (anger, independence). If you were a woman, you could never meet the standards of mental health, which by definition were correlated with being male.

Some women thought that my work lionized eccentric, dysfunctional behaviors and suggested that oppression caused these behaviors. As a result, many eccentric, dysfunctional women praised my work.

Here's what's true. Oppression and persecution of all kinds (sexism, racism, classism, homophobia) is stressful and traumatic. People *do* become disabled after they've been tormented and worn down. The normal human response to incest, rape, and battery may include hypervigilance, insomnia, paranoia, anxiety, phobias, disassociation, and the like. This behavior gets diagnosed as "mental illness," while allegations of physical or sexual violence are often disbelieved or minimized.

Sometimes people betrayed by their intimates or persecuted by society trust no one and thus are difficult to help.

Feminist knowledge, feminist support, feminist activism, and a purpose-driven life can often heal certain wounds; feminist therapy and bibliotherapy (reading feminist books) can also help. I argued for the development of a strong and independent self—strong enough not only to tolerate difference but to celebrate it.

Gloria Steinem kept asking me to help her learn how to express anger. She was terminally polite, genial, reserved, nice in a Midwestern kind of way. (She's from Ohio.) This amiable stability, this supercontrol—plus her appearance—contributed to people not viewing her as a threat. This also meant that she could be heard, which I thought was a great advantage. But Gloria said in despair: "This is why Betty Friedan hates me. She won't talk to me. I was in Bloomingdale's doing some Christmas shopping and bumped into Betty. I said, 'Oh, hi,' and she said, 'I won't talk to you,' and just walked off."

Gloria could not bear being disliked.

Betty Friedan was in a rage about all the media attention Gloria was getting; she believed that Gloria was unfairly stealing attention from her. Betty also did not believe that Gloria represented Middle America because she had never been married or had children.

Betty saw Gloria as a lightweight people-pleaser, a Jane-come-lately, a copycat. Betty did not value Gloria as someone who could preach Feminism 101, decade after decade, long after the rest of us had quit the stage in exhaustion or boredom.

Betty went on to accuse Gloria of being a CIA agent. To Betty's way of thinking, what else but a huge government conspiracy could have organized Betty's disappearance from the media limelight, not to mention the disappearance of all of our radical and visionary feminist activists?

Betty was not really being disappeared. She remained a force to be reckoned with. Journalists and politicians continued to take her calls. Her coterie continued to adore her and remained willing to suffer her bullying ways. Betty's wound was partly political and partly psychological. She did not agree with Gloria's overly sentimental belief that sisterhood would overcome all differences, and she was outraged that Gloria had begun to get so much media attention.

Betty viewed Gloria as the prom queen who made off with the captain of the football team, the girl everyone liked—the upstart who stalked Betty's nightmares.

Betty was a hot Jewish tamale, just like Bella Abzug, and they didn't get along with each other either.

The radical-feminist activists—mainly leftist, but also dangerously, wondrously feminist—*were* being preempted and disappeared by the media-enabled ascent of *Ms.* and its sisterhood party line. The radicals would soon attempt a public reckoning.

Gloria was troubled about something else as well, something she had shared with me in slightly different words a number of times.

"Betty's written a major book. You've written a major book. I haven't done anything like that and I may never do it," she told me. "I'm not an intellectual like you are. I delay, I miss deadlines, I need others to help me get organized."

"Gloria! I'm not going to hit the road in order to get candidates elected," I replied. "I'm not going to bear the burden of getting a feminist magazine funded and of sitting at a thousand and one meetings."

While Gloria may not have been an intellectual or a scholar, she was nevertheless supremely talented in other important ways. She was a tireless networker, capable of gladly suffering fools as she lectured everywhere, anywhere that would have her. She overcame the most profound stage fright in order to do this. She was also witty and charming.

Given all her gifts and talents, I'm puzzled, slightly on edge, when anyone, especially a woman like Gloria, wants to be somebody she's not.

I have often debated those on the other side of an issue. For example, in 1972 I agreed to meet on camera with the world-famous R.D. "Ronnie" Laing. He was known as the "antipsychiatry" psychiatrist. He believed that psychosis, including schizophrenia, does not need medication or institutionalization but rather needs a community of like-minded spirits and friends. Laing, a Scot, started a program at Kingsley Hall in London where patients and their therapists lived together. Laing published such works as *The Divided Self* and *Sanity, Madness and the Family*, whose ideas I challenged in *Women and Madness*.

We met at the Algonquin Hotel. Newspaper reporters and a videographer treated our meeting as a theatrical event. Later, some feminists criticized me because I had talked to a "sexist man." What's the point in talking only to those with whom you agree?

I talked to sexist women, too.

Five years later, I flew into Cincinnati in the midst of a blizzard to debate the great anthropologist Margaret "Maggie" Mead. She was best known for her groundbreaking work in Samoa, which at the time was seen as radically and unacceptably feminist. Eventually, it was criticized as flawed in its methodology. Among her many books were *Coming of Age in Samoa* and *Sex and Temperament in Three Primitive Societies*. Mead maintained an office at the American Museum of Natural History in New York City but often repaired to the University of Cincinnati to write.

Mead's task in our debate was to oppose feminism. To the chagrin of the one thousand feminists who had gathered to enjoy what they hoped would be a matricidal boxing match, Mead and I bonded instead. I presented first. Fifteen minutes into my speech, Mead got up, leaned on her walking stick, slowly and loudly clumped her way to the microphone, nudged me aside, and interrupted me.

"You, young woman, are obviously brilliant. But how many more are there like you in that movement of yours?"

It was a no-win moment. While I was pleased—even thrilled— that I had impressed her, I was also embarrassed and outraged that she had publicly demeaned the movement I represented. I told her: "Dr. Mead, no matter what I say I'm in trouble. If I'm not part of a worthy movement because, in your view, it doesn't exist, then I'm not that smart after all, am I?"

We laughed. Soon enough, we ran into some profound differences. She insisted that women deserve to be raped, that it never happens unless they have violated a taboo. Oh, how we disagreed—but respectfully. She would not budge. The assembled feminists had planned a reception to honor us both. However, given what Mead had said about rape, the sisters refused to allow her to join us. I had no choice; I spent the evening with Mead. (Looking back, I realize that she was seventy-six years old when we met, close to my own age as I write this.)

Ironically, Mead was castigated for decades for her view that gender was fluid, that culture influenced gender roles, and that in some so-called primitive societies girls were as sexually free as boys. One would have expected the feminists in Cincinnati to carry her on their shoulders. That was not the case because her view on rape was wrong—reprehensibly so.

Afterward Mead and I became friendly colleagues. She wanted to endorse my book *About Men* but only if I removed the two pages that dealt with rape. I would have loved her support but told her, "You know I can't do that. But thanks for reading the book."

Later that year, in the late fall, I was seven months pregnant and Mead insisted on coming to see me.

"Being pregnant is more fragile than being old," she declared. Her first question was, "What are you doing about your nipples?"

My own mother never asked me this question. Mead was blunt, forceful, and unbelievably kind to me. She told me: "Rub them with a rough washcloth, pinch them, toughen them up."

We talked at length about the problems that arise when an ambitious intellectual woman decides to become a mother. (She told me to buy a big house and to find a mother who already has children and needs a home and a family—and to never stop my work, no matter what domestic crisis may arise.)

We may not have agreed about rape, but how blessed I was that such a visible grandmother of our American tribe arrived in person to initiate me into the rites of motherhood.

I didn't know then that she had cancer.

———

I've previously described what I call the Chinese Cultural Revolution in Feminist America—the resentment and anger shown to any feminist perceived as more talented, more visible, or prettier than whoever resented this fact. Many feminists came to believe that feminist ideas and activism belonged to the movement, not to any individual, and especially not to the feminist who did the writing or organized the protest.

"Ripping off the movement."

This phrase was the angry, anguished rallying cry of many radical feminists. If someone wrote an article, coined a phrase, pioneered a method of organizing (such as consciousness raising), or planned a speak-out, she was judged to have "ripped off" what others considered intellectual property that belonged to "the people," the sisterhood, the boundary-less merging of one with all.

When certain feminists began taking credit for what they had not done, or allowed the media to conclude that they alone had originated such key phrases as "the personal is political" or "sisterhood is powerful" or had pioneered the idea of consciousness raising *when they had not done so*, rage and paranoia provoked a bitter and frustrated despair in those who had.

The feminist most often accused of taking credit for someone else's ideas—for their exact words—was Robin Morgan. I was her friend and ally. I did not believe this about her.

Robin Morgan edited the feminist anthology *Sisterhood Is Powerful*. It gathered together the earliest feminist writings, from 1967 to 1970. Robin devised a creative but cumbersome way of distributing royalties to fifty-five feminist authors and fifteen feminist collectives, but only if they were willing to donate their share of the royalties to a preapproved feminist group that Robin had compiled.

In 1973 Lucinda "Cindy" Cisler sued Robin and Random House, claiming she had plagiarized Cindy's *Bibliography on Feminism and Reproductive Rights*. For years Cindy could be seen at conferences and on street corners selling her thirty-six-page, single-spaced *Bibliography*; this was how she paid for her coffee and Danish.

Robin told me and everyone else that Cindy was a "crazy lady" whose lawsuit was intended to trash Robin in order to bring her down and, in so doing, "destroy our movement."

In a panic, Robin turned to me to help mediate the matter with Cindy. Robin wanted the royalties to go to "the movement." Alas, it was too late. Random House had made a settlement offer, and Cindy had accepted it. The Sisterhood Is Powerful Fund was ruined because Random House used Robin's royalties from this book and from her own book of poetry to pay the publisher's legal costs as well as Cindy's $10,000 settlement. Robin dissolved the fund.

I believed what Robin told me. Really, how could someone steal a bibliography?

Forty-three years later I am holding Robin's twenty-page, single-spaced 1974 "Report to the Women's Movement," which she apparently mailed to hundreds of feminist groups and to individual feminists, such as myself. She did not publish this but the matter became public in feminist circles. My hands are shaking. I had not read it before. In effect, it's a call for shunning, female style.

In it Robin names 115 feminist groups that were slated to receive small grants ($180 to $500) and explains that because Random House settled with Cindy, the Sisterhood Is Powerful Fund was destroyed. She sent this public indictment to every feminist and feminist group in her massive Rolodex.

According to Robin, Cindy's lawsuit cheated the entire movement of its money. Even if Cindy was right, even if her work was plagiarized, she did not have to sue over a bibliography.

Robin wrote: "I should have blasted the story all over the Movement six months ago—and let the Movement 'deal' with her."

Deal with her? How? By shunning her? Or by having her chained in the Tower of London—beheaded, perhaps?

Kate Millett was the first among us to become famous. When it happened to me, I didn't know what had hit me. No one had ever taught me how to ride this tiger or how to safely dismount.

People who didn't know me—people who *did* know me—either loved me or hated me. My life was not my own. Nothing was personal anymore. I flew to California to ask my older sister Kate-the-feminist-icon about what happens next. We were staying in Flo Kennedy's San Francisco apartment.

Flo dragged us around all day, first to meet Angela Davis, who was giving a press conference at the San Francisco Federal Building about Wounded Knee, and then to a press conference to protest cuts in the welfare budget for childcare. Then poetry. Ishmael Reed came on to me in an enticing and irresistible manner. (I barely remembered this, but my diary notes reminded me of it.)

Angela Davis was a revered household name among leftists, black nationalists, and feminists. I once marched for Angela when she was imprisoned in the Women's House of Detention in New York City for her role in a courtroom shooting.

The Soledad Brothers were three inmates accused of killing a prison guard. Angela bought the guns that Jonathan Jackson, the younger brother of George Jackson, one of the accused Soledad inmates, used in the armed takeover of a California courtroom. Four people were killed. A jury found that her purchase of the weapons did not mean she had collaborated in the crime. In those fevered times Angela became something of a cultural hero and had the support of, among others, the Rolling Stones, John Lennon and Yoko Ono, Kate Millett, and Robin Morgan. Angela joined the Communist Party and visited Cuba and Soviet Russia, where she was awarded the Lenin Prize. She retired as a professor at the University of California, Santa Cruz, where she was director of the Feminist Studies department.

Flo asked me to accompany her to the supermarket.

"Do you think this grapefruit is good?" asked the Queen of Retorts.

Said I: "I don't know."

Then she said: "I have to get a floor mop. What's a good one?"

"Are you kidding? I can make a good cup of coffee, but I'm no shopper."

So there we were, two feminist time bombs discussing grapefruits and floor mops in a San Francisco supermarket on a Saturday night.

Flo was sassy and savvy and should have been out there practicing law in a major way, but practicing law was difficult for a woman in the 1960s, and doubly so for a black woman. Flo was on the lecture circuit, but she sure wasn't living large. Her apartment on East Forty-eighth Street in Manhattan was tiny.

In 2000, as Flo was dying, I visited her. I sang to her: "Embrace me, you sweet embraceable you," and other cabaret love songs, and she smiled and laughed in appreciation and amazement—I'd never sung to her before.

Flo was the only woman I've known who had two memorial services plus a wake. The women who loved her, as well as her biological sisters, fought over everything. I dare not share what happened lest I be sued. Women fought to be included in the program. Some women paid to be included. Flo was laid out in state, dressed like an African queen. I attended her wake; I attended the first memorial service, at

Saint John the Divine; and I attended the second memorial service, on the Upper East Side, which some feminists actually picketed.

White feminists fought about who Flo loved the most, whose photos and artifacts would be displayed at the service, and who owned the rights to her archives. I wondered what Flo would have said about this—no doubt something wickedly witty.

But all those years ago in San Francisco, Flo left Kate and me in her apartment and warned us not to do anything illegal, like smoke pot. Of course, we locked the bathroom door and giggled with each drag.

Suddenly Kate started pawing me, telling me she was in love with me, that we had to become lovers.

"Kate, I'm a straight girl, I'm into boys, what is *wrong* with you? I'm here on a feminist matter of state."

I became rigid, unmoving. I said, "This is not what I want." She persisted. I was outraged and frightened. She was my "older sister" Kate, the feminist icon. After a while she stopped. I believe she arrested my bisexual evolution by a decade.

Kate did me and herself no favor by falling in love with me. She began a campaign of sending flowers and leaving phone messages. I hid from her.

I didn't break with her over this; we continued our intellectual and political friendship, but without special privileges. Our friendship lasted through many episodes of her truly bad behavior.

The truth is that I did love her—not sexually or romantically, but intellectually. I loved her for her ideas, for the energy they generated around her. I'm a sucker for women with exceedingly bright brains. I put up with their considerable bullshit for the sake of sparkling conversation.

John Lennon, Yoko Ono, Angela Davis, and now Kate all wanted Bill Kunstler to handle the case of the Trinidadian known as Michael X. Kate said she'd present his case to the Oxford Union, the British debating society. I told her that I didn't understand why she was spending her time on this case. What did it have to do with women's rights?

Michael X was a self-styled black revolutionary, but he was actually a criminal. He had been born Michael de Freitas but called himself Michael Abdul Malik or Michael X. He advocated the killing of any white man who "lays a hand on a black woman" and claimed that "white men have no soul." In 1969, Michael X founded Black House, a black power commune, in London.

Two members of his commune viciously beat and tortured a Jewish businessman in an attempt to extort money from him. In 1971, Black House mysteriously burned down, and Michael X was arrested for extortion.

John Lennon paid his bail. Michael X fled to Trinidad, where he founded another Black House, which also mysteriously burned down. The police investigating the fire found two bodies in shallow graves. Both had been hacked to death. Michael X then fled to Guyana. He was extradited to London, where he was found guilty of murdering the two black members of his commune for refusing to obey his order to attack a local police station.

Nevertheless, John Lennon et al., Dick Gregory, Flo Kennedy, and Bill Kunstler (hired by Lennon) were on Michael X's side and formed the Save Malik Committee. Kunstler pleaded for clemency, but in 1975 Michael X was executed.

This was what was occupying the fearless leader of the Free Feminist Forces. I don't know if this is an example of European-style leftist politics or guilty white radical chic, which views black criminality as justified resistance. In Kate's case it might simply have been a manifestation of madness. She was obsessed with death and torture and wrote a painful and powerful book titled *The Basement* (1979), about the torture-murder of Sylvia Likens, a sixteen-year-old American, and another book about state torture in general, *The Politics of Cruelty: An Essay on the Literature of Political Imprisonment* (1994).

Kate's lover, Maria, or Kate's husband, Fumio (I have two different stories about this), had her committed after she set fire to her bed in California.

Kate called me demanding that I rescue her from the loony bin in Minnesota, where her mother and sisters had subsequently put her. Kate had a battery of do-gooder lawyers. After a three-day insanity hearing, she was remanded to a psychiatric facility and medicated against her will. Kate was in a small room, and she was a serious claustrophobe.

"Buddy, come down and tell them that there's no such thing as madness. You're the expert, you wrote the goddamn book!"

I talked to Kate's ostensible helpers, trying to explain that it doesn't help to lock someone like Kate up against her will. Yes, she certainly needed help, but I doubted that imprisoning her, even "for her own good," would be helpful.

On the phone, Kate kept spewing a steady stream of political talk about Michael X, the Irish, "the prisoners," and all the "oppressed women."

I told her: "Look: you're in serious trouble. You have to deal with it seriously."

She said: "Why the hell aren't you here? Why aren't you testifying for me, getting me out? I know why. It's because you're not in love with me. You're ripping off the movement, you're ripping off mental patients, women, black people, Indians. You're a Jewish princess, you're too busy to come."

I became frightened for Kate only when she offered me a bite of her (not metaphorical) candy bar over the phone. But I did everything in my power to help. This included getting Gloria to call more lawyers. Finally, Kate was released.

She was coming to find me.

I flew to Washington, D.C., to meet with Peter Breggin, an antipsychiatry psychiatrist. Kate came to D.C. looking for me. She took the most expensive suite in the fanciest hotel and ran up a $200 phone bill hunting me down. I told her she was abusing me and that she was just plain nuts. But she was also crazy like a fox. Kate said: "If I'm going crazy, you of all people should understand and not abandon me."

"Kate, I'm not your doctor and you're not my patient. You've made everything so much harder by falling in love with me."

Kate started leaving abusive messages on my answering machine. Our friend Lila Karp told me that she had taken Kate to the beach and that Kate had "bloody freaked out. She was yelling at gas station attendants. She insisted that the beach had been dirtied by the Jews and that the Irish always have to clean up Jewish filth."

Whoa! Woe!

What is one to make of a mad genius? Kate's friends and groupies put up with it, thereby enabling it. It was the price they were willing to pay to be part of the revolution. No one wanted to break with her. It was years before her enablers-in-chief came to me for help.

I spent some time with Marge Piercy at her home in Wellfleet, on Cape Cod. I had rented a house nearby and spent my days writing. I was having some of my diaries typed up, and I had embarked on a new book, to be titled *Women, Money, and Power*. I spent my downtime with Marge.

Erica Jong arrived with an offering of a large grilled fish. Her hair flopped down over her face, which was also hidden by oversized glasses. Marge and I were movement heavies, we were already famous. Erica yearned for fame as if it were the Muse herself.

Awkward, overly eager, desperately serious—that was Erica when she was young. Like so many women of her era, Erica wanted to look like Marilyn Monroe. Erica wore expensive perfume, expensive shoes, and expensive designer outfits. She had her own money and she married money. Still, she fancied herself a bohemian. She later told me that she had been as depressed as any serious poet ever had been, had had a drinking problem, and had suffered from too many love affairs and marriages gone wrong.

Nevertheless, Erica was good-hearted and generous to those she loved. This included me. She was also quite hardworking, a good poet, and an outrageously witty comic writer with a grand literary imagination.

I love many of her novels, beginning with *Fear of Flying* but especially *Fanny: Being the History of the Adventures of Fanny Hackabout-Jones* and *Serenissima* (published in later editions as *Shylock's Daughter*), in which Erica's avatar has an affair with Will Shakespeare himself.

To my sorrow, Erica always sells out at the end of each novel. Boy marries girl, wife stays with husband, they all live happily ever after. Erica will keep writing sexy, funny, well-researched fairy tales.

I belonged to so many worlds: I moved effortlessly among academic, feminist, psychoanalytic, Jewish, Muslim, Christian, pagan, and publishing circles.

I remember Manhattan publishing when times were flush, when authors were wined and dined at three-martini lunches at the Four Seasons or similarly impressive spots. I remember a time when a meeting with an editor followed by a two- or three-page proposal was all that was necessary to obtain an advance, a time when deadlines were infinitely flexible and authors were not expected to pay back their advances if they failed to complete their manuscript—or if their work was rejected.

I remember even more fondly the women sent to meet the author's plane or train (they held up our books) in Boston, Chicago, Detroit, Los Angeles, Philadelphia, Seattle, San Francisco, or Washington, D.C., and who would gallantly or resignedly escort you from one radio or television station to another and to "just one more bookstore."

And I remember the feminist bookstores that sprang up almost overnight and stayed in business for as long as they could in Ann Arbor, Atlanta, Austin, Boston, Bridgeport, Cambridge, Chicago, Gainesville, Minneapolis, New York City, Portland, San Francisco, Seattle, Toledo, and Tucson. Most were run on a shoestring and volunteer labor. There were once over a hundred feminist bookstores in the country. As of 2014, there were twelve.

I remember appearing on television and radio programs to talk about a book before the stations installed security. People just waltzed right in. I remember how intellectual the talk-show hosts and print journalists were in Canada and all across Europe in England, France, Germany, Italy, Holland, and Scandinavia.

Most of all I remember all the book parties we had—like Christmas cakes they were, just filled with promise and possibility; how so many authors, literary agents, editors, publicists, and journalists showed up. I felt so "in," so Manhattan, so grown up—even as I contemplated feminist revolution pretty much day and night.

At the end of 1973, I got married. I had met the man in Eilat, at the airport. We had a lovely affair in Israel and I never expected to see him again, but he kept calling and writing and then one day he arrived and never left. Did we love each other? Perhaps. Did he want a green card? Yes. Were we destined to be together? Yes.

He told me that through his mother he was a ninth-generation descendant of the founder of Jewish mysticism, the Baal Shem Tov (Master of the Good Name). He was younger than me and one pretty boy.

He was always waiting for me when I got home from a meeting. That was so nice. He cooked for me and drove us everywhere. He began working odd jobs. I started talking to him about his career options. Seven months passed. By the end of the year we had decided to marry.

To officiate, I chose Sally Priesand, the first-ever American woman rabbi ordained by a rabbinical seminary. The night before the wedding my mother called to say, "It's not too late—we can get a real rabbi for tomorrow."

"Mom, I've waited thousands of years for a real rabbi, and now I have her."

Emily Jane Goodman, a founding member of the Center for Women and Law, wanted to call the *New York Times* to demand that the groom's photo appear rather than the bride's. I admonished her: "Emily, no photo, no announcement—this is a private ceremony, not a political statement."

"What shall we wear?" my groom asked.

"Whatever we want."

"Would you try a long white dress?"

"Sure, why not?" I said. And we went to Fred Leighton in the Village and I tried on a many-layered lacy Mexican wedding dress, but we agreed, laughing, that it just was not me.

I decided to dress as a Renaissance prince. I wore a long painted leather vest, a soft black suede blouse and pants, and tall turquoise suede boots. My groom chose a light-blue suit and no tie.

We were perfect together. We married in an Israeli restaurant, Kinneret, in Greenwich Village. The waiters all mock-crossed themselves when they saw that the rabbi was a woman.

We married on the evening of December 24. The Arabs had declared an oil embargo a few months back. My assistant had forgotten to fill up the car—and when she tried to do so at the last minute, there was no fuel to be had. However, she went to such trouble to finally get us fueled up that we ended up inviting her and her boyfriend along to the hotel I had chosen in the Catskills (because that's where Jewish girls used to go on their honeymoon). Suddenly I was Marjorie Morningstar.

A waiter complained to my husband about me.

"Why does she always bring a book to the table?"

"This is what she's like," he said most amiably.

7 Feminism Becomes International

By 1974 I rarely had time to go to museums or the theater. But I made an exception for the opening-night performance of the play *Yentl* at the Brooklyn Academy of Music. After it ended I sat there, rooted to my chair. Yentl's story was my story—and obviously also that of about ten other women who, similarly stunned, lingered long after the performance ended. Yentl cross-dresses in order to be admitted to a yeshiva (study hall), where she secretly falls in love with her male Torah study partner. But Yentl has to marry a woman—so she does.

Leah Napolin's play is magical, mystical, and mysterious. It's neither political nor sexual. It's a story for the ages.

I took the playwright out to lunch to congratulate her. We met at the Cookery on Eighth Street in the Village. Long before Barbra Streisand made the movie *Yentl*, this haunting figure appeared to us all, as if in a dream. Leah Napolin had written it and Bob Kalfin had directed it. They really deserved the credit for resurrecting *Yentl*.

"Let's toast to your work," I told Leah.

Leah smiled broadly and then surprised, even thrilled me. She said that when she'd heard me speak in Ohio, my words, as well as the times, had inspired her to finally take up Yentl's story. As they say, bread cast upon the waters returns to you tenfold.

———

Around 1973 or 1974, my friend Z (Zsuzsanna) Budapest formed the Susan B. Anthony Coven Number 1 in Santa Monica, California, the first feminist, women-only Wiccan coven. Z may have single-handedly introduced pagan spirituality and goddess-centered religion in America. In 1975 she was arrested for doing a tarot reading for a female undercover officer and found guilty of fortune telling. The California Supreme Court eventually overturned the verdict, agreeing with her lawyers' contention that Wicca was a religion and that Z had been persecuted in violation of every American's right to freedom of religion.

Z has published many books, including *The Feminist Book of Lights and Shadows* (1976) and *The Grandmother of Time: A Woman's Book of Celebrations, Spells, and Sacred Objects for Every Month of the Year* (1989).

Z is a "genetic witch"; her Hungarian mother and grandmother were also Wiccans.

"My Queen [this is how Z addressed me], you snapped me out of a long and terrible sleep," she once told me. "When I saw your photos of goddesses and Amazons [in *Women and Madness*], I knew that the female face of God was coming back. I got busy."

Z had a tinkle of a laugh and flirtatious gray-blue eyes. She was part peasant, part priestess. Z opened a local Wicca shop in Venice, California, where she did her tarot readings and dispensed candles and oils.

"The blazer dykes [academic or wealthy women] mock what I'm doing, but they all come through the back door for love charms and readings."

It was very California but enchantingly, redolently pagan. Z smoked a lot of weed and had a lot of lovers.

Sometime in the late 1970s, three Jewish lesbians picketed Z's home, accusing her of having treated the Holocaust disrespectfully. I happened to be in California at the time and she begged me to help.

I found her weeping in the bedroom of her Oakland home. Z had referred to the Inquisition's slaughter of millions of women as witches over three centuries as a "holocaust." I explained the problem to her. The term "Holocaust" had come to mean the specific systematic, almost industrialized, genocide of six million Jews by the Nazis during a period of only five years—the murder of Jews not because of any alleged crimes but simply because they were Jewish. Z was right to see parallels: both women and Jews have been maligned and scapegoated, as well as tortured and murdered. Like the witch-accusers of the Inquisition, Nazis, as well as neighbors, appropriated the homes, factories, fields, and possessions of their victims.

Historically, women have been viewed as witches, bitches, whores, and madwomen. Witches were seen as sexually dangerous women capable of causing impotence, famine, and crop failure. If you read the fifteenth-century *Malleus Maleficarum* ("The Hammer of Witchcraft"), you'll see that my description is something of an understatement. Those accused were arrested, tormented, and burned at the stake; their property was given to whichever neighbor had accused them or to their churchly torturers.

I suggested to Z that we needed to find unique words to describe these horrendous crimes. I said: "Each is different, one from the other, and we cannot piggyback on someone else's tragedy or fail to explain our own tragedies succinctly and carefully."

She was contrite. I went outside, spoke with the demonstrators, and suggested that they consider picking on someone bigger than Z. "Why not picket the Vatican? Or a major Holocaust denier?"

They finally left, also a bit contrite. Again and again, I saw feminist women turn on each other rather than on bigger, more dangerous, patriarchal foes.

In the mid-1980s, Z spoke at the public library in San Jose. Five hundred born-again Christians were there to protest "the witch." I believe in freedom of religion, so I stood with her in solidarity. The police escorted us in. Z wore a garland of flowers. As she spoke, some of the protesters spoke in tongues and threatened hellfire and damnation. The police escorted us out a back door and then drove us a mile away to a diner. Z told me: "Even when the Russian tanks rolled into Budapest, I was never this scared."

The theologian Mary Daly once implored me to help her empty her classroom at Boston College, which she had opened to "all women." Homeless, prostituted, and mentally ill women, along with lost feminists with major attitude problems, had taken over her classroom. I resolved her dilemma by flirting with her unwanted guests, charming the crowd, appealing for mercy for Mary-the-professor who was under almost permanent siege at her Jesuit college.

Mary was intellectually outrageous and courageous, but she was interpersonally tone deaf. For example, once she commanded the platform at a conference, getting her to stop was difficult, even when time was short, others were waiting, and the audience had grown restless.

I listed two of Mary's books in the bibliography of my 1998 book *Letters to a Young Feminist*. She was outraged that I had not listed all her books in all their editions, including their foreign editions, and she faxed me a rather daunting list of all her titles.

Oh, how wounded our warrior women were, how desperate we were for attention, how much we needed to be remembered! This made sense, because our work was routinely attacked or disappeared, and when that happened we were all soon forgotten.

When three women published a work of feminist erotica and political liberation, they were treated like witches.

In 1972 three Portuguese feminists published *Novas Cartas Portuguesas* (published in English as *New Portuguese Letters*). The work was inspired by the seventeenth-century classic *Letters of a Portuguese Nun*, purported to be by Soror (Sister) Mariana Alcoforado. It was said that her family had forced her into a convent when she was sixteen years old, from where, years later, she wrote to the French cavalier who had promised to love her but had deserted her. (It is now generally recognized as a work of fiction.)

The authors of *New Portuguese Letters*—who cannot be distinguished one from the other—write about sexually free women who reject men, marriage, motherhood, and the patriarchal social order. Writing as the "Three Marias" (Maria Teresa Horta, Maria Isabel Barreno, and Maria Velho da Costa), they accuse fathers, husbands, and brothers. They believe that real liberation will come about only when consciousness transforms all separations and all exploitative hierarchies, both physical and psychological. In their view, women remain "the last colonial territory."

In Portugal the book was seen as an affront to "public decency" and as "abusing the freedom of the press." The book was banned and the remaining copies confiscated. The authors were jailed and interrogated by the secret police, who especially wanted to know which of the Marias wrote the erotic passages.

Feminists worldwide campaigned on their behalf. We demonstrated in cities across the United States, in Brazil, in Europe (Belgium, France, Germany, Sweden, the United Kingdom), and in front of Portuguese embassies. NOW chapters organized demonstrations in Houston, New York City, Washington, D.C., Boston, and Los Angeles. International writers' groups also took up the authors' case.

Marge Piercy and I wrote a speech for the authors that was circulated widely and was reprinted in a 2010 annotated Portuguese edition of the book.

Their trial began in 1974 and dragged on; Prime Minister Marcello José das Neves Alves Caetano's regime fell in April, at which point the judge proclaimed the work to be one of "literary merit" and dismissed the case.

———

I've had an international perspective on feminist matters ever since I was held captive in Kabul. For a long time I talked about a feminist government in exile. I believe in feminism without borders in terms of feminist consciousness. I understand that women who live on different continents and belong to different cultures will transform feminist ideas to suit their needs. The campaign for the Three Marias was one of the first in which a large number of American and European feminists flexed their muscles concerning women's global concerns, and it was not sponsored by a government or by the UN.

It was followed in 1975 by an amazing tribunal in Brussels organized by Dr. Diana Russell, a South Africa–born American sociologist, and Nicole Van de Ven, a Belgian. Together they edited the proceedings of the International Tribunal of Crimes Against Women. More than two thousand women from forty countries participated in this conference, also a first of its kind.

The conference opened the world's eyes to the physical abuse of women, female genital mutilation, femicide, rape, forced sterilization, outlawed abortion, the persecution of lesbians, forced motherhood, prostitution, pornography, and the double and triple oppressions of immigrant women and women of color.

As I wrote of the proceedings when they were published in 1976, "For the first time in [thousands of] years, the enforced silence of women around the world has been broken. The testimonies are inspiring, dreadful, objective, and overwhelmingly moving."

Diana, known professionally as Diana E. H. Russell, was a pioneer in conducting groundbreaking sociological research on violence against women and girls, starting in the 1970s, about rape, incest, woman-abuse, pornography, and "femicide" (misogynist woman-killing). Diana has also been a radical activist in efforts to combat such crimes. Simone de Beauvoir described the International Tribunal on Crimes Against Women as "the beginning of the radical decolonization of women."

Born in South Africa, Diana also participated in the revolutionary underground organization the African Resistance Movement, which used sabotage to undermine the white-supremacist apartheid regime. Her book, *Lives of Courage: Women for a New South Africa*, was praised by Archbishop Desmond Tutu and Oliver Tambo. Her feminist and anti-racist activism resulted in her being arrested five times and sued once.

In 1970, Diana also pioneered Women's Studies courses at Mills College. She is one of the world's foremost feminist experts on violence, especially sexual violence.

I was already seen as a feminist leader when a new, young feminist appeared: Andrea Dworkin, whom I first met in 1974 when she was in crisis with her publisher. She turned to me for help, and that remained the nature of our relationship for more than thirty years.

We are *all* always in crisis with our publishers. We expect to change the world immediately with the power of our pen, and when a book doesn't garner good reviews, or any reviews at all, we panic; it feels like we're failing the revolution, not to mention our own ambition.

Like Kate Millett and Shulie Firestone, Andrea was a genius. Also like them, she was destructive, self-destructive, intense, demanding, paranoid, feared, despised, and misunderstood—but also deeply admired and loved, rather passionately, by her followers. Andrea was a fire-and-brimstone feminist preacher and was seen as *the* feminist advocate against pornography, prostitution, and sexual violence against women. Andrea was a daring and talented essayist and novelist. She conducted many campaigns against pornography and wrote many important books, including *Woman Hating, Pornography: Men Possessing Women*, and *Letters from a War Zone*.

When her first book, *Woman Hating*, was published in 1974, Andrea said that she could not convince President Jack Macrae at Dutton to advertise, promote, and distribute copies of the book in a manner that would ensure its visibility; she organized a sit-in at Dutton.

Through a third party I heard that Jack said, "Well, even important feminists like Phyllis Chesler don't like the book, so what can I do?" I had said no such thing; I hadn't even read the book. I called Andrea and asked her, "Why haven't you called me directly?"

Her answer was shocking. "Well, I suppose I thought you might have said that about my work, since I consider yours so superior."

By then I had read the book. I told her to come over and I gave her a resoundingly warm endorsement for her publisher to use. Her book deserved it.

Andrea and I became friends. Yes, of course, we quarreled—on matters of both style and substance, and on the nature of coalition politics, plagiarism, intimate partner choices, the dangerous consequences of bad-mouthing colleagues, the danger of cults—but we always made up. At least we did for about thirty years. I thought we had a privileged and rather tender friendship, and I cherished it despite the difficulties.

The first time Andrea met my mother was an unforgettable moment. My mother said to Andrea, who always wore denim overalls, like a farmer: "And who are you? The garbage man?"

Andrea and I were shocked and tried not to laugh. My mother broke the ice by declaring, "My daughter is no better than you. She doesn't dress like a professor. What is wrong with the women in your group?"

Now Andrea was shocked. "Mrs. Chesler, Phyllis is one of the most glamorous women in our movement."

Who knew that Andrea noticed such things?

I didn't think of myself as glamorous, but I did wear lipstick and I didn't try to look scruffy or like an adolescent boy. Sometimes feminists held my appearance against me.

Some of the sisters also objected to my being married to a man. In the mid-1970s a group of Australian lesbian academics invited me to speak, then rescinded the invitation when they learned that I was straight and married to a man, and probably planned to travel to Australia with him. (I had.) A radical lesbian-separatist Australian rock band came to my defense: "No matter who she sleeps with, she's still the author of *Women and Madness* and we want to hear her."

Sweet, sweet women.

8 Feminists and the Weather Underground and Lesbian Land on the West Coast

In the mid-1960s, young African, Hispanic, Native, and Caucasian American activists became a driving force for civil rights, free speech, and academic freedom. In manifestos, conferences, and teach-ins, young Americans also opposed the Vietnam War, capitalism, and racism; some eventually became willing to use violence. The mainly male leaders fought about socialism versus communism, totalitarianism versus democratic socialism, and whether Soviet Russia or the United States was more to blame for the Cold War and the nuclear arms race. However, the quarrelsome male socialists, Black Power, Native, and Latino activists shut most women out of significant roles in these debates. In 1965 and 1966, many male movement leaders expected women to make them coffee, do the typing and mimeographing, and provide sex.

As feminist ideas gained currency, women on the Left refused to be treated in this way. They began drafting manifestos of their own, which were treated with contempt. Some men also humiliated the women. When Marilyn Webb, a member of Students for a Democratic Society (SDS), tried to speak about women's liberation, the men yelled: "Take her off the stage and fuck her."

SDS morphed into the Weather Underground. Bill Ayers, Kathy Boudin, Bernardine Dohrn, and Mark Rudd, among many others, began a program of bombing commercial and government buildings and robbing banks. They held up a Brink's armored car and killed a police officer. Some blew themselves up by accident. Survivors went underground.

The FBI spied on the Weather Underground as well as on Martin Luther King's nonviolent civil rights movement, the Black Panthers, and SDS. Weirdly, the FBI also infiltrated nonviolent feminist groups and collectives; informers and agents provocateurs filed reports that many of us later obtained under the Freedom of Information Act.

The FBI had been scouring hippie and lesbian feminist communities in its search for radical left-wing female fugitives. They found no one. Then, in 1974, the Weather Underground fugitive Jane Alpert, who had been in touch with Robin Morgan at *Ms.* magazine, surfaced voluntarily and met with the FBI. Jane was ready to denounce male leftists. She'd become a feminist.

All hell broke loose.

In 1969 Jane had participated in eight bombings of commercial and government buildings in New York City. These bombs led to no deaths or injuries.

She was sentenced to twenty-seven months in jail. Soon after, the FBI arrested five more fugitives, all feminists with whom Jane had lived or traveled. Robin defended Jane by blaming some of the newly arrested women for not taking proper precautions.

Jane had one wish before she went to jail: she wanted to meet the feminists whose work she'd been reading. We gathered in Kate Millett's loft. When Jane arrived, Flo Kennedy and Ti-Grace Atkinson exited noisily and in a rage. They believed that Jane had named names and was therefore responsible for the arrest of one of her former underground comrades and for the imprisonment of several feminists.

In 1974, *Ms.* published Jane's "Ode to Mother-Right," which Gloria introduced. "Mother Right" was a theory that claimed that women are naturally nurturing and compassionate caregivers, biologically different from, and superior to, patriarchal men, who wage war against each other and against women, whom they victimize.

At the time I wanted to believe that this theory could be true. But if it was, how to explain women's cruelty to children, men, and each other?

Robin had formed a "Circle of Support" for Jane that divided the feminist movement in an ugly way: Either you believed in a matriarchy or you didn't; either you believed in class warfare or you didn't; either you were against the government or you were for it; either you sympathized with Jane and Robin or you viewed them as traitors.

Feminists had already fought about whether class warfare against the system or reform *of* the system would free most women. We had fought about whether lesbianism and identity politics were the cutting edge of feminism or the most reactionary, narcissistic, and self-defeating of positions. White feminists berated themselves constantly because women of color were not with us in droves. Some of us made genuine overtures to try to interest women of color in joining us; others made only token efforts. While there were many important individual exceptions, most feminists of color chose to fight for women's rights with other women of color or for racial-minority rights with both men and women of color.

Jane and Robin were supported by Gloria, whom Robin had persuaded to back Jane's position by having Gloria introduce Jane's article and giving it prime space in *Ms.* This led to a great division among feminists. It prepared us to believe the worst about each other: it unleashed demons, exposed fault lines, and was the training ground for what later came to be known as the great feminist sex wars about pornography, prostitution, and censorship. As I said at the time, the FBI could have saved taxpayers money by leaving us alone: feminists did not need agents to do us in. We did a pretty good job of that ourselves.

The Jane-and-Robin division followed me around the city. Once I was standing on a street corner in Greenwich Village waiting for a bus when two women suddenly materialized out of the urban mist. I didn't know them, but they seemed to know me. One stood in front of me, the other to my right. They were standing far too close.

They had come to confront me. They demanded to know whether I would be signing a petition for or against Jane. I refused to say. I don't even know which side they represented, only that they'd come not to have a discussion but to bully and frighten me.

Like most feminists, I simply pledged and maintained my long-time political alliances. I believed that Robin was trying to protect her friend Jane and I admired her for it. However, as a scholar I was uncomfortable with *Ms.*'s embrace of Jane's "mother right" doctrine. I thought that Ti-Grace and Flo had raised some real and worrisome points about it.

Even ideologues were diplomatic and pragmatic where Gloria was concerned. Flo viewed Jane as a pig, but she didn't cut her ties to Gloria over her support for Jane and Robin. I didn't agree with Kate's early support for decriminalizing all aspects of prostitution or Flo's continued support of prostitution, but I didn't cut my ties to either of them, either.

Some years later, Jane Alpert wrote an autobiography in which she accused Robin of using her when she was underground because, as a fugitive, Jane was sexy. Robin stopped visiting her in jail and eventually cut Jane off completely and denounced her as an inveterate man junkie. Jane approached me afterward. She was looking for support and sympathy, trying to get me to see that Robin was a chameleon exploiter. Jane was in anguish, but I didn't break with Robin over this.

Although I had single-handedly created a women's studies course for credit at Richmond College (later the College of Staten Island), the new women's studies program, housed at CUNY's Graduate Center, had never asked me to deliver a lecture. Oh, how I had hoped that when they heard me speak, they would ask me to teach at least one graduate course a year.

Years later, I was finally summoned. After applauding my words, the chair of the program told me: "Look, if we allow you to join us, we'll lose our program. You're too controversial. We can't afford to risk that."

I replied that if she couldn't have someone like me, her program would not be worth much. We were probably both right.

I went to Harold Proshansky, then president of the graduate school, to tell him that I wanted to teach graduate students. His response? "I understand that you're married. Surely you don't need the extra salary. Why, then, bother?"

As Aristotle said, "Revolution may also arise when persons of great ability, and second to none in their merits, are treated dishonorably by those who themselves enjoy the highest honors."

After Jane Alpert surfaced in 1974, left-wing feminists were always looking for FBI agents in their midst. The FBI did infiltrate feminist communities and collectives, ostensibly to determine whether they were hiding Weather Underground fugitives, but also because J. Edgar Hoover really believed that feminism was a threat to national security. If only.

The summer of 1975 was a hot one for feminists. An educational venture in Vermont called Sagaris—named after the weapon used by Scythian Amazons—was splitting the feminist world wide open. Feminists saw FBI agents behind every tree. The atmosphere was highly charged.

The radical-feminist group Redstockings accused Gloria of being a CIA agent. As a result Sagaris attendees split over whether to accept a much-needed grant of "tainted money" from *Ms*.

As I understood it, Sagaris cheerfully accepted grants from the Ford and Rockefeller foundations, so apparently robber baron money was acceptable, but feminist money was held to a higher standard. Robber barons had not presented themselves as feminists, nor were they interested in cornering the market on Brand X Feminism, which Redstockings believed *Ms.* was doing.

I do not believe that Gloria was a CIA agent. In 1959 and 1962, she had attended the World Youth Festivals in, respectively, Vienna and Helsinki. The festivals were largely underwritten by the Soviet Union. She knew that her attendance was partly funded by the CIA, but, according to the feminist historian Ruth Rosen, in *The World Split Open: How the Modern Women's Movement Changed America*, Gloria "naively believed that the CIA did so to help prevent wars, not as a systematic effort to contain and subvert Communism."

This fact would have died on the proverbial vine were it not for Betty Friedan, who kept talking about it and made common cause with those left-wing feminists who earnestly, honestly believed that Gloria was an antifeminist Mata Hari. Gloria took to her couch. She didn't get up for many days. I know because I visited her as her friend and unofficial shrink. I went there day after day until she rose and soared again. The Gloria I knew could not bear to be so disliked, so publicly attacked, the target of so much vitriolic rage.

Gloria was no spy. She was a sincere feminist. That the media preferred a pretty, dry-witted, and emotionally low-key woman must have gnawed at Betty nonstop. Gloria was so damn likeable, and Betty was a rare harridan constantly raging at everyone, including the women who adored and served her.

However, radical leftist feminists did fear that Gloria would water down their version of anticapitalist and antipatriarchal feminism, sell that inferior brand, and gain celebrity, influence, Democratic Party power, and funding, which in turn would enable her to buy off or reward those feminists who supported this approach while consigning to the dustbin of history all those who had been activists years before she began covering their ideas and activism as a journalist.

They had a point.

Feminists spent years accusing each other of being "male identified" and elitist. According to Ruth Rosen: "One of the strangest consequences of such anti-elitism was that activists pressured one another to write without bylines. Writing anonymously had been required of modest ladies of the nineteenth century. Now, in the name of solidarity, some women's liberationists asked that no woman take credit for her work."

My friends Kate Millett, Naomi Weisstein, and Robin Morgan were, like me, subjected to these insane pressures. Charges of plagiarism, especially against Robin, were fierce. But at the time it was impossible for me to know what or whom to believe.

That was what the radical feminists were doing—eating their leaders, destroying their own best minds.

Robin and I were friends. Robin was eloquent, charming, and a superb cook. We met for intimate coffees at Cafe Borgia in the Village and talked nonstop feminism. In one-on-one situations, Robin, who had been a child actor, acted the part of your best, most maternal friend. As one of our movement's many mother-wounded and mother-starved daughters, I was seduced, completely taken in.

Robin needed money and a job, and I suggested to Gloria that she hire Robin at *Ms.* Gloria loved the idea; she always wanted more color around her, both skin color and politically radical color. Robin fit the bill especially well because she was one of the radical-left "downtown" girls, a veteran of the feminist takeovers of the leftist underground newspaper *Rat*, the East Fifth Street Welfare building (where I once worked), and Grove Press, as well as a woman who had kept in touch with SDS members when they were underground.

A perfect cover for the haute bourgeoisie.

What about the grown-ups, the within-the-system reformers? How were *they* doing?

Friedan's book *The Feminine Mystique* had started second-wave feminism as a reform movement. The importance of founding the National Organization for Women must never be underestimated. NOW pioneered countless successful lawsuits, marches, demonstrations, press conferences, and lobbying campaigns.

Betty's volatile, abusive personality had the founding mothers of NOW constantly on edge. She viewed them as attempting to steal her rightful power, not as having normal human reactions to her off-putting behavior.

Then the radicals and the lesbians stole even more of the media thunder that Betty had counted on for herself.

And then came the ultimate indignity. Almost a decade after she had published *The Feminine Mystique*, six years after she had helped found NOW, along came Gloria and *Ms.*, and they stole the media limelight from both Betty and the radicals.

For years Betty refused to greet me; perhaps she didn't recognize me. Maybe she was nearsighted. I was not one of her NOW lackeys; was that why I seemed not to exist for her? Or did she perceive me as too close to Gloria?

I always made it a point to say, "Hello, Betty, how are you? I'm Phyllis." Absent-mindedly she might (or might not) say, "Oh, all right, Phyllis."

Sometime in the 1970s, we were on a panel together. She proudly held aloft a photo of the Pope inscribed "To Betty Friedan." I found that Pope to be exceptionally sympathetic, but had Betty completely forgotten the Catholic Church's record on women regarding abortion, birth control, and divorce? Maybe that was not as important as demonstrating that she moved in elevated circles.

When Betty's book *The Second Stage* appeared in 1981, it did not do well. Elinor "Ellie" Guggenheim gave Betty a book party to buck up her spirits. The living and dining rooms were filled mainly with women, but there were some men too. Our guest of honor wove unsteadily on her feet, talking mainly to the men. When the time came for Betty to say a few words, she waved the invitation and roared: "Why does this read, '*Women* support Betty Friedan'? Why doesn't this invitation read '*Men* and women support Betty Friedan'?"

She often spoke of herself in the third person. She didn't seem to care that we were all looking down, looking away, embarrassed, feeling like shit.

Still, Betty deserved to be honored, warts and all. Like many of the men who changed history, she was difficult: cantankerous, abusive, abrasive, outrageously demanding—and an out-of-control drunk.

Wounded women of genius bring out my maternal instincts. I tend to protect and support them, despite the lack of reciprocity.

For example, I defended Andrea Dworkin against all comers. But I also experienced Andrea as a demanding, domineering figure. She experienced herself as fragile, wounded, and vulnerable. When Andrea verbally laid you low or ordered you around, it was because *she* felt under attack. She was only defending herself. I refused to think of her as the battered wife or prostituted woman she claimed she was—one of patriarchy's ubervictims.

Andrea was a tough-minded tactician and an original thinker, but she demanded blind loyalty from her troops. Personally, she was shy and insecure. She'd sometimes ask me to accompany her when she lectured, together with her life partner, John Stoltenberg, and our mutual agent, Elaine Markson. On stage she threw down gauntlet after gauntlet, often to tremendous applause; afterward she felt that she'd failed, that her views were hated.

She said she was gay. She had no known female lover. John was also gay. Both were gay rights activists. But I saw how she looked at him, her tall, blond Aryan. He was gay and he was sexual. I was not sure about her.

In 1975 Andrea told me that she didn't get a teaching job at Hampshire College because someone in the administration had said that "any woman who would teach Kate Millett's work is intellectually incompetent." She also said that "the edge of my vision is darkening but not because of men. I hate what I see among women."

Although Andrea depended upon Gloria for support, Andrea despised *Ms.* magazine. She knew whom to badmouth (practically everyone), but she defended Gloria and John.

We happened to live near each other both on the Upper West Side of Manhattan and then in Park Slope, Brooklyn. Andrea was a serious European-style leftist, a serious nineteenth-century-style abolitionist, and a serious twentieth-century-style feminist. Andrea was very, very serious.

So there I was, a married woman living on the Upper West Side, writing and lecturing away but a bit weary of my bourgeois life. A young lesbian feminist offered to take me on a tour of the women's land trusts in Oregon and Washington. It was summer, I had some free time, and I left within days. (My poor husband!)

Lesbian feminists had gone "back to the land," not as survivalists but as utopians committed to all-female communities. I had long wondered whether this phenomenon was real and would last or was a charming but passing fantasy, something out of the pages of a feminist science fiction novel by Joanna Russ, Sally Gearhart, or Diana Rivers.

I found that some of the feminists who were living collectively were committed to it, while others seemed to be dropping out of school, work, and adult life, but only for a while.

My guide took me to a feminist collective in Seattle where the women owned guns, regularly attended target practice, and were building a house together in the country. We traveled by motorcycle. For years afterward I bore a faint indentation where I burned my leg on the exhaust pipe.

There, hours from Portland, I saw Amazons straight out of science fiction. I had never seen eight women working together to build a house. They were putting on a roof, sawing wood, measuring windows. I didn't see them as male identified. I saw them as mythic angels building a shining city in the desert.

Given the rampant anti-elitism among feminists, I decided to travel under a pseudonym: Buttercup. At lunch (peanut-butter-and-jelly sandwiches) we were expected to discuss "political apathy in the Left lesbian community." I said that I saw no such apathy here, that I felt I was standing on sacred ground. I was amazed by such a holy sight: women who so expertly put hammer to nail so that a glorious house would rise into the air from nothingness.

"Who the hell are you?"

At a farm I saw women planting, gardening, sitting in a sauna, building a shrine to "the goddess," and eating only what they could grow. Their beds were sleeping bags in colorful tents. It was medieval and fabulist.

"Is this land collectively owned?" I asked.

"Nah, we're renting it from some man."

At another location the answer was, "The land is owned by one of the women. Well, actually, her parents are loaded and they own the land."

The pioneers were not the owners. This didn't seem to bother them. They lived on money from home or on welfare and disability checks. This, then, was only a temporary New Land, a vacation paradise, not a serious, sustainable future way of life.

When I visited an Oakland collective, packed to the rafters with lesbian feminist poets, I noticed that it had too few towels and those they had were thin and always damp; that the fridge was practically empty and the ashtrays overflowing; and it was dark even at noon because the shades were always drawn.

"Why do rebel women choose to live on the other side of midnight?" I asked.

My friend told me, "We won't do housework, and we won't pay someone else to do our dirty work for us."

A group of women became core members of Kate Millett's Poughkeepsie Christmas tree farm and summer colony for artists. For half the summer day they planted Christmas trees (which Kate planned to sell in the city), repaired barns, and tinkered with the plumbing; for the other half they painted, sculpted, and wrote poems, and then swam, lounged, drank, dined, quarreled, danced, made love—and made off with each other's lovers.

I visited often but kept my distance. Although I loved them all, as a group they were far too promiscuous for me. They were also capable of surviving without air-conditioning in the most intense heat. This I could not easily do.

The farm and artist's colony was a charmed vision, its only flaw Kate's bouts of madness. But her writing and the kind of bohemian feminism she symbolized still had the power to lure the lesbian feminist artists to Poughkeepsie summer after summer, in search of utopia, their truest and only home.

In 1984, Simone de Beauvoir and her adopted daughter, Sylvie Le Bon, came to visit. Kate was going to write a book about her relationship with Beauvoir, but then illness struck and Kate did not get to do so. The philosopher Linda Clarke and the musician Joan Casamo exerted a graceful and stabilizing force over this madcap enterprise. I came to love them both.

I remember when Linda first left, in 1972, her incongruously long skirt dragging behind her impeccable blazer, her white-blond hair glowing like the sun. Kate begged me to ask her to stay. Clarkie hugged us both, smiled, and continued down the path and on her way to Mother India.

Now, back from the land of ashrams, Clarkie set and cleared a fine table and gentled the interns into washing and drying the dishes. The bathtubs were clean and even had some fluffy towels. Clarkie was now devoted to uplifting those assembled at Kate's: this was now her chosen spiritual practice. When she was not hard at work, Clarkie (who has a doctorate in philosophy) sat writing mantras in a thick notebook.

9 The Pornography Wars Commence, and I Host the First Feminist Passover Seder in America

In February 1976, the distributor Allan Shackleton released *Snuff* in a Times Square movie theater. The film depicted a naked woman being raped, murdered, and dismembered.

Antipornography activists went crazy. Andrea Dworkin called me and said, "I'm going to kill myself." The poet and activist Leah Fritz, the author of *Thinking Like a Woman*, said, "I can't stand it." Both Leah and Andrea sounded *personally* endangered by this film.

They ordered me to "get lawyers." I tried. I called every lawyer I knew and pleaded: "Some women are threatening civil disobedience. Others are threatening to destroy property or to physically prevent customers from going in." (Aka dyke tactics. They might be arrested.) This usually seemed to excite both journalists and lawyers.

However, the American Civil Liberties Union was having its national convention. Lawyers were in short supply.

At the Women's Coffeehouse Leah announced, Phyllis has called *all* the lawyers in town and no one will come.

I hadn't called all the lawyers—only those I knew and could reach. Two actually came to one of the demonstrations.

Filmed rapes, fictionalized rapes, and faked rapes are considered free speech protected under the First Amendment. Many feminists considered violent pornography to be speech protected under the First Amendment.

We held a meeting at the attorney Betty Levinson's apartment.

Betty specialized in representing victims of domestic violence and believed in their right to sue their batterers for damages. She employed the concept in the late 1980s, when she represented Hedda Nussbaum against Joel Steinberg, the man who battered her and killed their six-year-old non-adopted daughter, Lisa. Whether Levinson was able to recover money from a financially ruined Steinberg is irrelevant. She used Nussbaum to pioneer a concept that lawyers could use on behalf of other battered women.

After the meeting, four or five of us crowded into a small elevator. It got stuck. We started yelling for help and banging on the walls. The lesbian activist and author (*Out of the Closets*) Karla Jay said: "I think I can get us out of here." Andrea and I cautioned her not do anything crazy. Someone heard our screams and told us he would call the police. After half an hour Karla said, "I'm doing something," and she did. Somehow she got the elevator to move. At that moment the police arrived.

Karla believed in self-help.

Three hundred to six hundred of us demonstrated outside the movie theater for days, in the rain and the cold. The prominent anti–Vietnam War activist and author Grace Paley (*Enormous Changes at the Last Minute*), the civil rights activist Barbara Deming (*Prison Notes*), the antipornography activist Dorchen Leidholdt, the author Susan Brownmiller (*Against Our Will: Men, Women, and Rape*), Andrea, Leah, and me.

Grace had an amazing discussion with Allan Shackleton. He told her that he admired her stance on the Vietnam War and asked, quite sincerely, whether she thought the issue of the snuff film in any way compared to the war issue. Grace told him, "Absolutely yes." I saw his genuinely surprised face.

Grace made this point: just as innocent civilians were being wounded and murdered in Vietnam, women were being tortured and murdered—not only prostitutes, but also wives and girlfriends, because of the influence of sadistic pornography on men.

The feminist views about pornography then were diverse and highly charged. They still are. One faction feared state censorship, Puritanism, and patriarchy's history of controlling women in terms of whom they can sleep with and how they must have (or never have) orgasms. Another faction was concerned with how many incestuously abused runaways and battered wives were used in the making of pornographic films and viewed their false portrayals of pleasure as forced, not free, even if the force was mainly economic. A third faction was more interested in how pornography aroused people, lowered inhibition, and led to enjoyment they might otherwise not have had. A fourth faction believed that pornography might reduce rape and that it was also useful in terms of teaching young men "what to do." A fifth faction believed that pornography teaches boys to degrade women as living sex toys and to treat all women as if they were prostituted.

Andrea Dworkin and the legal scholar Catherine "Kitty" MacKinnon pioneered the idea that if a woman could prove, in a court of law, that she had been harmed by a particular man or group of men who had forced her to perform pornographic acts (the acts of a prostitute), that she could sue for civil (money) damages. But first, she would have to persuade a jury and/or judge and this might be hard to prove. However, this idea was defamed and defeated by a coalition of feminists, lawyers, and "pro-sex" activists.

I suggested that we petition the district attorney to close down the movie. We did and we failed. Women in other cities did get the movie closed down.

We eventually learned that no woman was ever murdered or dismembered during the making of the film—it was all trick photography.

More than forty years have passed since we demonstrated against *Snuff*, and it was nearly that long ago that I stood next to Andrea at NYU Law School's first-ever conference on pornography. I suggested that we consider pornography a form of harmful hate speech, one that may lead to or desensitize us against violence toward women. My idea inflamed the First Amendment lawyers present.

Andrea Dworkin and Kitty MacKinnon were royally pilloried for their crusade against pornography.

So what did we accomplish?

Not much. Images of women being debased during or through sex have gotten even raunchier and are now pandemic: the folks next door post videos of themselves having sex, and paramilitary barbarians, like ISIS warriors, demand that the child virgins they have kidnapped reenact the scenes of the most sadistic pornography or die.

But, to our credit, we were willing to take to the streets.

In 1986, we demonstrated outside Dorrian's Red Hand on East Eighty-fourth Street. This was the bar where the six-foot-five-inch Robert Chambers (the "Preppy Killer") was drinking heavily when he met the eighteen-year-old, five-foot-four-inch Jennifer Levin. He subsequently claimed that they had had "rough sex" and that he killed her by accident.

But dead she was—yet another young victim of an increasingly "lost boy" scene fueled by alcohol, cocaine, pot, and failing grades.

Andrea Dworkin, Dorchen Leitholdt, Norma Ramos, and I were distraught. We had to do something. So we stood outside Dorrian's and howled for Jennifer Levin, for all the young women who had been oh-so-casually raped or killed by young men all across the country and around the world. Chambers expressed no remorse, laughed at the accusations, eventually pleaded guilty to manslaughter, did hard time in prison, emerged with his longtime girlfriend on his arm, and was again imprisoned, this time for running a cocaine ring.

Dorrian's Red Hand settled a suit brought by Jennifer Levin's parents, who claimed the bar had served an excessive amount of alcohol to Chambers. Her parents also won a wrongful death lawsuit that prevented Chambers from keeping any money he might make from book or movie deals.

———

Male authors routinely review their friends' work. In the 1970s, women feared that they would be criticized if they did so—that they'd be seen as biased or sneaky and would never again be called upon to review a book. An editor once harshly interrogated me after I volunteered to review a book. "Do you know the author? Are you her friend? Do you have some ulterior motive?"

As a result, many women were reluctant to review a friend's book. For example, in 1976 the *New York Times Book Review* asked a friend of mine to review the book I wrote with Emily Jane Goodman, *Women, Money and Power*. My friend turned the opportunity down. She reported, "I told them that we're friends and that I cannot in good conscience pretend to neutrality here."

We both knew—we'd spent hours discussing it—how few women were reviewed and how few women were asked to write reviews for the *Book Review* back then; we knew that men who were colleagues, even friends, reviewed each other all the time.

Still, my eminently literary friend was above all that.

Ah, friends.

When I was in Israel in 1975, I had delivered standing-room-only lectures about feminism at the American Embassy in Tel Aviv and in Haifa, where the American feminist writer E.M. Broner heard me speak. She praised me—oh, how she praised my every word. I was hooked. Although E.M. slept little, she was always "on," always superenergized. We decided that once she was back in the States, I'd organize a feminist Passover seder for us and invite all the right people.

E.M. and Naomi Nimrod had begun drafting a counter-Haggadah (the book Jews read to tell the Exodus story about how we were liberated from slavery in Egypt). *The Women's Haggadah* would feature our long-missing mothers and not our omnipresent fathers; we envisioned a corrective to the male-dominated tale.

And so I invited the left-wing artists Edith Isaac-Rose and Bea Kreloff; the publicist and *Ms.* editor Letty Cottin Pogrebin; and the left-wing filmmaker Lilly Rivlin, all of whom became core members. I also invited Bella Abzug, Gloria Steinem, and Aviva Cantor Zuckoff, with whom I'd been organizing conferences about Judaism and feminism—and about anti-Semitism among leftist feminists—since the early 1970s. Aviva was also one of the cofounders of *Lilith* magazine, the first Jewish feminist publication.

Gloria had me pegged for a pagan and after the seder, asked me privately whether I really believed "all this stuff." I told her that this seder was my legacy—an intellectual and religious treasure that was meant for women too. "Gloria, we're feminists who want to take back our religion." She did not look persuaded.

The seder became an annual event that lasted for more than forty years. Over time, it became more concerned with important social justice issues than with divine intervention—and a ritual not necessarily specific to Jews. We became a celebrated clique, dominated by, as the Catholic Church might say, "particular friendships."

One reward of being a published author is that you get to meet other published writers. Our conversations were heady, as if we were members of a secret society. We got to know the person behind the book cover.

For example, in 1976 I was invited to meet the great French writer Monique Wittig at the apartment of the art critic and literature professor Gloria Orenstein. Monique was the author of two literary masterpieces: *Les Guérillères* ("The Amazon Warriors") and *Across the Acheron*.

When we met, she said, "You cannot be Dr. Chesler. She's a very tall woman, an Amazon."

I replied, "Monique, look at you—you're even shorter than I am. Perhaps Amazons are short people."

Monique was broke. "The Marxists drove me out of Paris," she said. She pronounced Paris as *Baris*.

I had often read passages from her books aloud before my lectures, so I insisted on giving her a royalty check.

"But," I said, "there's a catch."

Monique had created a wreath of women's names on some of her book's right-hand pages. "Phyllis" wasn't among them. "Please include my name."

She took out a pencil and did so immediately. I treasure this volume.

Monique was actually driven out of Paris by the zero-sum games played by feminists, especially lesbian feminists—and, yes, by Marxists too. I could never understand the French feminist movement, and I really tried. Some took a psychoanalytic approach to politics, refusing to consider any other approach. One feminist psychoanalyst even tried to trademark the name of the French women's liberation movement, Mouvement de Libération des Femmes.

Others believed only in class struggle and viewed women's liberation as part of, or secondary to, class struggle in Marxist terms. Still others viewed women as an underclass and men as an overclass to be overthrown. Different groups of radical lesbians challenged the gay movement for being primarily male focused and male dominated and the feminist movement for being primarily heterosexual. Some lesbians viewed straight women as collaborators with men on behalf of men as a class.

The same splits existed in the United States—minus the unique arrogance of French intellectuals and the beauty of the French language. However, French feminists were uniquely incomprehensible in the ways in which they adopted and transformed language.

Monique suffered all these splits. As I understood it, what drove

Monique out of "Baris" was a lesbian who made off with another lesbian's lover, which led to the dissolution of a group of feminists.

Feminists on both sides of the Atlantic were cruel to their more talented stars. Monique was a major star.

Some women who write tend to be high-strung and needy. Many of my friends were women who wrote. Our dramas were always high dramas.

Some of my dearest friends were demanding and difficult women. Would they say the same about me? Probably.

Marge Piercy is a great poet and novelist. I turned over to her some of the interviews I had taped for *Women and Madness*, and she used one of them to fashion a rather fabulous heroine, Connie Ramos, for her novel *Woman on the Edge of Time*. Marge was a puritanical leftist but she also loved gardening, cooking, and all the pleasures of the flesh.

When we were together, especially when she traveled down from the Cape to New York City, Marge needed me to serve as her faithful courtier. If she lost something, I was supposed to find it. She was anxious about being late to her poetry readings, so she always left early. Since I was expected to accompany her, I too had to leave early.

Once, when Marge was in a grave emotional crisis, I suggested that we try becoming ordinary friends and talking about personal matters, not just about our work and our ideas.

She replied: "You always come through when it's a matter of revolution. I count on you like no one else. But you're not able to meet my emotional needs."

Perhaps she was right. But I felt bad. I'd like to be there for her but I can't. Like me, she was too needy, too sensitive—and she was right. I always put my work first and relationships second.

———

The poet Martha Shelley's family name was Altman, but she used Percy Bysshe Shelley's last name. Martha wrote poems to me. We were the best of friends. But she wanted more. I prized our friendship, but the tension remained.

Once, Martha, Marge, and I came upon an enormous stash of pornography in the bathroom of a radical male comrade's home. Quietly and quickly we destroyed it. We burned some of it, tore some of it up, and hid some of it and later tossed it out the car window. We didn't rescue the women who had been trafficked for male pleasure; we didn't cut into the pimp's or pornographer's profits; we didn't even get ourselves arrested for destroying private property. What we did didn't constitute a political act, but it represented our gut-level revulsion toward both the pornography and the hypocrisy of that particular consumer.

In 1977 Jeanne Parr interviewed me and Gloria Steinem on CBS-TV about women and money. Afterward Gloria and I shared a limousine, and as I was about to get out, she suddenly turned to me and asked: "Should we be buried near each other? If so, where? What did Susan B. Anthony and Elizabeth Cady Stanton do?"

This was a heart-stopping and poignant question.

Gloria continued, "I know you have some attachment to Israel, but do you want to be buried there?"

Then, almost immediately, she asked: "Wanna come clubbing tonight?"

"Of course not."

We had had this exchange about nightlife many times before. After a long, hard day at work, the idea of dancing and drinking with the Beautiful People horrified me.

But Gloria was indefatigable. She attended theater and film premieres, art gallery openings, book parties, and birthday parties, and "took" breakfast meetings. I didn't comprehend how important this nonstop activity was in terms of becoming a familiar face among powerful people in the service of fund-raising and branding.

I also thought it was a bit early to be thinking about our burials. (About fifteen years later, my dear friend Merle Hoffman and I placed ads asking women who wished to be buried together with other feminists to contact us. Only a few replied.)

Later that same night, Gloria and I met for an early dinner at Elaine's, on the Upper East Side. Elaine's was *the* celebrity joint in town, known for its clientele of actors and authors. Joseph Heller, Gay and Nan Talese, Tom Wolfe, Sidney Zion, Nora Ephron, and Nick Pileggi were regulars. Woody Allen filmed scenes for two of his movies at Elaine's.

As she had before, Gloria told me that I was "a real heavyweight" and that she was a "real lightweight."

"What are you talking about?" I asked. "You're running a magazine, you're working politically—you've just gotten a Woodrow Wilson fellowship. Surely that will allow you to put together a collection of your essays."

"If there's a spare fellowship in someone's back pocket, might you want to come?"

"I'd be happy for the money and the time off, but I can't leave my teaching position to live in Washington for a year."

Did she just invite me to become part of her court, and did I just decline the honor?

Gloria didn't laugh at my ideas about gathering feminists together internationally and thinking of us as a kind of feminist government in formation and in exile. She listened carefully and asked thoughtful questions.

I was invited to conduct a grand rounds at the Langley Porter Psychiatric Clinic in San Francisco. I thought I was so smart. I found three women who had once been incarcerated there and asked them to join me in some political theater by asking each of them to describe what the psychiatric staff did to her.

The women were brilliant. They pointed at specific doctors and said: "You ordered shock therapy for me." "You gave me bad medicine." It was all so theatrical—until two of the women began to decompensate and started ranting about the Vietnam War, South America, and the voices in their heads.

I was embarrassed. The staff was embarrassed for me. I was embarrassed for the women. Afterward I had lunch with some young staff psychiatrists. They asked me: "What can we do? When the talk therapy and all the meds that we have fail, and when our patient is still suicidal or agonizingly depressed, we try shock therapy. Sometimes it works; it pulls them back. They go on with their lives. Should we avoid this treatment for political reasons?"

They were right. And from that moment on, I repeated their question whenever I spoke about the subject. I had nothing left to lose. I had long ago run afoul of the Mental Patients' Liberation Project people—poor souls, much sinned against, but also so lost in outer space.

I believe that madness does exist and that those who suffer from it have been punitively diagnosed, stigmatized, and mistreated. Nevertheless, I oppose those who attempt to romanticize depression or to view it as an art form. I view mania, depression, intrusive flashbacks, and schizophrenia as real, not imaginary; I do not think that a political revolution can cure such states of being.

However, these symptoms, which may also be caused by chronic or acute traumas, were not easily cured by medications or talking cures in the 1960s and 1970s.

Deinstitutionalizing public psychiatric hospitals was absolutely the right thing to do. But allowing vulnerable people to hallucinate and live on the streets is no kinder to them than incarcerating them against their will but failing to help them.

If you are a clinician and not an ideologue, and if you care about someone who is suffering (whether you are a family member, a friend, or a therapist), you will try anything and everything that might work. A number of public figures have come forward to claim that low levels of maintenance shock therapy (preceded by tranquilizers) was the only thing that helped save them from the most profound depression. Others insist that shock therapy led to their losing many memories for weeks or months, or even permanently. Some people with manic depressive, bipolar, or anxiety disorders extol the drugs that they say have saved them; others cannot bear the side effects, stop taking their meds, and soon begin another downward spiral.

Ideologues who mistrust physicians, therapists, and drugs, and those who have been incarcerated in hospitals where they have, in fact, been brutalized, do not want to hear any of this. Some people who suffer from a mental illness try to cover their considerable shame by insisting that mental illness does not exist, or that even if it does, they are not suffering from it.

Members of a Mental Patients' Liberation Project who considered my views traitorous (for an alleged liberator) targeted me. That I would find medication or even hospitalization, not to mention shock therapy, ever acceptable, under any conditions, was absolute anathema to them. One woman kept writing articles opposing all my views, not just these particular ones.

Once, a student of mine—not a patient—was actively hallucinating and on drugs. Her friends brought her to me for help. She'd been walking around all night in fairly treacherous neighborhoods half naked. Her preferred drug rehab center had no room for her, so I walked her over to a hospital (she was totally docile) and asked that they consider admitting her to the psychiatric ward.

"She's in danger out on those mean streets," I said. "She can detox more safely as an inpatient."

When I introduced myself, the young female psychiatrist on duty asked if I was the same Phyllis Chesler who wrote *Women and Madness*. When I told her I was she replied: "How can you of all people be party to an involuntary hospitalization? True, this woman is in no condition to accept or reject being hospitalized, but I do not see her as an imminent danger to herself or to others, so I cannot admit her."

Ah, be careful what you write. Or, rather, be wary of how what you write may be interpreted.

This student dropped out of school and I never saw her or heard from her again.

Another time the women who had spent years enabling Kate Millett's madness came to me, utterly distraught.

"She hasn't slept for days, maybe weeks. She's drinking and verbally, sometimes physically, abusing us and driving *us* mad. She needs some meds that work. She won't take anything on her own. Please help."

Big Shot here called a young female psychiatrist and told her that we had an important woman in need of help. "If you hospitalize her against her will, I want her out in one week, no matter what, and some of us must be allowed to visit her every day," I said. The psychiatrist agreed, but then managed to screw things up considerably.

She sent police cars and ambulances, and Kate—witty, brilliant Kate—read the officers and paramedics the riot act about her civil rights in the most lucid fashion, and off they all went.

Some time later, and more than once, Kate would look at me rather balefully and say: "Buddy, old buddy, you would have done that to me? How could you?"

Although I believed that I'd done the right thing, I still was ashamed.

After that, Kate voluntarily started talk therapy and began taking meds, which she always hated. And I? I helped her frame her arguments against psychiatry each time she insisted on debating psychiatrists in public.

———

I was frequently asked to speak to psychotherapists and psychoanalysts. Women members of various psychological associations often insisted I be invited; often I was the token feminist. One of these occasions was especially memorable.

I got to bear witness to two acts of courage at the Boston Institute for Psychotherapy. First, the audience, composed of both men and women, demanded that one of the panelists name the psychiatrist who had been censured by the Ethics Committee of the American Psychological Association for sleeping with his female patients. She took a deep breath and did so.

I immediately stood up and named him too. I asked the audience of five hundred to stand and name him as well. If he was going to sue, he'd have to sue all of us.

Second, a young woman associated with this institute bravely said that it didn't hire women. The institute invited outside women like me to come once a year, but that was all. She said that the institute claimed it could not find any qualified women. She continued: "I practice in this community. The men who are here have the power to hurt me in terms of nonreferrals or in other ways. Phyllis has asked us to be courageous, and that's what I'm doing."

She was applauded for a full five minutes. I had tears in my eyes. If you are invited to deliver paid lectures, your travel is also funded, and you can meet like-minded people in many cities around the country and around the world. On that same visit to Boston I had dinner with Rita Mae Brown. It was then that she confirmed to me Jill Johnston's anti-Semitism.

"Jill used to call me at two or three in the morning to complain that the Jewish mafia was taking over the women's movement."

"She may have only meant me," I said.

Robin Morgan and I were walking arm in arm one winter day. She talked to me about motherhood and about how many radical feminists disapproved of her becoming a biological mother and wouldn't help her in any way.

"If I needed a quart of milk for my baby and would ask someone who was already on her way over here for a meeting to pick it up, I'd get nothing but attitude."

We also talked about publishing. She thanked me for writing a letter to some publishers on her behalf. I talked to her about the importance of expanding our feminist vision internationally, creating an international feminist think tank, and thinking in terms of a future feminist government in formation.

10 Do Women of Color Have the Right to Kill White Male Rapists in Self-Defense? Do Lesbians Have the Right to Custody of Their Children?

In my pre-feminist days, sexual harassment and rape were so common, so pervasive, so accepted that they were virtually invisible. The shame, the stench, stuck to the victim or to the whistle-blower; the abuser almost never experienced the consequences of his actions. In fact, he was almost never even named, and when he was, all ranks closed to protect him and to destroy his accuser.

In the 1950s and 1960s, the great men (and the few token women) of the academy did not study sexual violence. Yet in the 1970s, they claimed to be the experts and characterized as exaggerated and man-hating the grassroots feminist exposés of sexual violence against women.

Back then, like most young women, I was sexually harassed—by professors, employers, and strangers on street corners. Also like others of my generation, I was bred to accept it, keep quiet about it, and blame myself if something about these peculiar arrangements bothered me. For years I did this, until the feminist movement in the late 1960s allowed me to analyze my situation in feminist terms.

As every woman knows, hell hath no fury like a man spurned.

In the late 1960s, after we had had dinner together, the head of a department at a prestigious medical school tried to rape me. I was a graduate student and we'd met at his suggestion (I'm guilty, I confess: I went, I ate) to discuss how he could assist me in getting my research funded. In the decidedly nonamorous scuffle that ensued I broke one of his ribs, and although I helped him to a nearby hospital, he never helped me get my research funded.

In the early 1970s a professor arrived to rate my college's curriculum for a national review board. I admit it; I did it again: I accepted his invitation to a dinner party with well-known intellectuals and their wives. My equally ambitious heterosexual male counterparts also accepted dinner invitations, but they didn't have to face sexual harassment at the hands of their heterosexual mentors. I had the audacity to reject this professor's every subsequent social and sexual advance. He retaliated by arranging for the publication of a scathing review of *Women and Madness*.

Neither of these professors were overcome with love for me. They treated me as they did because I was a woman.

It was nothing personal. Prejudice rarely is.

I will always remember the 1970s as the decade in which three important lawsuits tested a victim's right to self-defense against a rapist or a drunken neighborhood intruder and pedophile. These cases were about gender, class, and race. They garnered huge amounts of publicity and were understood as feminist causes.

I always tried to bring these cases into my lectures. My knowledge of them allowed me to understand the Aileen Wuornos case in 1991—allegedly, the first female serial killer. I was able to see Wuornos as a woman who may have killed a rapist in self-defense, not only as a prostituted woman who became a serial killer. I was able to assemble a team of experts on Wuornos's behalf using some of the legal work that had first been done in the 1970s.

All three of the 1970s rape and self-defense cases involved poor women of color: Yvonne Wanrow, a Native American in Washington State; Joan Little, an African American in North Carolina; and Inez Garcia, a Latina in California. Defense committees and pro bono lawyers sprang into action in all three cases.

The burning issue these cases raised was whether a woman has the right to kill a man who was "merely" trying to rape her or a child, and whether killing him to avoid being raped is ever justifiable. Traditionally the answer was no. But how does a woman or a child know whether the rapist or pedophile plans to murder them afterward?

Rape is a violent act that can also end in the victim's death. Nevertheless, jurors and judges, both male and female, once had more sympathy for the man on trial whose life might be ruined by a rape accusation than for the woman who survived the encounter—and who, they often believed, probably seduced the man anyway.

No woman wants to be raped. Even a prostituted woman has the right to defend herself against rape.

There is a long and buried history of Black American women speaking out against rape and braving considerable shame in order to testify, in detail, about the most terrifying ordeals.

However, such anti-rape and anti-sexual harassment campaigns have been repeatedly forgotten or ghettoized.

Although I was one of the keynote speakers at the first-ever New York Radical Feminist Speak-Out on Rape in NYC, in 1971, neither I nor the other mainly white feminists gathered there, knew anything about the 1944 brutal white-on-black gang rape of Recy Taylor in Alabama, or about the nationwide protest campaign that followed.

Taylor's story, only one among many, was carefully documented, *but only thirty-eight years later*, by historian Danielle L. McGuire in her powerful book *At the Dark End of the Street: Black Women, Rape, and Resistance—a New History of the Civil Rights Movement from Rosa Parks to the Rise of Black Power*. This book led to a 2017 documentary on the subject, *The Rape of Recy Taylor*.

Most white feminists had no idea that the NAACP, a host of other organizations, and thousands of individuals had once campaigned for justice for Taylor. Her rapists were six white men and their identities were known; one even confessed. But the grand jury refused to indict twice.

The lynching of Black men and the rape of Black women were normalized in the Jim Crow South. Any Black woman who dared "tell" was threatened with death—and the death of her family. White men were never held accountable for raping Black women, not during slavery, and not afterwards, in the Jim Crow South.

Taylor has many Foremothers, especially Celia, a Missouri slave. Historian Melton A. McLaurin published an elegant book about her case—but not until 1991. We did not know about Celia until twenty years after our Speak-Out.

In 1850, an aging widower and farmer, Robert Newsom, purchased Celia, a fourteen-year-old child. Newsom raped Celia on the way to her new home; by the time Celia was nineteen she had given birth to two of Newsom's children.

Celia warned Newsom to keep away. When he advanced upon her anyway, she killed him, burned his body in her fireplace, crushed his bones, and hid some of the ashes. Celia did not flee.

Boldly, Celia denied everything. Faced with evidence, Celia finally confessed. Newspaper reports claimed that the murder had been committed "without any sufficient cause." This lie was repeated in William Lloyd Garrison's *The Liberator*—which meant that other abolitionist newspapers paid little attention to the story.

Celia was tried by an all-white, all-male jury and judge. Four of the jurors owned slaves. Although the judge remained hostile, Celia's highly experienced white defense attorney, John Jameson, argued that Celia had the moral, and possibly the legal right to kill in defense of her honor and her life. According to McLaurin, this argument was both "as bold as it was brilliant."

This may have been the first time in American history that a woman, slave or free, was seen as having such a right.

Jameson wanted Celia acquitted. The jury found her guilty and she was sentenced to hang. On December 21, 1855, Celia was "marched to the gallows . . . the trap was sprung and Celia fell to her death."

Celia now has some descendants.

In 1972, Yvonne Wanrow, a Native American, shot and killed William Wesler, a known child molester and psychiatric patient, after he attacked her son. Wesler had also previously raped her babysitter's seven-year-old daughter, giving her a sexually transmitted infection. Wesler had advanced upon Wanrow and her children in a drunken state. At the time she was in her own home. Wesler was a white man who lived in the neighborhood. Wanrow had a broken leg, which was in a cast, and was on crutches. At first she pleaded guilty; then she changed her plea to guilty by reason of temporary insanity and self-defense. Wanrow was found guilty of second-degree murder and first-degree assault, and was sentenced to twenty years in prison.

In 1975 the state appeals court reversed the decision and ordered a retrial. The defense appealed to the Washington Supreme Court. This time Wanrow's attorneys were Elizabeth Schneider of the Center for Constitutional Rights, Susan B. Jordan, and Mary Alice Theiler. They argued that a woman's right to self-defense should be based on different criteria than those that govern crimes committed by men against men, and that an endangered woman's perceptions and her need for weaponry against a much taller and heavier male attacker have to be taken into account.

The case was remanded back to state court for retrial. On April 26, 1978, Wanrow ended her seven-year ordeal in the Washington State courts and was freed. Wanrow pleaded guilty to reduced charges of manslaughter and second-degree assault in Spokane County Superior Court. She was sentenced to five years' probation by Judge Harold Clarke.

I met Yvonne when we both spoke at a conference for battered women on the West Coast. I asked her what had kept her strong during her seven-year ordeal.

"I meditated on the American flag—really, on the eagle at the top of the pole," she told me.

One wonders whether she would have been found guilty if she'd been a white woman who had shot and killed a Native American known to be a child molester.

In 1974, Joan Little, a twenty-year-old African American who was in jail for petty crimes, killed a sixty-two-year-old white prison guard, Clarence Alligood, with a pickax. His body, naked from the waist down with semen on his leg, was found in her cell. Little herself was missing, but when she was found, she insisted that Alligood had threatened her with the pickax and demanded oral sex.

The demand for sexual favors, as well as the rape of female prisoners, most of whom are women of color, was, and still is, epidemic in American prisons. Morris Dees, a lawyer with the Southern Poverty Law Center, established the Joan Little Defense Fund; Julian Bond and Dick Gregory joined protesters outside the courthouse; Ralph Abernathy, president of the Southern Christian Leadership Conference, was quoted as saying: "If there was a white woman who had stabbed a black man who was attempting to rape her, would that white woman be on trial today? That white woman would be given a Medal of Honor."

Angela Davis, writing in the pages of *Ms.* magazine, saw Little's case in political terms—as did I. She called upon "whites and women to grasp the issue of male supremacy in relation to the racism and class bias" involved in Little's case.

Little was charged with first-degree murder, which mandated a death sentence. At trial she claimed that Alligood had entered her cell three times. When he was temporarily weakened after his orgasm, Little seized the pickax, killed Alligood, and escaped. A jury of six whites and six African Americans found her not guilty.

Inez García, a religious American woman of Cuban and Puerto Rican heritage, worked in the lettuce fields to be near her husband, an anti-Castro political prisoner doing time in Soledad Prison, in

California. In 1974 Miguel Jimenez, a three-hundred-pound drug dealer, held García down while Louie Castillo raped her. Soon after, the men began taunting and laughing at her; they also threatened to kill her if she didn't leave town. About twenty minutes later, at another location, Jimenez flashed a knife at García and she shot him dead with her son's rifle.

García was ashamed that she had been raped and initially claimed that the two men had only attempted to rape her. García's first lawyer was Charles Garry, who had defended the Black Panthers Huey P. Newton and Bobby Seale. García's husband had advised her to work with Garry, who was certainly no feminist; he did not even consider that a woman might have a right to defend herself against rape. Instead he argued "diminished capacity," namely, that rape diminishes a woman's mental faculties and that if García killed Jimenez it was because she had not been in her right mind at the time.

In 1974 the jury found Garcia guilty of second-degree murder and sentenced her to five years to life and imprisoned her. "Free Inez" defense committees sprang up all over California. Feminists began speaking out about the issues raised by her case and raising money for her defense. García began to insist that she'd been raped and had a right to defend her honor.

I had some inside insights into this case. Maria del Drago, a Latina-American academic administrator, was Kate Millett's lover at the time. Maria was livid at the behavior of García's mainly lesbian feminist defenders and told me that the man who raped Garcia had "raped many women in that community who are too frightened to step forward. Now who surrounds Inez? A group of all-gay feminists with denim coveralls on who keep changing their names and addresses but not their clothes."

Maria finally managed to get an appointment with Governor Jerry Brown; she wanted to ask for a pardon, or at least bail, for García. Maria confided in me: "I told [Garcia's supporters]: 'It's far better to do it with an appointment. If you want to wear all your Gay Pride buttons—Fuck the Pig! Down with the Mother!—fine, but let's do it with an appointment.' They refused. I am tearing my hair out."

García won an appeal and a retrial. Now she was represented by the feminist lawyer Susan Jordan, who dropped the diminished capacity defense and argued that García had acted in self-defense. The jury acquitted her. Lawyers viewed the case as establishing a woman's right to use deadly force against a rapist and would-be rapists.

Because more men—mainly of color—are imprisoned than women, the plight of women behind bars is not as visible. Often, the mainly battered, prostituted, and drug-addicted women—as well as the women who finally kill their batterers—are demonized rather than pitied, and they tend to draw fewer passionate advocates.

I was summoned, urged, begged to consult on the earliest high-profile, feminist-era lesbian custody cases in America.

One took place in San Francisco. In 1977 the lesbian activist Jeanne Jullion won physical custody of her two boys in San Francisco, but the judge ordered that her Italian-born husband keep their passports and allowed him to take the boys to Italy for a summer vacation. Jeanne's attorneys pleaded with the judge not to do this because of the danger that the father would not return them. Indeed, In July 1978 he left the boys in Italy with his mother.

Jeanne's "crime" was that she had come out as a lesbian at a time when lesbianism was still viewed as an illness or as a serious affront to patriarchy.

Jeanne traveled to Italy and found her sons. One of them was eager to accompany her back to the United States. Jeanne wrote about her struggle in her book *Long Way Home*.

When we finally met, I was impressed by Jeanne's cool but determined demeanor. She sighed as she shared the many difficulties involved in being a "public lesbian" and a single mother to a boy who was sensitive about being taunted.

In 1976, I was on vacation when lesbian feminists found me and insisted that I fly to Denver to work with two custody-embattled lesbian mothers involved in the Rachele Yaseen case. Prominent lesbians, including Rita Mae Brown, Adrienne Rich, and Jan Oxenberg donated money to the defense fund. Psychiatrist Richard Green also flew in to Denver to work with us.

In terms of patriarchal history, fathers "owned" their children. Custody to the father was also seen as in the child's best interest. A child had no rights (and still does not) but was entitled to a woman's care in its "tender" years; really, any woman might do—a nurse, a nanny, a housekeeper, a girlfriend, a paternal grandmother, or a new wife. No mother had the right to custody of her own child. This slowly began to change in the mid-twentieth century.

Mothers had obligations toward their children without any reciprocal rights. Child support was rarely paid. Most fathers did not want the burden of being the caretaker of a young child. However, mothers still had to fight very hard for custody when fathers contested it and, according to my research, what I'd termed "good enough" mothers still lost these battles between 70 to 82 percent of the time. This was true even when fathers were wife beaters and child abusers. In 1986 and 1988, I published two pioneering books in this area, and in 2011, I added eight new chapters to *Mothers on Trial: The Battle for Children and Custody*.

In a sense, both royal and slave mothers were treated as surrogate uteruses for the patriarchal family—simply as breeders.

While I was in Denver, a woman I did not know, Dr. Anne Wilson Schaef, a therapist, took me to lunch. She wanted to hire me to work with her in Boulder on the Women's Institute for Alternative Psychotherapy. "I know you've been fighting great battles and winning them even without a community," she told me. "We'll be your community, your home—we'll comfort you and recognize you for who you are."

What a sales pitch!

I agreed to work with Anne, but only part time and without moving to Colorado. I delivered a lecture for her that was covered by the *Denver Post*, and I joined the faculty-in-formation. Anne had promised me a small monthly stipend, but she immediately started making excuses about a lack of funding, a banking problem, a telegraph problem, a tax problem. Then she explained that she had been in bed for two weeks because someone had "hexed" her.

My antennae went way up, but I didn't yet know whom or what I was dealing with. At our next meeting in Boulder, Anne told me that she had begun to sleep with both her male and female patients.

I believed that she had lost all sense of right and wrong and therefore told her that she needed professional help and should close the institute. In turn, she explained to an eager-to-belong feminist faculty that "when women do the same thing that men do, it's not the same thing." She didn't believe she had done anything wrong.

I immediately quit. Most of the remaining feminist faculty stayed and tried to persuade me to do likewise. So much for principle. So much for sanity.

A Marxist feminist, an otherwise principled soul, remained as one of Anne's right-hand women. Years later I asked her why she had stayed with such a corrupt, perhaps even criminal, person. "I needed the money," she said.

In 1981, Anne began to publish best selling titles about self-help, codependence, and society's addictions, titles such as *Native Wisdom for White Minds: Daily Reflections Inspired by the Native Peoples of the World* and *Meditations for Women Who Do Too Much*. A few years later, Anne began to describe herself as a "recovering therapist" who had given up traditional therapy as misguided.

I thought this was an odd turn of events. It was actually a canny one. Now Anne was unstoppable; she claimed that she was no longer a psychologist or a therapist and wasn't licensed. She could not be held to their ethical standards.

Years passed. In 1991, Denver-based feminists asked me whether I'd be willing to testify on behalf of one of Anne's former patients. The patient's name was Vonna Moody. She was one of the "nonpatients" with whom Anne had slept. Anne had also moved Vonna into her home. Now, years later, Vonna was suing her.

Court TV was planning to cover the trial. I was ill at the time and couldn't travel, so Vonna's lawyers came to New York to depose me. Mainly they wanted to know whether, in my opinion, Anne's treatment methods were in any way accepted by feminist academics or therapists. Were such practices previously acceptable?

"Absolutely not," I assured them.

A few days later, Anne settled with Vonna out of court for $240,000.

The feminist longing for community has sometimes led to the creation of cults. Over the years women have consulted with me about their experiences in so-called therapeutic cults in which "patient-daughters" socialized intensely with their "therapist-mothers" and with each other. They experienced boundary violations orgiastically; the cults merged Demeter (goddess of the harvest) with her daughter, Persephone (goddess of both spring and the underworld) and divine madness reigned. I wrote about both goddess figures in *Women and Madness*.

I am sure that many more heterosexual and homosexual *male* therapists abuse their power in sexual ways. That is not an excuse for women, gay or straight, to do so.

Being on the road was both tiring and exhilarating. When I flew to California to deliver some lectures, I visited my friend Z, the feminist witch. She introduced me to her guest, Ana-Kria, an astrologer, who offered to cast my lunar horoscope. She told me that there was one special day, perhaps a block of days, when, should I choose to get pregnant, I'd be blessed with exactly the right child for me.

I gave it no further mind but I surrendered to the possibility of becoming pregnant. My superstitious unconscious arranged a romantic night at home. Within six weeks I learned I was pregnant. Pregnant! The astrologer's advice proved prescient; my son is the best possible child I could have had.

Z wanted me to give birth on top of a mountain with women chanting all around me. I thought otherwise.

"I'm thirty-seven years old," I told her. "I'll get a midwife and do natural childbirth, but in a hospital, not on a mountaintop, however enchanting that might be."

Kate Millett told me that we had to have dinner. We met on the Upper West Side at a restaurant aptly named the Library.

"Look, man, you're too important to our struggle to become a mother. You have to have an abortion," Kate declared.

I laughed.

Quickly enough, Kate changed her mind and demanded that I pose naked for the cover of *Vogue* while pregnant.

"It will be important for Cynthia MacAdams's career as a photographer. You gotta help us out."

Cynthia "Rosie Dakota" and Kate were ever-squabbling lovers. But they were oracles; they had this idea long before Demi Moore posed naked while pregnant for the cover of *Vanity Fair* in 1991.

Again, I laughed. "You're two crazy women—and I'm not going to do this."

Afterward Kate was contrite; she gave me a whimsical line drawing of my pregnant self. She drew my breasts as two huge sundaes. I framed it and hung it in my living room.

I may have been pregnant, but I still had a doctoral degree; I was still teaching my classes. I ran into an administrator in my university cafeteria.

"You look tired," he said.

"And how. Who knew that pregnancy could do this?"

I had given him his opening. He gleefully sneered at me and said: "Why don't you just decide whether you want to be a mother or a professor?" and slithered away.

Patriarchy was not my only problem. Some feminists also had a problem with pregnancy.

Once, when I was lecturing out of town while pregnant, the lights were too strong for me and I felt dizzy. I asked for a chair.

The feminist in charge said: "Why can't you just keep standing? If you sit, it'll ruin the video."

Back then, many feminists had a highly charged, ambivalent relationship to biological motherhood. They didn't want to repeat the lives their mothers had lived. They yearned to develop strong selves and, given the obstacles women faced, they may have needed all their energies to do so. Some feminists were afraid of being overwhelmed or trapped. Others feared being abandoned or impoverished—rational fears. Fathers leave, die, lose their jobs, get sick.

But I think there was another reason for this ambivalence. Psychologically, many feminists needed other feminists to mother them. Even though we were all sisters, the need for intimate emotional attention was great. Unconsciously, we didn't want our mother-sister to mother her actual child. When would she have time for us and for the revolution? Many of my feminist friends and I had been attacked daily by that starving child let loose in other women.

I subsequently explored the subject of motherhood in four books: *With Child: A Diary of Motherhood*; *Mothers on Trial: The Battle for Children and Custody*; and *Sacred Bond: The Legacy of Baby M*. I also wrote at length about the mother-daughter relationship in *Woman's Inhumanity to Woman*.

I had never fantasized about becoming a mother. However, once the astrologer cast my chart, it became clear to me that I would have a child, and this was why my husband and I had stayed together: it was the most important thing we could do.

Pregnancy isn't a disease. I felt like myself. I felt healthy. In the summer, when I was five months pregnant, we traveled to Athens, Crete, Jerusalem, and Tel Aviv. The heat was intense, but I visited the Palace of Knossos and viewed the amazing bull-leaper frescoes and the small goddesses in the Heraklion Museum. I dipped my swollen ankles into the Aegean.

I was in Israel when I learned that I was having a son. A son! I'd expected a daughter, but many feminists seemed to be having sons, not daughters; it was as if nature were challenging us to raise the next generation of male feminists. I was not disappointed; in fact, I was pleased. Was I betraying the feminist requirement to prefer daughters? Or had I already betrayed my unborn son by expecting that he'd be a girl?

I was not worried about child care, as my husband had promised to share half the responsibilities. Given my other obligations, I also planned to hire a babysitter/housekeeper so that neither of us would get worn out.

When I was seven or eight months pregnant, Robin Morgan gave me a surprise baby shower. How lovely! She went all out. I was surrounded by feminist leaders (Kate, Gloria, E.M., Letty Cottin Pogrebin) bearing gifts. According to my diary, we talked about a mysteriously destroyed printing press, a closed abortion clinic, and the Equal Rights Amendment. As I later wrote in *With Child*: "The greatest gift is these women, themselves. . . . For the respect and friendship of such women I would do anything. I have."

I continued working until the middle of my ninth month.

———

Eventually, when a woman has absolutely no more room to breathe, when there is no longer any space for both the woman and her baby, that baby, however reluctantly, emerges. After thirty-two-and-a-half hours of labor, I gave birth to a very blond baby boy who needed to be ritually circumcised according to Jewish custom. I was terrified. What if this tiny cut hurts or wounds him?

E.M. Broner calmed me down. She had two sons.

She offered to fly in from Detroit to conduct a women's ritual to bless my son right after his religious ceremony. I invited feminist friends (Erica Jong, Gloria Steinem, Aviva Cantor Zuckoff); publishing friends (the editor Pat Meehan and the publicist Selma Shapiro); some treasured former students, and my mother and other female relatives. We all gathered around as Ariel's godmothers. As we passed him around, we blessed him:

"May you never know any more pain than you've known today, on this day of your circumcision."

"May you be strong enough to be the son of a feminist."

"May your mother be your friend all your shared life."

"May you honor the women in your life as we honor you."

"May your parents have the courage to allow you to be yourself, and may they love you for it."

"Good health."

"Long life."

"May you be blessed by women all your life, as you are today."

Afterward my husband's friend Eli, who was from Yemen, exclaimed: "This is what the women do in Yemen! Where did you learn it?"

While I was pregnant (with a boy), I was working on a book about male psychology.

I thought it was important to look at the so-called opposite sex, this time with fresh feminist eyes. I wanted to understand why, if men are so privileged, they obey orders given by other men that often lead them to their deaths. I wanted to understand the father-son relationship as a way of explaining why mothers are so routinely scapegoated for paternal absence or abuse. I was interested in male bonding and male uterus envy.

I published *About Men* in 1978. The book was controversial and widely reviewed in the mainstream media—but not in the feminist media. My friend the sociologist Pauline Bart demanded that the radical-feminist newspaper *Off Our Backs* "do something." And so its reviewer wrote a fairly savage critique of my book. She wondered why I had even bothered to spend time on this subject. A number of otherwise absolutely terrific feminist bookstores hid the book. I know this because I made it a point to visit the feminist bookstores in and around New York City.

While promoting the book in Los Angeles, I met Judy Chicago, one of our most fabulous feminist artists, for lunch. Many feminists were drawn to her bold, outsized "theme park" art in primary colors, and many (mainly the envious) disliked her work. My darling friend Arlene Raven, among a handful of outstanding feminist art critics, was a strong supporter of Judy's work.

My agent had asked me to call her because we were expecting a review of the book in the *New York Times Book Review*. After listening to Judy talk about her work for half an hour, I excused myself to use the pay phone. (No cell phones in those days.) The review had appeared. It was written by Gail Sheehy, the author of *Passages: Predictable Crises of Adult Life*. The review was hot and highly quotable. My agent started reading it to me over the phone. After about three minutes, Judy marched over, arms akimbo, and demanded: "Are we here to talk about me, or do I have to sit around and wait while you talk to someone about *your* work?"

Only a woman so prize-fighter pugnacious and thick-skinned could have cracked the cement ceiling of the male-dominated art world.

I told my agent I'd call her back.

Extraordinary female artists have always existed, but they were never allowed to be towering heroes in their own time. Judy was the stuff of which heroes are made. In Chicago, her home town, Judy was one of the boys—the chick who was tougher than the men. She didn't identify with other women. That changed. Judy became a passionate feminist, utterly consumed by women's herstory and by the unacceptable disappearance of it. I love Judy's work. Her first major project was *The Dinner Party*, a huge installation that required the volunteer work of hundreds of people.

The Dinner Party is a large triangular glazed dining table with thirtynine place settings, each commemorating a guest. These include the Empress Theodora of Byzantium, Eleanor of Aquitaine, Sojourner Truth, and Susan B. Anthony. This epic art installation is now housed at the Brooklyn Museum. I also love her spectacular *Birth Project*, which used some words of mine from my book *With Child*, and *The Holocaust Project*.

In June 1978, I chaired the opening panel on women at the first-ever Middle East Film Festival, on Bleecker Street, in the Village. The films and filmmakers represented America, Egypt, Iran, Israel, Kuwait, and Syria. The festival was organized by Ilan Ziv, an Israeli, and Faye Ginsburg, an American.

I had a coffee date with Khalid Al Siddiq, the Kuwaiti filmmaker, and Laila Abou-Saif, the Egyptian filmmaker. Egypt boasted two leading feminists: Laila and Nawal El Sadawi, a physician and author, and perhaps the most famous Arab feminist of her time. They were not on speaking terms (both of them told me so), although I am not sure why.

Laila had a high-bridged nose, lustrous eyes, masses of dark hair, and like so many Arab women of the time, she was ultrasophisticated. I was moved by her description of her life as both a feminist and a Coptic Christian. Although her parents believed in education for girls, they forced Laila into an arranged marriage. When I met her, she was already divorced.

Laila's feminism and her critique of government policies had led the government to deny her access to theaters. I decided that Laila needed feminist protection. I called Gloria, who was well known for allowing women to move in with her. I don't know if this was because she was a saint, on the road so much that she didn't mind someone occupying an empty apartment, or simply lonely.

Gloria agreed, and so I took Laila and her luggage to Gloria's apartment on the Upper East Side. She was thrilled just to be meeting Gloria.

"Gloria, here's another future member of our feminist government in exile."

They hit it off. I also introduced Laila to my agent, who decided to handle a book Laila wanted to write. It took Laila a decade, but in 1985 she finally published *A Bridge Through Time: A Memoir*. Understandably, tragically, she felt she had to publish it under a pseudonym, Laila Said, to spare her family shame. She may have eschewed the veil, but she veiled her true identity.

Together Laila and I watched the controversial British film *The Death of a Princess*, a dramatized reconstruction of real events that was broadcast on PBS in 1980. It told the story of how in 1977, a nineteen-year-old Saudi royal, Mishaal bint Fahd, dared to fall in love with a twenty-year-old Saudi man, the nephew of the Saudi ambassador in Lebanon, where the princess was attending school. I doubt they risked having an affair. She tried to flee the kingdom dressed as a man but was discovered and returned to her family. Her fiancé was executed in the public square in a botched beheading; she, most mercifully, was shot to death.

Many kinds of marriages fail, and for many reasons; I'm not sure that wives who have careers or callings are any more vulnerable to divorce than non-career women are. My first husband (from Afghanistan) had much more money and power than I did; that was dangerous for me. My second husband (from Israel) had less money and power than I did; that may have proved dangerous to him or to his ego.

We had been married for six years when a cold wind suddenly blew across my grave. My husband and I had agreed that I'd become a mother if he promised to share half the mothering and some of the earning. He was not doing either. I wasn't happy about this, but I doubt I would have left my son's father if something else had not happened.

He might have said that I'd left him long ago for feminism, and he wouldn't have been entirely wrong. I kept hoping that he'd find himself, choose a profession, just get on with it. I was overburdened, and in my frustration I committed a capital offense: I told his mother that he'd refused to work or attend school and begged her to talk to him.

In doing so I had dishonored a Middle Eastern man, a dangerous thing to do. His rage and vow of vengeance took my breath away; I literally could not breathe. I suffered my first and only panic attack. He wanted money. He threatened to kidnap our son and take him to Israel. I might never see my baby again.

I was terrified, but calmly, very calmly, I negotiated a minimal cash settlement and agreed to move out of our rental apartment and split the proceeds with him when it became a co-op. This was an apartment that I had found and for which I alone had paid the rent. (He realized a huge windfall when we sold the apartment.)

I assumed that my ex-husband would remain in our son's life. I was wrong. He disconnected almost totally. That was his revenge. And it was a terrible one, meant to torment and inconvenience me for the next twenty years. Inconvenience? Try maintaining a schedule when your son's father turns up two hours late to visit his child and returns him an hour early. Try watching your son's face pressed to the window as he waits for his father to appear. I never stopped trying to include this man in our son's life as a responsible parent, and I never succeeded in doing so.

L to R: Unidentified woman, Bill Baird, Merle Hoffman, Phyllis, Sharon Wyse, unidentified woman, Mary Lou McKinley-Greenberg, and unidentified woman at the March For

L to R: Phyllis and Andrea Dworkin at a feminist conference, Israel, 1988.

L to R: Phyllis's son, Ariel, with Phyllis, Merle Hoffman, and Rabbi Balfour Brickner participating in civil disobedience in front of St. Patrick's Cathedral, New York City, 1989. *Bettye Lane Photos, Schlesinger Library, Radcliffe Institute, Harvard University*

Clockwise: Vivian Gornick, Phyllis, Alix Kates Shulman, Ellen Willis, Kate Millett, and Ann Snitow, the Downtown Radical Feminist Girls. Behind the scenes at a photo shoot for a *New York Times* magazine cover, 1990. *Photograph by Sara Krulwich/Jeanne Strongin.*

L to R: Phyllis, Rivka Haut, and Shulamit Magnus at JFK, bringing a Torah for Women of Jerusalem, Women of the Wall, 1989.

L to R: Phyllis, Pauline Bart, and Martha Shelley. Phyllis is lecturing while pregnant, California, 1977.

L to R: Nancy Polikoff, May Neuberger, Phyllis, Noreen Connell, Judith Des Roché, Sherry Brodsky, Deborah Luepnitz, and Sheila Hamanaka at a Mothers' Custody Speak-Out press conference, New York City, 1986.

L to R: Violet Cherry and Phyllis at the Custody Speak-Out, New York City, 1986.

L to R: Buffie Johnson, Phyllis, and Sandy Miller at a book party for Buffie's *Lady of the Beasts,* in Phyllis's home, 1988.

L to R: Gloria Steinem and Phyllis at a benefit for a Women's Law Center, held at Phyllis's apartment in New York City, 1974.

Above: L to R: Kate Millett and Phyllis on the roof of Kate's New York City Bowery loft, c. 1974–1975.

Right: L to R: Ruth Gruber and Barbara Seaman at a baby shower for Phyllis, 1977.

L to R: Phyllis and Marge Piercy on Cape Cod, 1973.

L to R: Phyllis Chesler and Florence Rush, keynote speakers at New York Radical Feminists' first Speak-Out on Rape in New York City, 1971. *Photograph by Dick Yarwood*

Phyllis writing *Women and Madness* at the MacDowell Colony, 1971.
Photograph by Bernice B. Perry, courtesy of The MacDowell Colony

Women's Reproductive Rights and against attacks on abortion clinics, New York City,

1988. *Courtesy of Merle Hoffman*

L to R: Z Budapest, Phyllis, and Kate Millett at a fiftieth birthday party, given by Merle Hoffman and held at Kate Millett's loft, 1990. *Photograph by Merle Hoffman.*

Right: L to R: Phyllis, Bella Abzug, unidentified woman, and Letty Cottin Pogrebin at a feminist Passover Seder, New York City, 1991. *Courtesy of Joan L. Roth.*

Below: L to R: Wanda Hensen, Merle Hoffman, and Phyllis (unseen are Brenda Hensen, Diana Rivers, and Susan L. Bender) in solidarity with Camp Sister Spirit, Ovett, Mississippi, 1994.

This was not an unusual scenario. I've interviewed hundreds of divorced mothers whose ex-husbands stopped visiting their children, as well as mothers who were forced to fight for custody of their children. Nonpayment of child support was rampant. While it may not be true for every man, many fathers abandon their first set of children (at least economically) when they remarry and have a second family.

Whatever money I was able to earn, whatever money I had saved, went to pay the live-in babysitters. I wish I'd been able to follow Margaret Mead's advice to buy a large house and barter room and board with a mother of young children in exchange for childcare. I did buy a house, but bartering was out of the question. So I had to hire the best babysitter I could find, pray that I had made the right choice, and be prepared for rocky times.

Back then, as now, high-quality, low-cost childcare was simply not available in America.

Once, I found my son wailing, unfed, hungry, his diaper unchanged, and the babysitter passed out drunk on the floor. Her minister begged me not to fire her; her wages supported eleven people in the Caribbean. But I had to let her go.

Even this Amazon warrior couldn't leave her baby, but his stay-at-home father could. Most women don't leave their children—a profound difference from men.

I now understood that motherhood changes you forever.

I had my work and I had my son, and both were blessings; but when a woman goes through a divorce, she depends on her female friends to see her through.

One of these friends was Erica Jong. She was worried about my financial future. From her point of view, I had none. She advised me to "write comic novels—because then the men won't kill you." This was a rather self-revealing statement, but point taken.

In 1987, Erica and Andrea Dworkin appeared on *Donahue* to debate sex. Beforehand, I persuaded Erica to find three positive things to say about Andrea's work and asked Andrea to do the same. Erica did what she'd promised; Andrea did not.

I spent many weekends with Erica at her home in Weston, Connecticut. Once, she took me to visit the actress June Havoc. She also introduced me to the acclaimed author Howard Fast and his wife Bette, Erica's future in-laws. After I gave birth, Erica and Jonathan Fast (her third husband) took me and my husband to Tortola in the British Virgin Islands and wined and dined us, both on board and on land. We visited Erroll Flynn's yacht. Erica and Jonathan seemed to want something—I was not sure what.

Erica finally told me, quite earnestly, that she was close to Phyllis and Eberhard Kronhausen, who were holistic sex therapists and collectors of erotic art. They had persuaded her that the only way to keep a marriage alive is to engage in friendly orgies. She told me that Jonathan had been lusting after my breasts. Six years later, in the throes of my own divorce disaster, I finally went to bed with them—and Erica, the queen of erotica, chastely, passively held my hand as Jonathan had at me.

I felt like a used tissue. Rich people really *are* different from you and me. Jonathan began calling me. This didn't end well for any of us, but when Jonathan challenged Erica for custody of their daughter, Molly, I stood by Erica.

11 Our Sorely Afflicted Feminist Geniuses

From the time I was twenty-seven years old, in 1967, I shared my ideas mainly with women, rarely with men. This was a complete turn-around, since for most of my life I had primarily read works by men, studied with male professors, worked for men, and fallen in love only with men.

Not talking to men was a profound loss, but few men were interested in feminism—and I was consumed by it.

Turning to women to discuss my most important ideas was psychologically and intellectually revolutionary. It was also paradise. For many of us rebellious and ambitious daughters, the wounds of maternal disapproval were temporarily healed.

However, Paradise inevitably is always followed by the Fall.

Only now, looking back, do I remember how much of the early years of second-wave feminism was painful.

Individual petty jealousies and leaderless group bullying were frightening and ugly. "Mean girls" envied and destroyed excellence and talent; in short, they ate their most gifted leaders.

Feminists who had left the Left brought with them its tactics of intimidation and interrogation.

Many radical lesbians were lesbian supremacists who demanded primacy in terms of victimhood. Some also outed other women in cruel and public ways.

Thus, right at the beginning of paradise, trouble rumbled both overhead and beneath our feet. Trouble drove many a good feminist far, far away, but many of us who could still taste paradise on our tongues remained for the duration.

The psychologist Naomi Weisstein told me that within three years of its formation, the Chicago Women's Liberation Rock Band turned on her in pretty much all the familiar feminist ways. The Chicago Women's Liberation Union, which she had helped found in 1969, had already trashed her as a "star" and demanded that she surrender her speaking engagements to less eloquent speakers. Band members followed suit, and, fraught with envy and untold hidden agendas, the band disbanded in 1973.

Here's what they were thinking: if all women were supposed to be equal, then no woman should be more appreciated or better known than any other.

Although unacknowledged, the trashing of the late 1960s and 1970s was ultimately the psychological reason our mass radical movement ground to a halt. The ideological disputes played out in breathlessly vicious ways. But it didn't stop me. Luckily, I was blessed with the ability to remain connected to women on both sides of many of our major wars.

Some feminists did sound the alarm about trashing. In 1970, the journalist Anselma Dell'Olio addressed this in an unpublished and incandescent manuscript that was later known as her "swan-song to the women's movement." Jo Freeman discussed it in two important articles, "The Tyranny of Structurelessness" and "Trashing: The Dark Side of Sisterhood," which appeared in *Ms.* in 1976 and provoked more reader response than any previously published article. In 1972, I discussed it in *Women and Madness*. Our words didn't lead to a feminist reevaluation of sisterhood. Few feminists wanted to look at how they treated other women. And fewer still wanted to consider the possibility that the movement was not both "breast and womb."

I once convened a panel at the annual meeting of the National Women's Studies Association at Spelman College. The panel's title was "Horizontal Hostility among Women: Race, Class and Gender Issues," and it nearly tore the roof off the place. Because my invitee and copanelist bell hooks and I publicly agreed on so incendiary a subject, some audience members—many of whom were African American—accused the much-younger hooks of being my "mammy." But mainly the audience wanted to tell their own stories of woman-on-woman betrayal and heartbreak. When we were finally forced to leave the auditorium, I sat outside on the lawn for a long time listening to them speak.

Something rather different happened when I presented my views on psychological matricide and sororicide at a national conference of feminist therapists. Therapists had difficulty acknowledging that women can also be sexists. One African American therapist insisted that this is a "white girl's problem"; one lesbian therapist insisted that this is a "straight girl's problem"; one heterosexual therapist said that she hadn't known that "women even *had* a mother goddess or that we had killed her." She urgently wanted to know the goddess's name.

Perhaps we were tame compared with our suffragist foremothers. According to Kathy Barry in her riveting work *Susan B. Anthony: A Biography of a Singular Feminist*, conservative suffragists demanded that Anthony disinvite the famed Ernestine Rose as a speaker "because of her avowed atheism." They also rejected Victoria Woodhull, the first woman to run for president of the United States and passed a resolution that clarified that, unlike Woodhull, they didn't believe in free love.

Unbelievably, they also voted to disassociate the National Woman's

Party from Elizabeth Cady Stanton's critique of religion in *The Woman's Bible*. Barry writes:

> *Susan B. Anthony, in the chair as president of the association, was astounded and for a moment struck dumb. It was one thing to disagree with Mrs. Stanton over priorities but never would she consider that either Stanton or her critique of religion would be censored. . . . Never had their movement censored thought. Now these young women who were "unborn when Mrs. Stanton called the first Woman's Rights Convention" proposed to censure her. Anthony was eloquent in her anger: "When our platform becomes too narrow for people of all creeds and of no creeds, I myself shall not stand upon it."*

Anthony was heartbroken and considered resigning the presidency of her own association. She told her protégées, "I see nothing but the beginning of a petty espionage, a revival of the Spanish Inquisition," and that she was "sick at heart" because of their violation of the right to exercise one's judgment and for wronging Stanton personally.

By the mid-1970s, Betty Freidan, who claimed to have lost control of both NOW and the National Women's Political Caucus, concluded that NOW was suffering from a "power struggle so acute and so vicious that, finally, only those who can devote twenty-four hours a day to the movement can play—women who have made the women's movement their sole profession, their career, their sole road to glory, even their personal life."

Many NOW members had married NOW psychologically; they had turned it into a total institution, the equivalent of a family or a religious order. When they lost, they lost everything for all time. This was not a game. It was all they had, everything that mattered, and they had no rules of engagement or disengagement.

Sonia Johnson, a former Mormon who was excommunicated for her support of the Equal Rights Amendment and the author of *From Housewife to Heretic*, told me that seventeen NOW women who didn't want her to run for the NOW presidency had ganged up on her in her hotel room. Sonia withdrew her candidacy.

Ellen Hawkes, in her book *Feminism on Trial*, quotes the lawyer and former president of NOW Karen DeCrow:

> *Until you've seen a contested NOW election, you haven't seen anything. I had a bodyguard with me when I ran for reelection at the 1975 Philadelphia conference, and I thought, my God, am I going to need armed guards to be head of the sisters! When I left in '77 I felt I would have no trouble being a litigator because I'd been through the NOW wars. I'm frequently in a legal situation where someone will say, "How can you stay so cool?" I smile sweetly and think back on NOW. If you can live through NOW, you can battle both the Fortune 500 and the worst sex discrimination cases.*

According to Hawkes, Shelly Mandell, a California NOW member, was competing with another California NOW member, Ginny Foat, for the presidency of a NOW chapter, and got rid of her rival by reporting Foat to the police on a suspected murder charge. Ginny had been battered by her husband and was accused of killing him. She was eventually acquitted at trial.

According to my dear friend Arlene Raven, *Chrysalis* magazine folded in 1980 because women

> *gave each other too much grief as we all worked for no money. Everyone, including the leading feminist lights of the day, felt entitled to criticize and insult us. Editors who doted on a particular writer's work were devastated when that writer turned out to be nasty, cruel, petty, insane. Women only*

complained, few thanked us for being there. Once you stick your neck out, women think it's okay to take pot-shots at you. And the editors wanted approval from the very women who were criticizing them.

Once, a fight in a California gay bar about control of a woman's studies program and a feminist bookstore spilled outside, and in the altercation that followed a woman died of a heart attack.

I've been told that some feminists had a fistfight about pornography and prostitution on the street outside Columbia University.

Feminism as a philosophy or as a political movement cannot guarantee ethical behavior, nor can it save individual feminists from being undervalued, kicked to the curb, or impoverished. Feminism is a vision in whose service we enlisted. It couldn't give us most of what we wanted: victory in our lifetime, a lifelong loving community.

On the contrary, for most of us our lives became harder, not easier, because we were feminists. No one gave us the equivalent of boots and guns; most of us were rarely embraced as heroes. More likely, we were hazed—and the war was never over.

Most feminists were also women. As such, we carried extra baggage.

When a human being has been diminished by heartless prejudice daily and victimized by sexual, physical, economic, and legal violence, she can become disabled, just as veterans of combat and torture victims can. Some such people are able to carry on valorously, but even so, being wounded may lead to fits of weeping, bursts of bad temper, paranoid accusations, and disappearances without notice.

Add to this mix runaway egotism, the ideological demand for uniformity, envy of those perceived as more talented, and women's unacknowledged sexism and inhumanity toward other women and you can begin to understand what we were all up against.

I've never before written what I'm about to write here. I didn't even dare *think* it. But a recent conversation in 2016 opened this tightly shut door.

I was reminiscing with my friend Bob Brannon, a cofounder of the National Organization for Men Against Sexism and longtime feminist leader.

"Do you know X?" he asked.

"Of course I do. And how! She was totally nuts."

"Tell me about it," Bob groaned. "She once visited and went through my things, stole stuff, lied about it, and then she turned on me, accused me of being a sexist pig."

As we spoke, I realized that just as I was once afraid to admit—even to myself—that mental illness plagued my high-functioning mother and members of her family, so too have I denied the extent to which so many of the most charismatic and original of feminist thinkers were mentally ill.

I don't mean neurotic, difficult, anxious, or eccentric. I mean clinically schizophrenic or manic depressive, suicidal, addicted to drugs or alcohol, or afflicted with a personality disorder. Thus, quite apart from ideological differences, some of our most beloved geniuses were unstable and wildly needy. No more so than people in general—including socialites, artists, or members of other social justice movements—but no less so either.

Feminism isn't crazy, and feminist ideas aren't crazy, but some of the feminists I've known and loved have suffered from mental illness. I'm reluctantly willing to admit that mental illness may have been one of the many problems that dogged our movement.

However, I'm also writing about historical figures who must be judged for what they accomplished. That's why I'm writing about them; it's why they matter. At the time, however, even I refused to think of feminists (or of women) as mentally ill. That phrase had been used against women so unjustly that I simply did not want to repeat this calumny. Those among us who were not clinically or theoretically educated about mental illness, as well as those who were mentally ill, did not recognize or consider that certain behaviors (nonstop talking, yelling, paranoid accusations, drinking, stealing, pathological lying) might be evidence of mental illness. We all preferred to consider dysfunctional behaviors as ideological opposition.

Many great male artists have also been mentally ill. Baudelaire, Blake, Coleridge, Hemingway, Robert Lowell, Eugene O'Neill, Pound, Shelley, and Dylan Thomas all immediately come to mind. They attempted or committed suicide; drank to excess; were deeply, darkly depressed; spent time in lunatic asylums. Of the feminists, first came Shulie Firestone, the author of *The Dialectic of Sex: The Case for Feminist Revolution*. Oh, was that a breathtakingly brilliant book. For a long time our movement was haunted by her absence. But she was very much alive. She was either holed up in her apartment in the East Village or in a psychiatric facility.

I remember reading *The Dialectic of Sex* when it first came out in 1970. I was writing *Women and Madness* and her book electrified me. Her work is fierce, as sharp as a diamond—logically precise, somewhat frightening, offensively utopian, but extremely liberating.

Years later, Shulie called and asked me to visit her at home in my capacity as a psychotherapist. She said, "You're the only one I can trust." I immediately agreed to do so. Then she added: "But you'll need to come to the fifth floor by climbing up the fire escape. I'll talk to you through the window."

I told her I couldn't do that, that I might fall to earth and shatter, but I couldn't persuade her to open her door.

Her book *Airless Spaces* is a small and tender gem. Humbly, carefully, she writes about her schizophrenia and her time in various hospitals. When it was published in 1998, she asked a small group of us, including me, to read aloud from it at her book launch. I remember Shulie's standing off a bit to the side, watching, listening, but silent, at a remove, always removed.

Then came Kate Millett, another brilliant intellectual, whose productivity was miraculous given her crippling mental illness. Kate's first book, *Sexual Politics*, came out the same year as Shulie's, 1970. It too lit up the night sky.

I once offered to try and share my tenured professorship with her. Ha! But when I shared a lecture podium with Kate for the first time, all hell broke loose. She made no sense. She ranted and railed, talked about the Irish "troubles" and wouldn't stop rambling. Ultimately, to everyone's horror, she had to be physically removed from the stage.

Kate had a shitload of charm and, in the beginning, a commanding presence, but she also had periods in which she didn't sleep, raged at others, attempted suicide, and exploited her groupies—all the while feeling victimized by them (which she was). She couldn't be counted on to remain lucid at a press conference. She also fell in love, and tried to have her way, quite aggressively, with woman after woman (including me).

Once, I saw how frightened Gloria Steinem became when Kate freaked out at a press conference. French feminists had organized something at the United Nations on behalf of the imprisoned Madame Mao in China. Our girl Kate began talking about the Irish Troubles and simply wouldn't stop. She was off message and out of her mind. Gloria turned pale—her defense against chaos is to keep herself under tight control, never an emotional hair out of place, so to speak. She mumbled to me "You'll take care of this" and rushed away.

I did take care of it. I didn't desert Kate; I gallantly accompanied her home. However, this did not amount to therapy. It was merely an act of kindness.

Unlike Shulie, Kate hotly denied being mentally ill. She denied that mental illness existed. And even if it did, she insisted that she didn't suffer from it.

The point is that Kate wrote despite her mental illness; she kept going, she never stopped working, not even when other illnesses laid her low. It was also almost impossible to work with her or to have a stable or genuinely reciprocal relationship with her.

Andrea Dworkin—oh dear God, what can I say about Andrea? I valued both her work and our friendship. I was so protective of her because she seemed so fragile. But eventually, ultimately, I was forced to see that, although Andrea was a complex and strategic thinker, she was also a fanatic, a terribly wounded one, who felt that she was always the victim, even when she was on the attack, like picketing a bookstore reading when Rebecca Chalker and Carol Downer published *A Woman's Book of Choices: Abortion, Menstrual Extraction, RU-486* in 1992. In the book the authors had written: "Only in desperate situations—such as women may find themselves in the future if states ban abortion except for certain reasons such as rape—should women even consider resorting to faking rape," and then went on to warn about the potential this had for "undermining the gains of the movement against violence against women." Nevertheless, Andrea was enraged because she believed that this advice would weaken all rape allegations. She called a number of feminists to try to convince them to join her on the picket line outside a Brooklyn bookstore where Rebecca was doing a reading. Barbara Seaman, Rebecca's supporter, received a series of threatening phone calls in which a female voice said: "You're dead meat." This sounded very Andrea-like, and Barbara was convinced that Andrea was the caller.

Writers. Great writers. Revolutionary thinkers like Andrea and Kate are often shy and awkward in intimate gatherings, comfortable only on history's large stage.

My pal Jill Johnston, who inspired so many lesbian activists, described her nervous breakdowns as "stepping out" of her mind. She never hid this, nor was she ashamed of it. She was half British, and they're known for tolerating extreme eccentricity.

In 2005, at a memorial service for the lesbian feminist writer Bertha Harris, who apparently drank herself to death, I sat with Jill. She kept writing and wouldn't look up. I said, "Jill, this is our beloved community, our friends." She admonished me: "No, Phyllis. These are my competitors. All the lesbian writers here are my competitors, not my friends."

The authors Elizabeth "Betty" Fisher (*Women's Creation: Sexual Evolution and the Shaping of Society*) and Ellen Frankfort (*Vaginal Politics*) both killed themselves. I know that Ellen felt that our movement had failed her and also naively believed that she could forge a lifelong career as a writer-activist. Could this have had anything to do with her suicide? She had also been the one who found Betty Fisher's body. Or were the causes of these women's suicides simply genetic or neurochemical in nature?

Ellen and I became close friends. In the mid-1980s, she had found me a house near her in the Hamptons. That was where she told me how disappointed she was in Flo Kennedy for continuing to support black nationalism and the Left and how hurt she was by Flo's condemnation of Ellen's 1984 book, *Kathy Boudin and the Dance of Death*, which denounced the American Left. She said: "Phyllis, our movement has lost all dignity. Movement women are all bullshit artists."

A few years later, Ellen threatened to kill herself. I visited her immediately and tried to persuade her to get off all her prescription meds. She had seen so many different psychiatrists who had prescribed so many different medications. Red pills, blue pills, yellow pills, pink pills all tumbled out of her handbag. I told her, "These pills have messed with your mind."

"Phyllis, the book you're working on right now should be my book. I write about working-class women and the ways in which they're screwed."

"Ellen, get yourself together and perhaps we can coauthor this book."

I didn't really mean this—the deadline for *Sacred Bond: The Legacy of Baby M* was bearing down on me—but I said it because it meant so much to her.

As close as we became, I still didn't know that Ellen had a twin sister who had committed suicide. And perhaps I hadn't understood how deeply she may have been traumatized by having found Betty Fisher's body.

Although Ellen lived with a wealthy man, she still hoped to be able to support herself as a feminist writer within the context of a dignified feminist movement. I understood that Ellen was bereft, both of such income and of movement.

I could not save her. No one could.

I was the emcee for Ellen's memorial service, held in the courtyard of Westbeth, an artists' housing complex in the West Village. There was a gospel choir—she had left a suicide note and it was her choice; its members were her friends. I saw many pale, shocked feminist faces among those gathered in her honor. I can easily name twenty more feminist pioneers who were dear to me and produced extraordinary work but were disadvantaged, wounded by depression or other psychiatric afflictions. Were they depressed by how often they were on the losing end of ideological battles, by the everyday sexism that sapped their vital juices, by having to fight so hard to obtain so little because they were women? Were they at a perpetual disadvantage due to incest, rape, economic insecurity, overwork, or homophobia?

I know one brilliant feminist author who became so increasingly anxious that she was finally truly unemployable. She lost her home, her money, and even more of her mind. Today she's still brilliant, but she lives below the poverty line and spends her time writing long letters to newspapers that are rarely published.

I know several feminists with bipolar disorder or severe depression who are also gifted and accomplished but hard to be around. One of them used to turn up at my door weeping inconsolably and threatening suicide.

One of our early lesbian rights activists, Sidney Abbott (*Sappho Was a Right-On Woman*), was always disconnected and inappropriate but cheerfully, harmlessly, so. Luckily she found a psychiatrically challenged feminist billionaire who gave her a home, food, horses, dogs, and a caretaker, and that's how things stood until she eventually refused to ever get out of her armchair. There she sat, for nearly two years, until she accidentally burned herself to death.

I was there when yet another feminist completely freaked out under the pressure of success. She was on her way home from a television program when she tried to punch the TV show's driver, rushed into her apartment past a group of journalists and feminist friends awaiting her, slammed her bedroom door shut, and simply refused to come out. Maybe it was just as well. She was raving, crying, and had taken off all her clothes. It was a while before I could talk her down— and she was usually the sweetest soul.

African American feminists had problems of their own. I served as a therapist and confidante to a number of extremely accomplished African American feminists whose self-esteem was paper thin and who viewed themselves as ugly and perhaps unlovable. They were subject to periods of depression and self-imposed isolation. Many of them scapegoated white women for the considerable crimes of the African American men these women loved but who had betrayed them—perhaps slavery's long legacy.

Activists and artists are an at-risk population. Feminists are human beings. Some are normally competitive; some are bullies; some hide their viciousness by operating only in mobs; and a few are sociopaths, such as women who want to be able to brag to others about their own (unearned) importance. One feminist used to sneak up behind a feminist celebrity while the celebrity was speaking and had a friend quickly snap a photo of the two of them. This woman has a rather disassociated affect as she follows the camera. After watching her performance over many decades, I concluded that it was beyond merely eccentric, perhaps even beyond diagnosis.

The "celebrity selfie" taker merely appears to be in the center of things. Worse are the identity thieves, who take credit for work they've never done. This puzzled and disheartened me the most.

12 Rape at the UN and an Unexpected Betrayal by the Inveterate Scene-Stealer

Being raped is something that a woman never forgets—especially if she understands that rape is an act of violent domination, meant to humiliate and traumatize a woman. Being sexually harassed and raped by your employer—when you need to keep the job—consigns a woman to a special circle of hell.

A rape victim bears up under the weight of it, absorbs the blow, and tries to move on. Some women cannot do it; they break down and break apart. But even someone who can numbly, dumbly move on may still be dimly and occasionally haunted by shame or sorrow for ever after.

A child who is raped by her father can also move on, but an incest victim never forgets and never forgives the *mother* who did not protect her, sold her for rent money, refused to believe her, and ejected her from the family when her protests became too public. Most incest victims do not rage against their rapist fathers as much as against their mother's intimate betrayal.

Such traumatic events are difficult to discuss. The victim herself is reluctant to reenter the memory swamp. It can literally make her sick. The eyes of non-therapists and non-feminists glaze over. Feminist therapists are trained to listen—but good therapy takes a long time, and the details really matter—they're all that matter.

The rape victim requires a knowledgeable listener she can trust, someone inclined to believe that what she is saying actually happened and that it had real consequences that gathered increasing force over time.

Recovering from the trauma of sexual violence is especially difficult if the family blames, slanders, and exiles the victim. This includes the "family" of feminist leaders.

Davidson Nicol was a tall, dark, married man from Sierra Leone. He obtained a Ph.D. from the University of Cambridge and a medical degree from the London School of Medicine. From 1972 to 1982 he was an undersecretary general at the United Nations, when the secretary general was the former Nazi Kurt Waldheim. When I met Davidson, he was also serving as the head of the United Nations Institute for Training and Research.

Davidson heard me lecture in 1979. I'm no longer sure where this was. It might have been at the dramatization of my book *About Men* at the United Nations by the director Sue Flakes, or it might have been at one of my lectures about motherhood.

I had just published *With Child: A Diary of Motherhood*. Perhaps we met at the hours-long reading of the entire book at the Bloomsday Bookshop on the Upper West Side. This was a signal honor because the only all-day and all-night readings the proprietor, Enrico Adelman, had staged until then were by James Joyce.

Davidson introduced himself, told me that he was impressed with my work, and invited me to a dinner that he was hosting for fifty people to honor J.H. Plumb, the distinguished British historian.

Davidson encouraged me to share my feminist vision with him, saying he was fascinated and wanted to help. He saw a career for me at the UN.

He liked my idea about holding an international feminist conference under UN auspices and hired me to organize one. And he promised to pay me well at a time when I desperately needed the extra money.

My conference idea was simple: I wanted to find the most educated, prominent, and courageous feminists on every continent and to connect them right before the UN's second World Conference on Women, which was slated for the summer of 1980, in Copenhagen. That way, we might get to know each other and travel to Copenhagen together, and test out our ideas at an even larger forum. Davidson told me that Oslo would be the perfect venue for my international feminist conference; his contacts would arrange it. He especially wanted me to publish the proceedings of the Oslo conference and write the foreword for it. "I rely upon your publishing contacts," he said.

I envisioned a feminist government-in-formation and an observer post at the UN. This conference might be a first step.

I hired my friend and colleague Dr. Barbara Joans to assist me in researching feminists around the world who had some measure of power or prominence in their countries. We narrowed five hundred names down to about fifty and recommended some for invitations to the conference.

I was excited. I did not stop to ask myself why such a powerful man would want to help so radical a feminist. I was blinded by my own ambition and perhaps by the illusion that I was no longer subject to a "woman's fate." Just after midnight on December 25, 1979, four days after we signed my employment contract, my bell rang. I opened the door and my six-foot employer barged in. He was drunk. My infant son and babysitter were sleeping one room away. He declared his love for me, said he had waited long enough, and then, despite my most ferocious efforts, raped me. He could not ejaculate, but he tormented me with his attempts for nearly an hour.

I did not scream. I gritted my teeth and bore it. I thought about how a feminist government might handle rape. Life in prison? Execution? Radical rehabilitation?

Before he left, he went into my son's room and put his hand down the sleeping babysitter's underpants. She awakened, terrified. (I did not find out about this until later, when she told me.) Then my son awakened, crying. Davidson hastily left.

I wanted to call the police, but Davidson had diplomatic immunity. I considered quitting. No, I wasn't going to allow this man to drive me off my field of dreams. So I chose to endure an extraordinary campaign of intimidation, hostility, and terror. All I could do proactively was make sure I was never alone with him again and hope for feminist support and solidarity. Otherwise I was helpless. Vulnerable.

The following day I told both Barbara and my assistant what had happened. I have no memory of whom else I told. Over the years, Barbara has insisted that I tried to tell everyone about it, but I believe she's referring to what I revealed *after* the Oslo conference, not before it. Barbara said, "No one wanted to believe you; no one took you seriously."

Back then most people did not believe that a married woman could be raped by her husband, nor did they believe that someone with whom a woman had had sex before, a boyfriend or a date, could rape her. Sexual harassment on the job was well known but barely talked about. In 1975, the feminist journalist Lin Farley used this phrase when she testified before the New York City Human Rights Commission. Because of all the media coverage, the phrase became known both nationally and globally. In 1978, Farley published the book *Sexual Shakedown: The Sexual Harassment of Women on the Job*.

It changed nothing.

In the 1980s, corporations instituted rules about on-the-job sexual harassment that were rarely enforced. In 2017, Farley wrote in a *New York Times* article that this phrase was "co-opted, sanitized, stripped of its power to shock, disturb, and galvanize."

So there I was in early 1980 without any legal way to allege either rape or sexual harassment.

I stayed on at the UN. I felt that I had accepted the terms of battle and therefore deserved whatever came my way? I asked myself how important was it that I'd been raped. I thought of all the other women who had endured unwanted sex or had been forced to navigate the shoals of keeping their job and steering clear of their boss's filthy, leering eyes and hands.

Davidson let me know that he was still patiently waiting for me to become his mistress. After I finally convinced him that this would never happen, he created an even more hostile work environment for me. He assembled a steering committee that opposed my objectives. Many committee members had no expertise in feminism and simply wanted to be invited to Oslo—or they had contempt for American-style feminism. (After all, it was the United Nations.)

Although he was black, Davidson did not want too many dark-skinned women at the conference. He vetoed many of my African American and African candidates. He claimed he didn't have enough money, though he managed to come up with money for white women with blond hair. I have no idea whether Davidson had internalized skin-color prejudice or just liked being surrounded by blondes. The hypocrisy, the tyranny, was unbearable. Gritting my teeth, I hung on.

From time to time I invited a few blonde celebrities to attend steering committee meetings as a way of signaling to the barbarian that I had powerful friends with media connections. Once Gloria Steinem attended, as did Erica Jong.

And then things began to get really scary.

Davidson casually stopped by my desk and almost dreamily told me a story about Sierra Leone. He described how young girls there are lined up along the road to be sold. They are usually naked and their legs are splayed. The buyer or potential husband can decide whether their genital mutilation suits him.

This scene was so horrible that I've never written about it before. Was it true? I'll never know. But it terrified me to think that this was a man for whom little girls were like so many chickens in the marketplace, like silent slaves whose mouths were forced open to inspect their teeth in order to gauge their age; whose breasts, bellies, and genitalia were rudely inspected as a way of measuring their sexual attractiveness and child-bearing capacity.

Davidson's anecdote has haunted me ever since.

One day Davidson stayed home sick but wanted me to bring some paperwork over for his signature. His wife was there. I brought my assistant along. Still, he ordered me into another room and exposed himself to me. I looked at him with disgust. He said calmly, carefully: "I do not think that the UN should fund travel for your assistant."

I now understood that I was dealing with a demon.

Because I'd been talking to Gloria Steinem about forming an international feminist government for years, and because of her position at *Ms.*, I invited her to the conference. Since she is also a white blonde, Davidson did not oppose funding her travel. However, at the last minute Gloria informed me that Robin Morgan would be taking her place. That was fine with me. Robin was my sister, my comrade.

My Feminist Conference in Oslo

In July 1980, women from every continent gathered in Oslo. Some were high-level UN officials (Lucille Mair); one had served as a prime minister (Maria de Lourdes Pintasilgo of Portugal), another was a former Zambian ambassador (Gwendoline Konie), one was a newly elected member of New Zealand's parliament (Marilyn Waring). Women arrived in Oslo from Africa, Asia, Oceania, the Middle East, Europe, and North and South America.

I had invited three women I knew: E.M. Broner; Dr. Teresa Bernardez, an Argentinian American psychiatrist; and Robin Morgan.

Davidson was perpetually drunk. He knocked on my door at all hours of the night and sexually intimidated three other conference participants. I assembled a group that included black women from

Africa and revealed the details of my rape. We decided to confront him privately.

But Robin thought it wouldn't look good for a white feminist to charge a black man with rape and sexual harassment. "It will look bad for feminism," she declared. Marilyn Waring—Robin's admirer and shortly afterward her lover—strongly agreed.

"But Robin," I said, "there's no way I can sue him legally. This is the only justice I'll ever have."

Two black African women said, "Let's go and get this dirty dog." Our former prime minister said worriedly, "I always knew something like this could happen." Maria Pintasilgo told me that she had never seen a black African woman who was willing to back a white woman against a black man. "Your feminism must really be cross-cultural in appeal."

Robin insisted that confronting Davidson would make the *American* feminist movement look racist. I was confused by what she was saying, as well as by her vehemence. What happened next was even more incomprehensible to me. Robin abandoned the feminist workshop that I had cobbled together and spent more and more time with my rapist.

Clearly Robin did not have my back, and she had seemingly abandoned all feminist principles—and I didn't understand why.

Back in New York, something felt off, but I was so busy that I barely noticed that my allies at *Ms.* magazine had stopped inviting me to their events and parties. I was not invited to be on their Advisory Board of Scholars; I was no longer asked to review books or films. When Letty Cottin Pogrebin recommended me for a Wonder Woman grant, I was told that there was a quota on women who had "already been recognized for achievement."

Then Robin Morgan was announced as the recipient of a Wonder Woman grant.

———

Out of nowhere, Kate Millett sent over our dear mutual friend Clarkie to badger me into talking to Robin.

"C'mon, she's crying her eyes out. Just get over whatever is bothering you and kiss and make up."

"Clarkie, you don't know what you're talking about. If Robin really wants to kiss and make up, she should contact me. She'll have to make public amends for what she did in Oslo."

"You shouldn't let your concern about Israel come between feminists."

Ah, the disinformation campaign was underway. According to Robin, what happened in Oslo wasn't a matter of the betrayal of feminist principles but a difference of opinion about the Middle East. Robin and I did disagree about U.S. policy in the Middle East, but even I refused to believe that she'd side with my rapist because of this. Or would she?

I now wonder whether I should have talked to Robin anyway. But I was incensed that she was coming at me indirectly, sending others, whom she'd already disinformed.

In late August 1982 I nearly died in a car accident in Vermont. My assistant lost control of the car and we tore through a guardrail, plunged thirty feet, and landed upside-down in the shallows of a river, where I was trapped. I had broken bones and torn ligaments, and I faced several surgeries—but oh joy! I was alive. My assistant sustained only a few scratches.

Although I had received none of the Oslo participants' papers, I was still planning to edit them and write a foreword for the proceedings.

Davidson and his minions kept calling and sending me letters telling me that the publication had been delayed but that they still expected me to write a foreword.

Letty had questioned E.M. extensively about what happened in Oslo. E.M. considered Robin's actions to be unforgivable. Still, Letty tried to get Robin invited to our annual feminist Passover seder. But E.M. refused to normalize our relationship with Robin in this way. I agreed with E.M. and was grateful for her principled support.

In 1983, Letty, E.M., and I met by accident at the Conference on Women Surviving: The Holocaust. We talked quite intensely about what had happened in Oslo, and Letty seemed shaken. At some point, as I remember it, Letty implored me not to ask her to choose between me and Robin, because Robin was close to Gloria, and Gloria remained Letty's priority.

After our seder, to which Gloria often was invited, she and I talked about Oslo for the first time. Gloria looked strained and sickened. She said that what happened was beginning to remind her of an early-1960s tragedy in which a white female civil rights worker was raped by a black man. No one would support that woman in pressing charges.

"Well, Gloria, this is our 1980 version of that, only this time your close friend Robin opportunistically collaborated with my rapist, and it was feminist women—Robin and you—who silenced my cry of rape. This betrayal is even more significant to me than the rape was."

Two days later, Gloria called me and told me that she was concerned that I was so distressed. *She* was distressed about the possibility of a public battle and offered to help in any way she could. She said that, anyway, no one will ever read that Oslo book—"I understand that there are only six hundred copies in circulation." I barely heard her urging me to feel free to call her anytime for support, saying that she loved me and cared about me, how she had wondered why I hadn't called her sooner.

"Book?" I asked. "What book?"

Robin Was Wearing My Skin

I thought I was going to faint. I was holding a bright-blue book in my hand: *Creative Women in Changing Societies: A Quest for Alternatives*. This is the book for which I was supposed to write a foreword. Robin did so in my place, the same Robin who had cooled out the group confrontation with my employer-rapist. Without telling me, Robin had written the foreword to the proceedings of my conference. She had borrowed my bloodied skin and was wearing it. Robin didn't even mention me. In his preface, Davidson wrote glowingly about my invaluable involvement, my "considerable knowledge of the field," and my "dynamism and familiarity with the feminist literature."

My *rapist* thanked me for my contribution. My feminist *sister* Robin avoided mentioning my very existence.

At this point I threatened to sue. The last thing Robin and Gloria wanted was a lawsuit and the negative publicity it would bring. I didn't even know if I had grounds for legal action. Even if I did, I didn't really want to sue; I wanted feminist justice behind closed doors. I wanted Robin to admit what she had done and to atone for it in a feminist way. *I wanted us all to confront my rapist so that he didn't go to his grave thinking he could divide the likes of us.*

I suggested a feminist tribunal at Gloria's apartment. She agreed.

I composed a fifty-page document in which I exhaustively described what had happened and sent it to both Robin and Gloria.

I now understood that Robin had started a disinformation campaign about Oslo. Gloria thought that only four Oslo participants were included in Robin's own upcoming global feminist anthology and that two of them were known to *Ms.* before Oslo.

What global anthology?

Gloria wanted to have us both go over "our very different narratives." Unbelievably, she said: "Robin has done nothing wrong. It's true, I wouldn't have written a foreword to your conference proceedings, but, then again, it'll make no money and hardly anyone will read it."

What I think Gloria was really saying was that *Ms.*'s financial and political investment in Robin's global anthology (a work in process that was unknown to me at the time), and Gloria's dependence on Robin as one of her advisers, editors, and writers, was far more important than justice for a rape victim—even if that victim was me; that her personal and political friendship with Robin made it impossible for her to be part of exposing Robin in any way.

We set a date to meet. I invited three allies: Charlotte Bunch, the founder of *Women's Liberation* and *Quest: A Feminist Quarterly* and director of the Center for Women's Global Leadership at Rutgers; Letty Cottin Pogrebin; and Shelley Neiderbach, a psychotherapist and expert on crime victims.

The Feminist Tribunal on East Seventy-third Street, July 13, 1983

We gathered in Gloria's apartment, on the second floor of a brownstone on the Upper East Side. It occupied the entire floor and was generously proportioned but was really only two rooms: an office and small bathroom in the back, and a living room with a loft bedroom in the front. The kitchen was tiny. I had been visiting this apartment since 1971. Gloria said that the Warhol superstar "Baby Jane" Holzer had been her interior decorator.

Everyone except Robin was appropriately grave. Robin reclined theatrically on a chair, hand over her forehead. She claimed that she had not received my document and had only just read Gloria's copy. She affected a pose of weary boredom. She was not outraged by my accusations, but rather ever so slightly amused by the drama of it all.

At issue was not only what Robin had done to me but how she had shut out other feminists on behalf of *Ms.* magazine's territorial ownership of international feminism.

Charlotte spoke about how Robin and *Ms.* had consistently kept her out of international feminist meetings and had gone so far as to literally delete her name when covering an international event that Charlotte had organized.

Robin insisted that she had actually defended my honor by making a deal with my rapist: that she wouldn't write the foreword unless he mentioned my contribution to the conference in his preface. She admitted rather blithely that she had had an ongoing series of lunches and dinners with Davidson.

Robin claimed that Davidson also sexually harassed *her* in Oslo, and then she said that the feminists from Africa hadn't wanted a confrontation.

"Robin," I asked, "why didn't you tell me that Davidson wanted you to write the foreword in my place?"

"Because I was very busy. My mother was dying. I had marital and financial problems. It wasn't the most important thing to me. Anyway, no one will ever read the proceedings. Frankly, I didn't have time for the four-hour conversation with you. I can only apologize for how badly my own life had been going."

Then, incredibly, both Robin and Gloria said that they'd assumed I'd had an affair with Davidson.

"But even if a lover or a husband had raped a woman, that would be terrible," Gloria added.

Back then, people had very stereotypical ideas about who a rapist might be. He was a monster, a stranger, a loser—not the boy next door, definitely not someone who was a celebrity, a diplomat, the employer of hundreds. Why would Bill Cosby or Bill Clinton, Charlie Rose or Harvey Weinstein, need to rape or sexually harass a woman? How could a man of God—a priest or a rabbi or an imam—allow himself to do so?

I could see that Robin was going to stonewall. There was going to be no apology, no admission of guilt, no redress for me whatsoever.

I said, "Well, I might as well just publish everything."

Gloria immediately replied: "Don't threaten us. You're making me angry."

Finally, Gloria was expressing anger directly. When her reputation and the moral character of a friend so closely associated with the *Ms.* empire was threatened, Gloria was able to express anger.

Lips tight, Gloria asked: "Phyllis, what do you *want*?"

"What I want is to have Robin tell every Oslo participant why I didn't write the foreword and what exactly happened to me and to the other Oslo participants who were sexually harassed. *And I want us all to confront him so that he doesn't go to his grave thinking he can divide the likes of us.*"

Gloria agreed to all this and promised to have Robin do her part, which included writing a letter to the Oslo participants about what had happened.

I was patient. But in November, four months after our meeting, I wrote to Gloria to tell her that Robin had not written the letter.

I was really heartbroken that I was having to wait so long for a smidgen of sisterly solidarity.

Oh, what was the big deal? I was not dead. I was still teaching and writing. I was still a feminist leader. And yet, I was not quite right. I was a bit sad. I had absorbed three, perhaps four major betrayals within a nine-month period. My second husband had walked out, threatened to kidnap our son, demanded money before he'd go away—and then, after I'd agreed to his financial demands, took off and never looked back. Within a month of his departure, Davidson raped me and made my life hell on the job.

My Rapist Is Never Confronted as Promised

Robin's letter—bland, smooth, and vague—did not go out until February 1984, seven months after our tribunal.

I kept asking Gloria when we were going to confront my rapist. Time passed. She said that she had placed several calls to his UN office that he had not returned. More time passed. She said she couldn't find him.

Many years later, because she thought the information would comfort me, Gloria told me that she had run into my rapist on a small college campus in the South where she was lecturing. She said that I ought to feel good that this major diplomat and UN section chief had clearly been sent off to a place far from the dazzling city lights. As I recall it, Gloria told me, rather proudly, that she had said to David-son that she knew he had "hurt" her friend Phyllis.

Is that what rape and sexual harassment on the job are—some kind of hurt, like scraping a knuckle or bruising a knee?

Gloria said nothing about Robin's betrayal of feminist principles and of me personally—about the kind of hurt that is.

In 1991, when Gloria publicly stood by Anita Hill's side, I finally realized how much I would have wanted her to stand by my side as we confronted Davidson. I understand that Gloria goes where the media goes, and that she often gets the media to follow her. There would have been no media at a private confrontation with Davidson, although I would never have ruled out a public one. I also understood that Davidson was not about to be appointed to the U.S. Supreme Court. And yet, by Gloria's inaction, or her failure to find him, she was, in a sense, enabling him to continue preying upon an untold number of other women.

I have never collaborated with a rapist on behalf of a "larger" cause. I had absolutely no idea that another feminist leader might do so.

After many years, I came to believe that Robin and Gloria, two feminists I had unwisely trusted, had sacrificed someone else—me— to defend their brand of feminism and their control of international feminist networks.

So what was the big deal? Prostituted girls and women are raped twenty times a day for money. Women in war zones are gang-raped as a way of driving them and their families out of their minds. Compared to all the evil and cruelty in the world, this single rape, this particular workplace harassment, this feminist betrayal of trust seem to pale in comparison.

But when the people we trust betray us, we're wounded more deeply than we can be at the hands of strangers. When a woman finds a band of sisters who proclaim that we are all for one and one for all, what do we do when it turns out not to be true? Imagine being part of a movement that's on record as being against sexual violence and on record as believing the victim; a movement that earned its credibility and enormous following for holding precisely these views. Imagine finding out that your feminist allies don't really mean it—or, rather, that, like politicians, they will sacrifice one principle (believe the woman who says she was raped), for another (back the man or the political party that will keep abortion legal).

It took thirty-seven years for the mass media even to begin to critique the dual and duplicitous roles that institutional feminism played in the sexual harassment wars. While Gloria and Robin benefited from the feminist movement's analysis and exposure of rape and sexual harassment, they opportunistically covered for "their" men and also criticized some of the victims.

Towards the end of 2017, in the pages of the *New York Times*, Maureen Dowd called out Gloria for defending Bill Clinton's abuse of power and priapism. Dowd wrote: "Institutional feminism died when Gloria Steinem, Madeleine Albright and other top feminists vouched for President Clinton as he brazenly lied about never having had a sexual relationship with 'that woman'—Monica Lewinsky."

Were Clinton's other known victims believed? Did they receive justice? Were there also unknown victims?

Also toward the end of 2017, an article by Peggy Noonan in the *Wall Street Journal* described Gloria's role in protecting Bill Clinton. She cited an article by Caitlyn Flanagan in the *Atlantic* that said that by the 1990s, "The [feminist] movement had by then ossified into a partisan operation." Flanagan reminded us of the famous March 1998 op-ed piece Gloria wrote for the *New York Times* in which she "slut-shamed, victim-blamed, and age-shamed" the victims and "urged compassion for and gratitude to the man the women accused." She pointed out that Steinem characterized the assaults as "passes."

This is similar to the Gloria I had encountered so many years earlier when I described being raped and harassed. In my case, Gloria's larger cause was not the Democratic Party but rather her investment in Robin's work on behalf of *Ms.*'s brand of global feminism.

On November 30, 2017, Gloria unwisely responded to these critiques in an interview in the pages of the *Guardian*. She is quoted as saying that "what you write in one decade you don't necessarily write in the next." I interpret that as her saying that the times were different then, that we didn't know then what we know now. This is not true. Feminists knew all about rape and sexual harassment back then.

To me, Gloria's attitude is analogous to that of sexual predators who insist that back then, everyone was doing it, no one stopped them, the rules were different.

Gloria told the *Guardian* "I'm glad I wrote it in that decade." And why? "Because the danger then was we were about to lose sexual harassment law because it was being applied to extramarital sex, free will, extramarital sex, as with Monica Lewinsky."

Gloria did not acknowledge any wrongdoing or any awareness that by covering up what a judge later described as Clinton's "boorish and offensive" behavior, she might have hurt some women.

This was the Gloria whom I had encountered in the early 1980s. Back then, she covered up Robin's opportunistic collaboration with a rapist and her betrayal of his victim; she knew that I viewed her, Gloria's, failure to confront Davidson together with me as a failure of feminist courage, feminist principle, and personal loyalty. She knew that I thought that a man like Davidson would keep preying on women. This all made no difference. It was easy for me to say that Davidson had raped and sexually harassed me, and I said as much to those close to me. What Robin had done was far more devastating, complex, and consequential. I had no simple words to describe it.

Robin's campaign had already preempted anything I might have tried to say. As I came to understand it, Robin had told different mutual feminist allies different things. No one told me what she was saying, and no one asked me whether or not it was true.

Gloria and Robin and I were not ordinary friends. Were it not for a feminist vision and movement, I would have had little to do with either of them. Their betrayal might be the equivalent to Susan B. Anthony's refusal to stand up for Elizabeth Cady Stanton when she was under attack by younger feminists. What matters to us and to history is not whether Stanton and Anthony were "besties" but how feminist leaders behave in battle, in the breach, under pressure, when they have political choices to make.

Robin and Gloria and I did not hang out together, go to movies, double-date, take vacations, travel, or engage in small talk. I never discussed my husband with Gloria and she never discussed her boyfriends with me. Robin did not talk to me about her marriage to a man or her lesbianism.

Gloria and I attended feminist press conferences and meetings, did media together, and introduced each other to feminists worth knowing or women in need of help. We asked each other to sign petitions and told each other about new organizations, marches, and demonstrations. When we were together there was always a feminist agenda.

When Robin and I met for coffee it was always and only to discuss feminist issues. Yes, Gloria attended some of my birthday parties; Robin gave me a baby shower; and Gloria came to my infant son's Brit Milah and Blessing ceremony. But this only signaled that she and I were ranking members of a political clique.

It was all show biz, baby. And we were grand.

Was Robin always an actor (she had been a professional child actor), a chameleon, a scene stealer, someone who borrowed other women's roles, ideas, phrases, actions, tried them on, tried them out, claimed credit for the role, the imitation, then moved onto a new role? Was all the world a stage for her? If so, how could I have liked and trusted her? How could the seemingly mild and moderate Gloria keep her so close?

What was the big deal, really?

Well, for starters: I never heard a single word from any one of the women who participated in the Oslo conference—not a word since the summer of 1980 until today, as of this writing. That is a haunting silence.

A year or two after the Tribunal, Gloria sent me a loving note when I had surgery. She wrote, "Let me know if there's anything I can do to help, large or small."

Oddly, touchingly, as I look over my correspondence with Gloria, I see that it remained affectionate in tone for nearly twenty years after Oslo, right up until the twenty-first century. We signed our letters *Love*, and she continued to endorse all my books. I am not entirely sure why we stopped writing to each other, but we did.

Is Sisterhood Really Global?

It was 1984, Orwell's year, and I was holding Robin's 815-page anthology *Sisterhood Is Global: The International Women's Movement Anthology*. The anthology had seventy-one contributors. I was afraid to open the book. When I did, I discovered that almost 40 percent of the feminists Barbara Joans and I had found and brought to Oslo were in it. In her 2000 memoir *Saturday's Child*, Robin writes about how important the Oslo conference was to her: "The networking was indeed fantastic. At the week-long UNITAR conference . . . I also met for the first time a number of extraordinary women who were to become friends, allies, anthology contributors, and long-term colleagues."

I wonder what, if anything, Robin ever said to any of them about my sudden and total disappearance.

———

Robin was an inveterate scene-stealer. Why would anyone want credit for something she has not done? Perhaps someone who does this is insecure about her accomplishments, feels she's only making it up as she goes along, "winging" it, dancing as fast as she can; or perhaps she feels that she is an imposter, not legitimate, not who people think she is. I think that evil people do this too.

Robin's first anthology, published in 1970, was titled *Sisterhood Is Powerful*. Forever after, feminists, journalists, and even scholars assumed that the title was a phrase Robin coined. In fact, Kathie Sarachild coined the phrase at a demonstration against the war in Vietnam on January 15, 1968. What kind of sisterhood fails to attribute to its true author a phrase that becomes so popular?

In 2005 *New York* magazine quoted Robin in an article about Andrea Dworkin, who had recently died. The journalist Ariel Levy described Robin as "a great coiner of slogans for the movement, [such as] 'The personal is political.' 'That became rather well known,' [Robin] says drily, drinking wine in front of the fireplace of her West Village apartment. 'But for me it was always very true.'"

Robin did not coin the phrase "the personal is political." According to Carol Hanisch, this phrase was also coined by Kathie Sarachild and was brought to Hanisch's attention by Shulie Firestone and Anne Koedt. Hanisch also takes credit for this idea and for how it was used to organize women. Levy may have attributed this phrase to Robin out of ignorance, and Robin could have smoothly allowed her to do so without correcting her. Conceivably Robin clarified the matter and Levy unilaterally memorialized it this way.

Robin and Gloria did win the franchise for international feminism. Gloria became the sole face of second-wave American feminism. The *Ms.* magazine brand prevailed, although it watered down radical feminism, kept rewriting second-wave feminist history, and monetized a movement so that a handful of feminists would live well, remain in the public eye, and be able to support certain feminist causes and the Democratic Party.

Gloria and Robin's unfulfilled promise to support me in confronting my rapist silenced me. Why did they distance themselves from me? Did I remind them of their failure? Was it because I could, at any time, "tell"?

Well, I'm telling. I've been trying to do so for the longest time. Maybe now someone will actually hear me.

13 Whistleblowing and the Inevitable Blowback

Robin's unforgivable conduct and Gloria's collaboration with her pained me, but I remained in service to my feminist work. Their behavior did not become my darkness at noon.

Arthur Koestler's 1941 novel *Darkness at Noon* depicts the arrest, torture, and execution of a former Communist true believer who has been falsely accused—just as he had, in the past, falsely accused and betrayed other Communists for the sake of "the revolution." He finally understands that this ideology—especially as put into practice by its younger proponents—is even more brutal than the regime the revolutionaries had overthrown.

While feminist cliques did obtain enormous power and influence in academia, media, and politics, no clique ever obtained full state control. Therefore, feminists could not arrest or execute their ideological opponents or competitors—but they used the power they had. They eliminated other feminists by discrediting and shunning them and by disappearing their work in the eyes of the media, in the histories the victors wrote, and in the films they produced or for which they served as consultants.

In her 2000 book *Tales of the Lavender Menace: A Memoir of Liberation*, the lesbian feminist activist Karla Jay wrote: "It seemed to me that once a person fell under suspicion, it really didn't matter whether she was guilty: She could never undo the rumors flying around her."

If a rumor, however false, had made the rounds, recalling it was impossible. Even if someone knew that a rumor was false, breaking ranks with a ruling female clique is far too dangerous for most women to risk.

Women, including feminist women, risked being shunned and defamed by their own group if they adopted a "wrong" point of view, the "wrong" kind of friends, or by looking or acting in too independent a way. The consequences may be economic, political, social, and life-long.

Blowback?

The one time I named Davidson as my rapist and sexual harasser, someone who claimed to be his relative called me and threatened to have me killed if I did so again.

Blowback?

The Egyptian feminist Laila Abou-Saif, whom I had introduced to Gloria and my literary agent in 1978, at the time of the Middle East Film Festival in the Village, simply disappeared from my life post-Oslo. Years later, we finally met for drinks at the Plaza—Laila loved the Plaza; she said it reminded her of the Shepheard Hotel in Cairo. She talked about how much she had missed me. I asked her whether the rumor I'd heard was true: *Had* she denounced me to Davidson as some kind of Israeli spy? She blushed, laughed, and admitted that she might have said that I had divided loyalties.

"But Phyllis, didn't you have an affair with him?"

Laila might have talked to Gloria or another person who'd thought I'd had an affair with him. When Laila published her memoir, *A Bridge Through Time*, in 1985 (under the name "Laila Said," to protect her family), she did not send it to me for an endorsement or as a courtesy.

Blowback?

Years later, I showed Andrea Dworkin the dossier I'd kept about my involvement with the United Nations Institute for Training and Research.

She read it from beginning to end without stopping, sighed deeply, looked up, and said: "I have no doubt you were raped. Many rapists cannot ejaculate. Your story rings true. But drop it, let it go. It'll only keep hurting you. Robin believed that accusing a black man would make white feminists look like racists. That was her priority, to protect feminists."

Am I not a feminist? If you prick me, do I not bleed? Andrea, who knew how to make huge mountains out of tiny molehills; Andrea, who accused practically everyone of high crimes, never mere misdemeanors; Andrea, who obsessed about how cruelly she'd been treated by other feminists, including by those who, according to Andrea, were getting all the credit for Andrea's ideas; Andrea, who left no injustice unscorned—yes, that Andrea—knew on which side her bread was buttered. Just as Gloria protected Robin, she also steadfastly protected Andrea, who was a pariah among feminists who supported pornography and prostitution as First Amendment, sexual, and economic rights.

As I recall, there was one exception.

Alice Walker, the author of *The Color Purple* and *The Third Life of Grange Copeland*, and an activist in the effort to end female genital mutilation, was the only feminist in *Ms.* circles who supported me in my right to denounce my rapist. I'll never forget her principled kindness.

Thank you, Alice, from the bottom of my heart.

After the little feminist tribunal that failed, Gloria kept endorsing my work. In 1986, she commended my 1986 book *Mothers on Trial: The Battle for Children and Custody*; in 1988, she participated in a press conference that I organized when I published *Sacred Bond: The Legacy of Baby M*; and blurbed my 1998 book *Letters to a Young Feminist*.

Davidson died in late 1994, almost fifteen years after he raped me. Now we would never be able to confront him together. Robin's craven feminist collaboration with a rapist and sexual harasser, and Gloria's decision to side with Robin, stand; they are part of the historical record. My unspoken and never-promised agreement not to expose this episode no longer applied. Since Robin and Gloria had not done what they'd promised to do, my lips were now unsealed.

In 1995, with enormous help from Ellen Cole and Esther Rothblum, two other professors of psychology, I coedited *Feminist Foremothers in Women's Studies, Psychology, and Mental Health*. It told the personal stories of forty-eight "feminist foremothers." Ellen interviewed me for the book. For the first time, I briefly described what had happened to me at the UN and in Oslo, changing the names of the guilty parties. But, as Gloria might say, this volume would never become a best seller, so only a few people would ever see it.

That same year, I again briefly described this episode in a piece I wrote for the feminist progressive magazine *On the Issues* called "Rape in High Places." I had gotten John Stoltenberg, Andrea Dworkin's partner and the author of the book *Refusing to Be a Man*, a job at the magazine, and for years John had been after me to write about the "shit that feminist women do to each other." In the article I had again changed people's names and tried to disguise them. Nevertheless John took me to task. He said that I had not disguised Gloria and Robin well enough, that some people might still be able to recognize them, and that Robin was going through a hard time.

Maybe my writing about this, even without naming names, had begun to unsettle them, and I was experiencing the blowback.

Yes, my chest tightened when I learned that I'd been excluded from a gathering of many of the Oslo participants in New York City to celebrate Robin's *Sisterhood Is Global* anthology—but the universe of *Ms.* magazine was not my only, or even primary, world.

Would I have attended *Ms.* events that I was now being excluded from? I don't really know. This dilemma is similar to whether I would or could have written a foreword to the Oslo proceedings without mentioning the rape and sexual harassment. In both cases I was deprived of the opportunity to decide.

The real blowback did not begin to gather force until the late 1990s and early 2000s, and only after I'd begun to write about what had really happened.

In 1998, I had published *Letters to a Young Feminist* because I thought I might be dying—I had undiagnosed Lyme disease, which was eventually also diagnosed as chronic fatigue immune dysfunction syndrome, or myalgic encephalomyelitis—and wanted to transmit something of a legacy. Gloria had both endorsed and recommended this book in interviews. Three years later, two of Gloria's protégées, Jen Baumgardner and Amy Richards, published *Manifesta: Young Women, Feminism, and the Future*. In the *Women's Review of Books*, the reviewer described how my book is "discussed at length" in *Manifesta* because the authors thought it "epitomizes the way conflicts play out between Second and Third Wave feminists." The reviewer went on at length about how the book had singled me out for scorn. She notes that the authors "valued Chesler's other work" but find *Letters* to be "patronizing." I was surprised, because they'd interviewed me at length in my home and had been warm and respectful.

But when I read the book, I seemed to be the *only* second-wave feminist the authors had used as the straw mother for my entire generation.

The authors were angry because they and others of their generation felt that second-wave feminists were not reading their work, only telling them to read ours. They may have been right. Nevertheless, something strange seemed to be going on psychologically. My generation never sought our biological or ideological mothers' approval. Their generation seemed to need it. From a psychoanalytic point of view, they were biting the breast that feeds them. The book contained a "Letter to an Older Feminist," which they say is a response to my book title. In it they wrote: "You're not our mothers. Now you have to stop treating us as daughters. You're responsible for raising your own consciousness about what Third Wave feminists are thinking. Engaging with [us] rather than knocking [us] down. Read our books, buy our records. Support our organizations. Don't treat us as if we're competitive with you."

If I had received a letter from Elizabeth Cady Stanton, Isabella Baumfree (Sojourner Truth), Matilda Joslyn Gage, or Charlotte Perkins Gilman, I would have treasured both our similarities and our differences. But these nineteenth-century foremothers are long gone. Perhaps our greatest crime was that so many second-wave feminists were still alive—some of us, including me, still pioneering away.

I suggested to Jen Baumgardner that we meet. We did, at a coffee shop on the Lower East Side, but the conversation was stilted. A year later, at one of Kate Millett's book readings, Jen sidled up to me and asked whether I thought what happened was "like a mother-daughter thing." I replied, "Perhaps, but *Gloria* is your mother; I'm not. Why don't you challenge *her*? Why scapegoat me?"

She didn't answer.

Gloria had mentored and positioned these two journalists. They were a part of her third-wave inner circle.

Blowback?

Like Carol Gilligan, the author of *In a Different Voice: Psychological Theory and Women's Development* (1982), Gloria and Robin had invested a great deal in promoting the myth that all women are sisters, that sisterhood is both powerful and global, and that women are more compassionate, more moral, and more sensitive interpersonally than men. That this isn't true—or, rather, that it *is* true but in a more limited way is something that, in my view, Gloria could not bear to hear.

I had no idea how strongly she felt about this until my agent, Fifi Oscard, sent a copy of the manuscript of *Woman's Inhumanity to*

Woman to Gloria. Awkwardly, and in a somewhat shaken voice, Fifi told me the following: "Phyllis, you know I was once in a Women in Media group with Gloria. I've never seen her this upset. She said that she couldn't continue reading your book. That it had made her ill. She insisted that she *herself* had enjoyed a wonderful relationship with her mother and couldn't stomach what you were writing about mothers and daughters."

I was totally shocked. I knew something about Gloria's caretaker relationship to her mentally ill mother—everyone did. Gloria herself has written and talked about it at length. In her 1983 article *Ruth's Song (Because She Could Not Sing It)*, Gloria described her mother in an eloquent and moving way. Her mother, she wrote, was

> someone to be worried about and cared for; an invalid who lay in bed with eyes closed and lips moving in occasional response to voices only she could hear; a woman to whom I brought an endless stream of toast and coffee, bologna sandwiches and dime pies, in a child's version of what meals should be. . . . In many ways, our roles were reversed: I was the mother and she was the child. Yet that didn't help her either, for she still worried about me with all the intensity of a frightened mother, plus the special fears that came from her own world full of threats and hostile voices. . . . [She was] someone who was afraid to be alone, who could not hang on to reality long enough to hold a job, and who could rarely concentrate enough to read a book. . . .
>
> After many months in a sanatorium, she was pronounced recovered. . . . But she was never again completely without the spells of depression, anxiety, and visions into some other world that eventually were to turn her into the nonperson I remember. And she was never again without a bottle of . . . chloral hydrate. . . . Our lives, my mother's from forty-six to fifty-three, and my own from ten to seventeen, were spent alone together.

Perhaps, as we grow older, we become even more protective of our mothers' memories.

I now understood why Gloria was such a passionate champion of my book *Women and Madness*, why she'd published two excerpts from it in *Ms.*, and why she'd turned to me, again and again, for my expert advice. She may have felt that I'd redeemed her mother's reputation in the eyes of the world, that patriarchy drives both healthy and unhealthy women into dark places.

Why did Gloria reveal these feelings to my agent? She could have said that she was too busy to read the manuscript. How had I gone from being the woman near whom Gloria wanted to be buried to the woman whose work made her ill?

Was it that I had begun to break my silence?

Around this time, another feminist said: "This has been preying on my mind, and I have to tell you. The reason some feminists won't talk to you is because Robin has spread the rumor that you are too dangerous to talk to, that you will sue at the drop of a hat."

What a relief to learn precisely what Robin had been saying.

Blowback?

At Barbara Seaman's memorial service in 2008, I got into the elevator with my son and daughter-in-law. There stood Letty Cottin Pogrebin—the woman who had asked me not to make her choose between me and Gloria. Letty was with a close associate, a major Democratic Party operative. They both literally turned their backs to me. I was appalled by this behavior and called Letty the next day.

"Can't we agree to park our weapons outside when one of us has died?"

"No," she said. "You are too dangerous to talk to. You are dangerous to the women's movement." I think she was talking about my lack of loyalty to *Ms.* magazine, but that's a story for another day.

———

Blowback?

In 2014, Kate Millett—my buddy, my sister—and I were having dinner at the Bowery Bar and Grill. Kate said she wanted to give me an award at the next conference of the Veteran Feminists of America. I agreed to accept it. But then she and her partner, the photographer Sophie Keir, asked me whether I'd be willing to "make up with Robin." What? Is this still dogging my every step? I replied, "Sure—as long as she first confronts my rapist with me as promised and repairs the disconnect between myself and the feminists whom I invited to the conference in Oslo. And publicly admits what she did."

Kate looked both puzzled and pained; Sophie looked disapproving. I added: "Kate, I understand your problem: you can't afford to do anything that might get you in trouble with Gloria, whose goodwill you and Sophie depend upon. Why not give me this award in the bathroom or right here at the B-Bar? I don't need an audience of veteran feminists."

Kate withdrew the offer of the award. Sophie told me the award was being discontinued.

These are all small things. If only one or two such things had happened over a long period, they would hardly have mattered. But many small things eventually add up; they confirm an atmosphere of estrangement—an eerie silence instead of bubbling feminist voices.

I doubt that Gloria ever did much to actively hurt me. She didn't have to. When someone is powerful, all that person has to do is stop inviting someone to events at which it is important to be seen and heard and stop recommending that person to reporters, foundations, filmmakers, and award givers.

What can I say about Gloria? Only this: My generation of feminists needed Susan B. Anthony but we got Mary Tyler Moore. We needed Harriet Tubman but we got Jane Fonda. We got the blonde, blow-dried feminist in the aviator glasses, the one in the skinny jeans, the feminist who posed in a bubble bath for *People* magazine. As glamorous as a movie star, Gloria repeatedly gave the same pseudo-apology: "I'm not that attractive. I'm only attractive . . . for a feminist."

Pause, laugh.

Like Mary Tyler Moore, Gloria is spunky. She's also terminally nice, polite, witty, and—although appearances can deceive—not overtly combative or sexual. Gloria was disarming; she was not seen as a threat because she did not resemble any of the antifeminist stereotypes. Gloria did not look like an angry, man-hating lesbian and did not sound like an ideologue.

Gloria published her first full-length feminist book, a collection of her previously published articles, only in 1983, twenty years after Betty's *The Feminine Mystique* and sixteen to seventeen years after the first radical feminist articles appeared. Gloria's books are charming but not intellectually formidable.

Gloria's real contribution consists of teaching, year after year, and branding a relatively palatable version of feminism. To her credit, doing this allowed her to create the Ms. Foundation, which donates millions of dollars every year to worthy feminist projects.

Many left-wing radical feminists viewed Gloria's foundation "give-aways" as diversionary tactics rather than as underwriting a revolutionary struggle. They meant that the Ms. Foundation was funding individual, not collective, solutions—the equivalent of administering humanitarian medical treatment to miners with brown lung disease instead of funding a struggle to shut the mines down.

I do not agree with this criticism. Money to keep a domestic violence shelter or an abortion clinic open is money well spent.

Issues that other feminists pioneered—abortion, rape, sexual harassment, incest, domestic violence, women's economic, political, and social inequality—were made more visible, even acceptable, by her pleasant appearance, unfailing good humor, and Midwestern calm.

Gloria has done the best she can—and she's been tireless. Gloria can't sit still, can't stay in one place for too long; she is, indeed, her "father's daughter," as she writes in *My Life on the Road*. Her father was a classic Jewish peddler-salesman, a man who lived out of his car and felt most at home among strangers on the road. (Gloria actually depicts her father as a version of Johnny Appleseed or Paul Bunyan, as some kind of indigenous Native American nomad, not as the Jew he was.) In any event, perhaps her very genes are suited to a life of constant motion, travel, and change.

Gloria has also kept feminism (and herself) fashionable by positioning and repositioning an ever-modified brand of feminism, one that is always in sync with the next media-favored movement.

Over time, Gloria's brand of institutional and media iconic feminism was increasingly less about violence against women and more about racism, prison reform, climate change, foreign "occupations," and nuclear war—all important issues but not exactly "on message," or likely to appeal to women of all political persuasions.

Here's another helpful perspective: the feminist who brings a lawsuit that lasts for fifteen years for equal employment rights or against a hostile workplace environment, during which time she is fired as a whistleblower and becomes unemployable, is not the same as someone who supported her right to do so *once*—as I have—at a press conference.

The feminist who introduces sex harassment legislation and lobbies for it, against enormous opposition, year after year, is not the same as someone who is quoted once or twice in the media as supporting such legislation.

The feminist who runs a shelter for battered women, who works seven days a week for forty to fifty years, who embraces poverty as if she were a nun, is not the same as the feminist who does a one-time fund-raiser for that shelter, which is something I have done.

The feminist who spends a year organizing a speak-out, a march, a sit-in, a demonstration, or a conference is not the same as the feminist who is asked to join them for the photo-op.

However, the media anoints a handful of spokeswomen for all women's issues; we are led to believe that the feminist who is quoted most often in the media is the leader of that struggle. Over the years, this media-generated phenomenon has dispirited the troops.

I've known feminists who have been slandered, threatened with death, beaten up, and fired from their jobs because of their feminist beliefs; feminists who have risked jail sentences; feminists who have gone to jail to protect women's rights and to save children, both their own and those of other mothers. I've known feminists who have embraced lives of poverty, insecurity, and danger in order to keep shelters for battered women open. I've known feminists who have had to flee their families and their countries because their ideas and behaviors were unacceptable at home.

Just sayin'.

Gloria was moved by her prefeminist trip to India in the late 1950s or early 1960s. Ever since then, the developing world, filled with people of color, has always been on her mind and in her heart. As the academic and media worlds increasingly focused on race, ethnicity, and the evils of colonialism, Gloria increasingly positioned the history and focus of *Ms.* magazine accordingly.

Although I was out of the country when the 2017 Women's March took place, I was thrilled to see millions of civilians marching for women's rights on such a cold winter day. I was less thrilled by the "pussy hats," and the headscarves or hijabs (sometimes fashioned from American flags).

As to the hijab: I know too much about girls and women who are beaten, even murdered by their families for refusing to cover their head, face, and body properly; thus, I view veiling as the sign and symbol of women's subordination. The sight of American women virtue-signaling by donning headscarves or hijab (a symbol of oppression) as if it were a gesture of solidarity with freedom fighters and opposition to alleged Islamophobia was both alarming and Orwellian.

Confusing conformity with resistance is unwise. I personally have no objection to wearing a hat, a headscarf, or a wig, since it does not mask identity or prevent social interactions from taking place, but I do not view them as badges of courage or a protest against racism.

Gloria's most recent book, *My Life on the Road* (2016), is laced with homilies, witticisms, one-liners, heartfelt advice—and total misinformation. Even if it is meant only to entertain, there is little excuse for insisting that second-wave feminist consciousness raising had its origin in ancient Southern Africa. She writes: "From the Kwei and San in Southern Africa, the ancestors of us all, to the First Nations on my own continent, where layers of such [talking] circles turned into the Iroquois Confederacy.... A wave of talking circles and 'testifying' was going on in black churches of my own country and igniting the civil rights movement. I certainly didn't guess that, a decade later, I would see consciousness-raising groups, women's talking circles, give birth to the feminist movement."

It is unfair, perhaps even useless, to impose a scholarly critique upon a popular work. Nevertheless, it is sometimes important to do so. Celebrities are now our cultural arbiters, the only experts upon whom the uninformed rely. I realize that criticizing Gloria is like criticizing Jackie Kennedy.

Gloria *is* the Jackie Kennedy of the feminist movement, the only symbol, the sole torchbearer, of second-wave feminism.

Barbara Seaman taught me that being a feminist leader cannot save us from what can happen to any woman. Barbara said that her divorce from her second husband was a painful one, and she told me that her third husband beat her very badly—he broke bones. She said she kept this a secret until she feared that her life might be in danger, at which point she turned to me and to a lawyer.

This story broke my heart. Barbara left her third husband and faced reduced circumstances with courage and without complaint. But Betty Friedan, her longtime friend, feminist ally, and a known man junkie, socialized with Barbara's third husband after Barbara had left, even after Barbara had made her allegations public. Her third husband denied having beaten her.

Barbara suffered from Betty's betrayal more than from the abuse. This was the only time I ever saw Barbara get angry. "People will think I'm making it up if someone like Betty, who was my friend, is hanging out with him."

I understand how betrayal by one's feminist allies can cut more deeply than patriarchal violence.

What happened to me in Oslo is a behind-the-scenes tale about the second-wave feminist leadership. If this could happen to me, then far worse things must have happened to others.

However, what happened to me could not stop my pen or my ability to inspire and strengthen other women. That it cost me dearly is secondary.

14　Mothers on Trial and on the Run

First-wave feminism focused primarily on a single issue—getting the vote—and it took our brave foremothers seventy-two years (1848–1920) to accomplish that goal. Second-wave feminism focused on multiple issues: reproductive freedom, equal pay for equal work, the abolition of sexual violence and woman battering, lesbian rights, and so on. Mainstream feminism focused more on the right *not* to bear an unwanted child and less on the right to social and financial support to bear a wanted child.

Most second-wave feminists did not view child support or child-care as burning issues. When pressed, many of them even said that men deserved custody because women had always had it. They did not understand that, historically, in the rare cases of divorce, fathers (including violent fathers) were automatically given custody and that a "good enough" mother never was because children were considered property and women were not allowed to own property. Mothers had *obligations*, not rights, and were held to a much higher standard than fathers were.

Most feminists of my generation did not focus on motherhood (pregnancy, childbirth, the mother-child relationship) as sacred rites of passage or as feminist issues. I and a handful of other feminists did.

Nevertheless, custody is not a new issue for feminists. In the nineteenth century, Susan B. Anthony helped hide Phoebe Phelps, a severely battered runaway mother from a prominent New York family whose husband had locked her away in an insane asylum because she'd exposed his cruelties. Upon her release, she fled with her child; she knew that, as a woman, she had no legal rights to her child.

Anthony agreed to help her. Anthony escorted Phelps and her daughter to New York City and obtained refuge for them there. Charles Phelps, a Massachusetts state senator, threatened to have Anthony arrested during one of her public lectures. Anthony's colleagues claimed she was endangering both the women's rights movement and the anti-slavery cause. Some of Anthony's abolitionist friends chastised her for helping the runaway wife. Anthony disagreed. She said: "Don't you break the law every time you help a slave to Canada? . . . Well, the law which gives the father the sole ownership of the children is just as wicked and I'll break it just as quickly. You would die before you would deliver a slave to his master, and I will die before I will give up the child to its father."

I was first called into service on the issue of contested custody in the mid-1970s. I have already described some of the high-profile lesbian custody cases in which I was involved (see chapter 10). Thereafter, three heterosexual mothers came to see me. They were stay-at-home moms who had done absolutely nothing wrong. Shockingly, all had lost custody to fathers who were primarily absent or violent but who were high earners. Judges viewed these pro-father custody decisions as progressive and proudly attributed them to the feminist movement. Some prominent feminists agreed with this way of thinking.

A new mission, a new crusade, had claimed me.

I spent more than six years working on my book *Mothers on Trial: The Battle for Children and Custody*. I looked at this phenomenon historically, globally, and psychologically and then conducted hundreds of interviews and some original studies. I then spent nine months organizing a speak-out on the subject. Many of the mothers I had interviewed came to New York City to participate, either as speakers or as workshop participants.

I was in the final stages of preparing for the speak-out when two police officers visited me.

"Have you seen this woman?"

They showed me a blurry photo. I denied having seen her. But I had. She was one of my "protective mothers," a woman on the run with two young daughters who were being repeatedly raped by their father in a small town in upstate New York.

I am not exaggerating. Once a mother alleges that the father of her child is sexually or physically assaulting that child—especially if it's true—that mother invariably, incredibly, loses custody. Most people find this incomprehensible. They do not understand the nature of pedophilia or incest. Preying upon children is repugnant to most people, which is why they do not want to believe that a father, who is supposed to protect his family, would behave so destructively. It is easier to believe that the woman is lying or crazy or out for revenge.

Most police officers, mental health professionals, lawyers, and judges held such attitudes, and still do.

Imagine going up against many high-powered matrimonial lawyers while having to represent yourself. This is what most relatively poor mothers faced in high-conflict custody battles.

Fathers are men; by definition, society usually viewed them as more believable, more stable, even more charming than mothers. These men also tended to have more money and better access to an old-boys' network than most women did. This is still true today.

Maria, a stay-at-home and battered mother, lost custody of her daughters to a small-town, well-connected fiend. She was already on the run when she found my book in a feminist bookstore and called me.

I told my assistant to wire the woman money and to send it in the name of Susan B. Anthony. When Western Union asked my assistant to whom they should return the money if no one picked it up, my assistant gave them my real name but didn't tell me, which is how the police officers found me.

Maria arrived, children in tow. I sent her to a shelter and thereafter across the country through a feminist underground railroad.

"Just never mention my name," I told her.

Soon the FBI summoned me to appear before a grand jury to testify as to the whereabouts of this woman, who had been deemed a felon.

At the time, few feminists seemed to understand what was going on. Those I specifically asked to help (two feminist lawyers, a feminist therapist, and a movement leader) refused to get involved. Only a private criminal attorney and the left-wing Center for Constitutional Rights understood what going up against state power meant. One of the criminal attorneys, Margaret "Margy" Ratner, was in charge of the grand jury project at the Center.

I vowed never to talk about the women I'd helped. But I could face jail time for my refusal. This frightened me. I feared that feminists would not understand that my silence was political resistance. This frightened me even more.

Six months later, only days before I was supposed to testify, the FBI told me that they had captured Maria. I was advised to have nothing to do with her. She was sentenced to two years for trying to save her daughters from court-enabled incest. I immediately wrote to her in prison. She apologized for having gotten me into trouble. I told her: "You have nothing to apologize for. You've given me an opportunity to follow in Susan B. Anthony's footsteps."

When Maria finally got out of jail, she spent some time with me. She planned to open a shelter for other battered mothers facing similar circumstances. She was drinking too much and suffered from illnesses related to stress and her jail stay. Her dream of a shelter never came to pass.

Years later, Maria called me to ask for help on behalf of her younger daughter, who still lived with the father who was molesting her and jeering at Maria's efforts to save the girl. Sadly I had to tell her that I could not take on the FBI again and that she'd have to find another way.

Maria's husband had swatted away her pro bono lawyer, the best lawyer in her godforsaken rural town, because *his* best childhood friend owned the town. Literally. His friend's family employed most of the local citizenry and controlled or influenced the police force and the judiciary. The judge discounted the most horrifying forensic evidence that supported Maria's agonized allegations.

Maria has since died. I have her handwritten memoir. One day I may publish it.

I've interviewed many American mothers like Maria and reviewed their court documents. This phenomenon has gotten far worse in the twenty-first century.

Because my ex-husband had no interest in custody, I was spared having to flee with my son and never faced a life on the run and the possibility of incarceration. My problems were different, and they were hardly unique. All single mothers who also have high-powered careers or callings, and who are without the support of extended family, face the same thing.

First, my son's father refused to take him for more than a few hours at a time or for longer than an overnight. I had no respite, no break.

Second, he refused to pay a penny toward our son's clothes, toys, books, lessons, babysitters, vacations, or, after fifth grade, for private-school tuition.

I never asked for that penny until I became ill, couldn't work, and was in danger of losing our home.

The other side of the great American custody battle is the great non-payment of child support battle. I'm talking about the 1980s and 1990s (not that much different than the 1880s or 1890s), when divorced, widowed, and single mothers were on their own economically. Courts were reluctant to force fathers to pay anything, or more than a minimal amount, at best, equivalent to welfare. Those fathers who did pay child support often stopped within a year or two. In any event, most fathers didn't earn enough to support two families, and they tended to remarry and have more children.

Yes, there are exceptions. Some fathers have been unjustly ordered to pay excessive amounts of child support, but far more often mothers have been forced to depend upon their own, lesser earnings or upon the arrival of a new partner who is both able and willing to share economic and childcare responsibilities.

This injustice will not let go of me. It was not enough that I'd researched, written, and published a book on the subject; I'd also taken to the airwaves from coast to coast to discuss the scandal of women losing custody battles unjustly. The television programs were a joy to do, and as often as I could I brought some custody-battle mothers along with me.

Once, on AM San Francisco, one of the other interviewees was a judge who removed custody from a "good enough" mother because he disagreed with her politics. He was shocked that I was familiar with the details of the case.

On March 1, 1986, CUNY's John Jay College in Manhattan was the site of our Speak-Out on Women and Custody of Children. Five hundred women attended. Mothers flew in from all over the country; some were facing prison, some had just been released from prison. A handful were still living underground. I was sure that the FBI was watching us.

The mothers were magnificent. Their stories of horrendous injustice were poignant, compelling, heroic, devastating.

I will never forget the sari-draped woman from South Africa, now a longtime American citizen and an accomplished professional, who described how her husband had joined a cult and steered her son, her only child, into it, and how the court system had approved this removal of a son from a stable, competent mother. Nor will I forget the testimony of highly traditional stay-at-home mothers who lost custody to abusive and largely absent fathers who earned more money than they did; of loving lesbian mothers who lost custody because of their sexual orientation; of racially marginalized women who lost custody to brutal men who happened to be white. Never will I forget the heart-wrenching testimonies of mothers whose ex-husbands were granted joint or sole custody and who promptly kidnapped their children, whom the mothers never saw again; the story of a mother who tried to rescue her son from a pedophile father but was not believed by the courts. That mother now had limited supervised visitation, and the father had sole custody.

My feminist allies, most of whom were *not* mothers, had nevertheless come to speak. They understood that this matter was important to women. Ti-Grace Atkinson, Andrea Dworkin, and Kate Millett all spoke, as did the poet Toi Derricotte, who *was* a mother. The lawyer Nancy Polikoff and the psychologist Dr. Paula Caplan (*The Myth of Women's Masochism* and *Don't Blame Mother*), feminist mothers both, were wonderful.

Bella Abzug saw me in the bathroom and said: "I feel like crying. Their testimonies are so sad."

Outside, a noisy fathers' rights demonstration was taking place. They and their second-wife handmaidens were opposed to what we were saying. A shouting match broke out and there was almost a fistfight.

A columnist for the *New York Times* was told that she could not cover this event. She attended anyway and ended up writing two columns about it. We had enormous media coverage. It changed very little.

Sharon Murphy, a good mother who had flown to the speak-out, went directly to prison when she left the conference. According to Sharon, whom I've interviewed, her mother-in-law, the writer Maya Angelou, protected her own batterer-son, not her daughter-in-law and not her grandson. When Sharon could take no more abuse and fled the jurisdiction with *her* son (Maya's grandson), Maya paid to have Sharon hunted down, arrested, and imprisoned as a kidnapper.

Sharon tried to tell her story, but magazines rejected her articles. In 2013 she self-published an account of her ordeal, *Disappearing Act: A Mother's Journey to the Underground*.

Sharon tried hard to reconnect with her adult son. She was not successful.

Sharon's story was sadly typical and not unusual. I'd interviewed many mothers who ran, were caught, and paid a heavy price for trying to protect themselves or their children from serious abuse. Such mothers were both poor and rich; career women and high school dropouts; white Americans and Americans of African, Native, Hispanic, and Asian descent; and of all ethnicities and religions.

Their stories were heartbreaking and always slightly unbelievable, especially when they were true. With a few exceptions, none of these women started out crazy, and most did not alienate their children from their fathers. But by the time these women turned to me for help, many were traumatized, beaten down by all that had happened to them.

With the help of the best feminist publicist in town, Karin Lippert, who was my lecture agent at Doubleday before she became *Ms.* magazine's main publicist, we organized a congressional briefing on custody. Chuck Schumer and Barbara Boxer were on board, but they favored a gender-neutral presumption for custody. I feared that this could hurt traditional stay-at-home mothers. I preferred a presumption that custody should be awarded to the primary caretaker. Since we could not resolve this, we instead held a congressional press briefing in 1986. It was still an important moment in feminist history.

In the summer of 1986, I flew out to Watsonville, California, to meet with members of the sanctuary movement. This was a religious and political movement that sheltered Central American refugees in flight from civil war. I wanted to know whether the sanctuary movement would offer shelter to American mothers and children who were fleeing our own court system, who lived in hiding right here at home and needed shelter and new identities. The former nuns and priests and I talked and talked, but we resolved nothing.

With Paula Caplan's help, I traveled to Toronto for a speak-out on custody.

Some belligerent fathers' rights activists invaded the event. Two mothers who had planned to speak fled in tears because their husbands were in the crowd and were armed with tape recorders. Someone placed a dead animal outside the door of my hotel room.

A year or two later I was privileged to be part of a feminist legal team in Toronto that represented a battered mother who had kidnapped her children. She had fled across the border and opened a candle and Wicca shop in New England. Eventually one of the children revealed her whereabouts, and she was extradited to Canada. We faced a jury. After other experts soberly covered everything else, I argued something novel, namely, that a mother has a moral right—perhaps even a natural mandate—to protect her children from harm.

"Where can a mother who is being beaten and whose children are being beaten or sexually abused find asylum? Canadians gave asylum to Americans pacifists who didn't want to fight in the Vietnam War. What about mothers?"

The jury found her guilty, but the judge, a woman, imposed no sentence. We believed that our arguments had persuaded the judge, and we were overjoyed. On the courthouse steps, in full view, according to one of the lawyers, the woman's ex-husband threatened her again. We formed a protective circle around her—but soon enough she turned on us. She accused us of having betrayed her, having only taken her case for our own reasons—and she yelled and yelled.

These battles take a terrible toll on high-functioning, mentally healthy mothers. Toss in serious and prolonged domestic violence (which was the case here), a trial from hell, and an impoverished underground life, factor in someone who was traumatized in childhood, and you get a self-sabotaging human being. I have seen this happen again and again.

I was eager to get *Mothers on Trial* out in paperback. An obscure fathers' rights group threatened to sue my publisher, which then withdrew the book from auction for its paperback rights. Impatient and frustrated, I brought it to a small feminist press that immediately scooped it up. I was enormously relieved. However, within a month, before the small press had incurred any production costs, I got an offer from a large commercial house for much more money and the promise to print 100,000 copies of the book.

I *begged* my feminist daughters to let me go. I said I would return their advance—with interest—and I offered them *Women and Madness* in perpetuity. They refused. They said that they'd already told everyone they'd acquired me. In their hands, the paperback edition of *Mothers on Trial* did not reach its audience.

In my view my feminist daughters kept this book out of the hands of at least 100,000 mother-readers. It was my fault. I chose not to stand up to them.

When the small press finally let me go five years later, I found another publisher, but too much time had passed; I had moved on to other subjects and could no longer generate the same public attention or ignite a movement.

Mothers and their advocates, such as the psychologist Maureen "Mo" Hannah and the attorney Barry Goldstein, would, over time, create such a movement against every conceivable obstacle. I'm honored that they still consider my book their bible.

When I first wrote about how hard juggling childcare and my multiple careers was *for me*, I was attacked and shamed. One reviewer of my 1979 book, *With Child: A Diary of Motherhood*, wrote that I was too demanding in having expected that my mother would help out. Another reviewer wrote that she was surprised that even though I was a feminist, I still shared the same concerns that most (normal?) mothers do.

My mother knew I was drowning. I was working six jobs (full-time professor, full-time researcher and author, part-time traveling lecturer, therapist, consultant on court cases, and media interviewee). I had worked hard for the privilege of being able to do intellectual, activist, and world-changing work. I was the sole support of my household and was responsible for all child-related costs (including a babysitter-housekeeper who lived in five days a week). I also employed an assistant, without whom I never would have been able to do everything. I do not know how most single mothers with demanding careers manage. Even if you're a stay-at-home mother, I think the task of caring for children requires superhuman skills and strength.

As I struggled to spend time with my son, as I struggled to keep up with it all, my mother remained critical. She believed I should stop working and stay home, as she did, at least until my son was older. She wanted me to be more like her, to put family and children first, to not try to have it all, and if I insisted on trying to do so, she was not going to help. Moving in for the kill, she said: "If it's too hard for you, give him to me. I'll put him in a religious school and I'll manage him. I'm willing to take over if you're not up to the job."

Chilling words.

No, I wasn't going to part with my boy, but the truth was that even with hired help, the burden of being both a caregiver to my child and managing the people I hired to help me was crushing me.

In 1980 I purchased a heavily-mortgaged brownstone in Brooklyn. This was long before Brooklyn became trendy, and it cost me far less than it would have cost to buy a one bedroom co-op in Manhattan. I needed a studio apartment to offer a live-in babysitter-housekeeper and another studio apartment for a tenant to help offset the mortgage and taxes.

Looking back, I realize that I had followed Margaret Mead's advice. I also moved to Brooklyn so that I'd finally have a "room of my own" to write in instead of only a corner of the living room. I wanted to be nearby when my son needed me (or I needed him). I wrote on the ground floor, overlooking the garden. When I absolutely did not want to be disturbed, I hung a sign on the door: MOM OFF-DUTY.

My clever boy burst in anyway, saying, "Mom, you're not a taxi!" Sometimes I laughed and took him in my arms; other times, when I was in the midst of a particularly compelling sentence, I lost my train of thought, cursed my fate, and wondered why we had no high-quality, low-cost childcare in this great country of ours.

We still don't.

I had nights of agonizing loneliness. I took my son out to Seventh Avenue for dinner—pizza, pasta, or hamburgers—and prayed that someone interesting would stop by for a moment of adult conversation. That rarely happened.

My son's narrative of this time suggests that he had two mothers. Alas, he has one mother—myself, a divorced and single mother, whose husband took no further responsibility for his son. My first female partner did not choose to function as a co-mother once she no longer lived with us. My second female partner had absolutely nothing to do with my wonderful son until after he became a lawyer. Thus, he was alone with me from the time he was one-and-a-half years old until he was six. My first female partner really helped the full-time live-in housekeeper until he just turned thirteen, and then she walked out. They saw each other at Christmas. From then on, he had only me.

Until my mid-forties, I lived with men. Then, in the "middle of my life," finding myself in a "dark wood," as Dante once did, a forest crowded with unwilling and unworthy potential stepfathers, I consciously chose to live only with women. Perhaps, one day, I will write a book about sexuality and identity, eros and motherhood. This is not such a book.

Although custody was not my personal issue, it continued to draw my attention.

In 1987, I got involved in the high-profile Baby M case. To me it was primarily a custody battle. It took my work on embattled motherhood to another level.

Mary Beth Whitehead was a New Jersey mother and housewife who had signed a contract to be a surrogate mother for a married couple, Dr. William and Dr. Elizabeth Stern. Her family needed the money. In my view she may have wanted a third child even more than she wanted the money, but her husband had had a vasectomy, and Mary Beth was a practicing Catholic who did not want to commit adultery. Choosing to bear a child for someone else would also be seen as an act of heroic, sacrificial altruism. She used her own egg, underwent artificial insemination at the Noel Keane Infertility Clinic with sperm provided by the husband, was pregnant for nine months, and followed a carefully proscribed nutrition program during her pregnancy.

Mary Beth had been interviewed by a psychologist, who warned the clinic that she might have trouble turning over her baby. The Sterns were never shown this report.

According to Mary Beth's lawyer, Harold Cassidy, "the baby was born on March 27, 1986. When the baby was born the hospital personnel did not know there was a surrogacy contract. When the Sterns visited at the hospital, Mary Beth was tearful because she felt that she could not part with her baby girl. Mary Beth gave the baby to the Sterns on March 30, 1986, when the Sterns came to Mary Beth's house to pick her up. That day Mary Beth was grief-stricken, cried, could not eat and could not sleep. The next day, March 31, Mary Beth went to the Sterns' home, cried and told them of her deep suffering: the pain of separation was too great for her to bear. The Sterns agreed to let her take the baby back to Mary Beth's house, Stern explaining he feared she would otherwise commit suicide, such was her despair. The agreement was that Mary Beth would have the child for a week to make a better goodbye."

Under the adoption laws of New Jersey, Mary Beth was within her legal rights to change her mind. However, her decision led to a firestorm.

All during April of 1987, the Sterns and Mary Beth talked on the phone. Mary Beth said she could not surrender her child. Mary Beth continued to breastfeed her daughter. She refused to take the ten thousand dollars or to sign the adoption papers. By April 12, Mary Beth informed the Sterns that she could not surrender Sara to them. She had her baptized in the Catholic Church.

In the same interview, Cassidy said, "After a few weeks, the Sterns went into an in-camera meeting with a judge, without Mary Beth knowing about the hearing—no notice was given to her—and Judge Sorkow signed an order directing Mary Beth to turn the child over to Stern. The order had no provision for Mary Beth to visit the child."

On the evening of May 5, the Sterns, accompanied by the police, arrived at the Whitehead home with an order for "Melissa Elizabeth Stern" (the name the Sterns had picked for Bill's genetic child). The Whiteheads showed them the birth certificate, which identified Mary Beth's biological and her husband Rick's legal child as "Sara Elizabeth Whitehead." Then Mary Beth went into the bedroom and passed the baby out the window to Rick. When the police discovered that the baby was gone, they handcuffed Mary Beth and led her into the back seat of a squad car. The police, with no legal basis for arresting her, released her. Within twenty-four hours, Mary Beth and her family fled to Florida and took refuge with her parents.

During this time, the judge froze the Whiteheads' bank account; the bank was about to foreclose on their mortgage. Detectives hunted Mary Beth down. Baby M was weaned the day the police took her away. The judge would not allow Mary Beth to see her child for five and a half weeks, and thereafter she was allowed only supervised visitation twice a week for an hour, only in a public institution, and with an armed guard present. She was also forbidden to breastfeed her daughter.

I had to act.

After meeting with Mary Beth's pro bono lawyer, Harold Cassidy, and with Mary Beth's previous lawyer, Bob Arenstein, I began organizing demonstrations outside the Bergen County courthouse in Hackensack. Many feminists supported what I was doing, including Gena Corea (*The Mother Machine*), Andrea Dworkin, Barbara Seaman, and Dr. Michelle Harrison (*A Woman in Residence*).

Mary Beth cried when she saw that women—*feminists*—were supporting her at the trial.

At the second demonstration a woman I'd never met was suddenly at my side. She remembered seeing me standing beside an empty crib and making a speech; this poignant prop had been Michelle's idea.

The next day a check for $1,000 was hand-delivered to my home. The mystery woman was Merle Hoffman. She wanted to honor my "cutting-edge" activism. I had never, ever had another feminist fund my activism.

And this was how I met the feminist entrepreneur and visionary who would become one of my closest friends.

Merle's is a restless, searching intelligence; she reads widely and constantly, loves philosophy, history, art, theater, travel, horses, dinosaurs, interior decorating, and classical music, especially opera. We often go to the opera together. If our hair doesn't catch on fire, we don't stay; but when our hearts and minds are ablaze, we remain until the last of the ovations has died down and much of the audience has departed.

Merle founded the first legal abortion clinic in New York City; it is now the leading women's medical facility in the country, serving 45,000 patients a year. She also founded and funded the best feminist magazine of the late 1980s and the 1990s, *On the Issues*. I became editor at large.

Many feminists favored surrogacy as an option for infertile women and gay men. They also viewed adoption as both high-risk and fraught with interminable red tape. They or someone close to them may have endured years of painful fertility treatments that failed or years of anguish waiting for an adoption to come through. Single people who wanted to become parents and gay couples, male and female, were not seen as worthy candidates for adoption. Many undertook a desperate search for some way, any way, to parent a child.

That was why many feminists remained silent about Mary Beth's plight—until headlines quoted psychologists and psychiatrists who had insisted in court that Mary Beth was an "unfit mother" who suffered from a "narcissistic personality disorder" and played patty-cake incorrectly. These were outrageous accusations that many mothers feared could be leveled against them, too.

This was the opening I needed.

Together with media-savvy feminists, I helped write a statement— "By These Standards We Are All Unfit Mothers"—that 135 prominent feminists signed. The *New York Times* wrote about it, and it was discussed in *People* magazine. The signatories included Margaret Atwood, Nora Ephron, and Meryl Streep.

This letter cheered me enormously because I knew that many feminists supported surrogacy for another reason too: They believed that women own their bodies and therefore have the right to an abortion, the right to sell sex, the right to rent out their wombs, and the right to sell the fruit of their womb's labor.

Betty Friedan told me that she was "up in arms, outraged" by what the media and the courts were doing to Mary Beth. Betty sent me a telegram addressed to Mary Beth. It read: "Your courage to fight is amazing and admirable. Keep up the fight for all of us." Betty kept repeating: "Where are the feminists? Where are the feminists?"

When the Pope came out against surrogacy, one feminist accused me of "being in bed with his Holiness."

"That's an interesting image," I said.

On March 31, 1987, Judge Sorkow severed Mary Beth's parental rights and conducted an impromptu adoption proceeding. Eighty members of the media from all over the world were there. Every television show wanted to talk to Mary Beth or her lawyer, and sometimes me. She appealed the case to the New Jersey Supreme Court.

According to Cassidy, "On February 3, 1988, after the N.J. Supreme Court granted us direct review, bypassing the Appellate Division, after all extended briefing and oral argument, the Supreme Court reversed Sorkow, declared the contract unenforceable, vacated the order of termination of Mary Beth's rights, stripped Betsy of her legal status as mother, reinstated Mary Beth as legal mother, placed primary custody in Bill Stern and remanded the case for a hearing to fix visitation for Mary Beth. Mary Beth was never paid any money and never requested such payment.

Sorkow ordered the Sterns to pay the agreed upon contract price into court. The Sterns made the payment and the court held the funds for Mary Beth, but she repeatedly refused to accept the payment."

Mary Beth's parental rights to her infant daughter were restored. Betsy Stern's adoption of the girl was revoked. The Sterns retained custody—but Mary Beth was entitled to visitation, and she would not be *legally* redacted from her daughter's life. All three adults were ordered into counseling.

For me this case raised the following questions:

Do low-income and less educated mothers have a right to their biological children, or, by definition, are wealthier, higher-income, better-educated mothers always better parents and therefore entitled to the children of the poor?

Is a mere donation of sperm equivalent to nine months of pregnancy (with all its attendant risks) and the labor of childbirth?

Are all contracts enforceable—even, say, one in which a person agrees to become a slave or to sell one's only remaining kidney?

How do surrogacy arrangements psychologically affect birth mothers *and* the children who are targeted for adoption before they've even been conceived?

As I'd noted in previous works, I believed in adoption. I also saw it as a high-risk proposition for everyone. More important, I viewed the choice of surrogacy over adoption as complicated, and sometimes, even as racism in action. Abused and discarded children of African descent were remaindered in group homes. Social workers made it difficult for Caucasian parents to adopt them. Early childhood abuse, fetal alcohol syndrome, being born addicted to heroin or with AIDS: adoptions of children with issues like these are primarily the province of saints.

Wealthy Hollywood celebrities were able to adopt children from Africa: Angelina Jolie, Madonna, and Sandra Bullock all did so. This takes money. Thus, the red tape involved in adoption, the sound of one's biological clock ticking, the increase in infertility for both men and women, discrimination against adoption by single parents or gay parents, especially of modest means—all make surrogacy an understandable and tempting option. I'd heard of *private* surrogacy arrangements without a middle man, arrangements in which no money changed hands. I knew several stories with happy outcomes which involved gay male sperm and grateful lesbian mothers, and a grandmother who bore a fertilized embryo for her womb-less daughter. I also knew stories that are private but had ended tragically, in hotly contested battles for custody, visitation, and for real or imaginary sums of promised money.

Still, much of what I feared would happen in terms of a *commercial* surrogacy industry has come to pass. Beginning in the late twentieth century, commercial surrogacy gained an enormous following among Hollywood actors, infertile women, gay male couples, and both single straight and gay men and women. Much of this business had been outsourced to India, Thailand, and Mexico; these breeders were sometimes prostituted women in brothels or impoverished women who bore babies for primarily Caucasian or Asian customers. Increasingly these women were not always genetically related to the infants they were bearing. This was deliberate: using the egg of a different woman was regarded as diminishing the gestational mother's claim to the infant if she changed her mind.

The media rarely cover failed surrogacy arrangements. In some cases, birth mothers have died or nearly died of complications during pregnancy. Sometimes such birth mothers incurred major medical debt for long-term illnesses for which the sperm donor or contracting couple were not responsible. Also, when some sperm donors and adoptive mothers-to-be learned that their surrogate was carrying a less-than-perfect baby or multiple babies, and if the birth mother refused to have an abortion or a so-called reduction in the number of embryos, the hapless surrogate faced sole responsibility for child care and earning a living.

Harold Cassidy still represents birth mothers all over the country who signed surrogacy contracts. He and I remain in touch to this day.

Another late-1980s custody case stands out in my mind—that of Dr. Elizabeth Morgan. I think she had good reason to believe that her daughter, Hilary, was being sexually abused by her father during visitation. Hilary's therapist at a distinguished Washington, D.C.–area institute confirmed to me that this was true but said that the institute did not allow her to get involved in any court case.

Elizabeth's father had been a CIA operative. He and his wife managed to get their granddaughter out of the country and to New Zealand, a country that had not signed a reciprocity agreement with the United States. Elizabeth would not reveal Hilary's whereabouts to Superior Court Judge Herbert Dixon, Jr., so he jailed her for contempt. She remained there for more than *two years*. Perhaps Dixon wanted to make Elizabeth an example of what can happen to a mother who dares to defy the law, even to save her own child.

I organized petitions and demonstrations on Elizabeth's behalf outside the U.S. Department of Justice. National NOW was quite helpful to me in this matter.

Hilary's father consistently denied any wrongdoing, and no court ever found that he had sexually abused his daughter. However, a Virginia judge did prevent him from seeing Hilary's half-sister, Heather, from a previous marriage; Heather's mother had also accused him of sexually molesting their daughter. Dixon refused to consider this as relevant to the Morgan case.

Unlike Mary Beth Whitehead, Elizabeth Morgan, a plastic surgeon, was an insider in terms of class and education. But as a woman, she was still an outsider. Would a *male* physician be allowed to sit in jail so long without some old-boys' network springing into action? Elizabeth was freed only after Congress approved a special bill and President George H. W. Bush signed it into law in 1989. It states that in the future no judge can imprison a resident of Washington, D.C., for more than twelve months without a trial by jury for specific stated crimes. The case of Minnesota's heroic Holly Collins also haunts me. Holly was seriously battered by her husband, whom she (and her now-grown daughter) claimed also physically and psychologically abused them all. Eventually, in 1994, Holly, an American citizen, fled, and in 1996 she obtained asylum in Holland under the European Treaty on Human Rights.

Holly had a suitcase filled with legal documentation—and she had my book. The Dutch authorities determined that both she and the children had been injured and remained at risk. In 2011, Garland Waller directed a powerful and disturbing documentary about Holly's case called *No Way Out But One*.

I've spent hours talking to Holly and to her daughter Jennifer, who works with other children who live underground. I have absolutely no doubt that Holly is telling the truth. She is now back in the United States. While her story is unique (in that she gained political asylum abroad as a battered *American* mother), in general, it embodies the plight of many other battered American mothers whose batterers have challenged them for custody of their children.

By the turn of the twenty-first century, I understood that mothers engaged in custody battles had it harder, not easier, than their predecessors. My updated 2011 edition of *Mothers on Trial* has eight new chapters. The mothers still write to me. I wish I could do more. I've learned my limitations even as I've learned the power of writing the books I have.

Although I had been interviewing birth mothers for the Baby M case, I could scarcely imagine the horror that one such mother, Michele Launders, must have felt. Michele was Lisa Steinberg's birth mother, and she had just learned that Joel Steinberg, the lawyer who had promised to have Lisa adopted by a good, middle-class, two-parent family, had not done so, nor had he arranged for a legal adoption.

In November 1987, Joel killed five-year-old Lisa, the child he had also been physically and sexually abusing. After beating her with a hammer, he stormed out of the apartment he shared with his partner, Hedda Nussbaum. Hedda did not call 911 for many hours. The hospital confirmed that Lisa was dead; at Joel's apartment, the police found another child, a boy, chained up and covered in his own feces. Cocaine was everywhere.

For twelve years, Joel had battered and terrorized Hedda, a book editor who had turned to drugs. Her face was smashed in and looked lopsided, like a boxer who had lost all her fights—and like a boozer, too. I found it painful to look at her. Granted immunity, Hedda testified against Steinberg.

The question remained: How could any woman allow a helpless child to be tortured and then murdered?

Many feminists felt that Hedda should have protected her two young children and rescued them from that hellhole. Both Susan Brownmiller and Judge Harold J. Rothwax viewed Hedda as an accomplice.

However, some feminists viewed Hedda as a traumatized victim—morally culpable, yes; criminally liable, maybe not.

I understood both points of view. This was an important feminist controversy. Are women responsible for what we do (or for what we fail to do) if we too are victims? Or do women have agency, a moral choice, even if we ourselves are being held captive?

As previously mentioned, in 1987, I had become editor-at-large for *On the Issues* magazine (*OTI*). In my view, *OTI* was the most wide-ranging, iconoclastic, and culturally sophisticated feminist magazine of its time. Merle Hoffman always wrote bold editorials on both predictable subjects—abortion clinics under siege, sexual harassment by American politicians—and unexpected ones—Queen Elizabeth I, a trip to Khomeini's Iran. Merle also chose the most creative covers.

I wrote some of my best pieces for *OTI*: about women in prison and on death row; in psychiatric asylums and in courtrooms both here and in Europe; in war zones such as Bosnia, North Africa, South

America, and Mississippi. In *OTI*, I published my first piece about our legendary feminist religious struggle in Jerusalem, where we were known as Women of the Wall (now Original Women of the Wall). I also wrote about opera and reviewed films and books.

I had been aware that John Stoltenberg (the author of *Refusing to Be a Man*) supported Andrea Dworkin economically and that they lived frugally, and I persuaded Merle to hire him as her managing editor. He seemed agreeable and had the skills for the position. I had no idea how arrogant and domineering John was—he was quite the bully.

And then something rather shocking happened. A group of young gay feminist men, all of whom said they'd been seduced and abandoned by John, found each other and wrote a group letter about his abuse of power. They sent it to antipornography activists, including me. They accused John of mesmerizing them with his preening proximity to Andrea, swearing each to secrecy about their sexual relationship, and then cutting each one loose.

John had committed no crime in the eyes of the law, yet he had abused his power. This was disappointing in someone who held himself out as a model of the new feminist man and as the feminist gay man.

But this was not half as disappointing as what Andrea did. She wrote to everyone who had received this letter to defend John with all the power of her mighty pen.

From that moment on, whenever Andrea and I made a date to meet, John always accompanied her. Andrea and I talked while John watched. On the surface it was always sociable, but it felt creepy. When I finally said that I'd like to have coffee with Andrea alone, she wrote a long letter hotly defending John and the importance of their relationship.

At this point I allowed myself to understand that something was very wrong with Andrea and with her primary relationship. I was too heartsick to mention this at first, but when I did, other people who cared deeply about Andrea agreed that she had apparently found another kind of dangerous relationship from which she absolutely would not be parted.

A small band of Andrea's friends, including our city's major mavens on domestic violence, finally met and agreed that Andrea was the kind of woman we could not rescue, that she would never, ever leave John. So there we were, the alleged liberators of womankind, and there was This. Sick. Thing.

As an author, I'm lucky. *Women and Madness* has never been out of print. One fine day an editor rang my doorbell. His name was John Radziewicz. He uttered the most sublime words: "We publish Virginia Woolf and T.S. Eliot, and we want to publish you."

"Come in, dearest of men."

And so I moved to a new publisher, Harcourt Brace.

In 1989, I appeared on *Geraldo* to talk about my revised and updated edition of *Women and Madness*. When I arrived, I was shocked to find that Kate Millett was part of a group of female former mental patients who had agreed to appear on camera. Each one, including Kate, insisted that she had never been mentally ill and that the psychiatric establishment had brutalized her. This may have been true. However, Kate went a step further and insisted that her family had "turned her in" because of her "radical feminist politics."

This was a lie, part of whatever mental illness Kate suffered from. Perhaps all the women gathered with Kate in the TV studio that day were also mentally ill and also in shamed and defiant denial about it; perhaps all were stigmatized and mistreated. Both things are often true.

I walked a fine line here. I sympathized with those who had been mistreated, but the other mental health expert on camera, an elegant, high-heeled, European-born woman psychologist, scornfully mocked these former mental patients for denying the truth and tried to persuade them that they needed help. Afterward, she assumed that she and I would go out for a drink. Instead, I joined Kate and her little band of woebegone deniers. I thought it was the more honorable thing to do.

15 I Travel the Wide World, Pray at the Western Wall, and Come to the Aid of Lesbian-Feminists Under Siege in Mississippi

Despite Oslo and its aftermath, I remained among the most privileged of feminists. For nearly half a century, I had been continuously published and interviewed by the media on every continent, my work had been translated into many languages, and I was asked to speak at conferences from coast to coast in North America as well as abroad.

Over the years, I've been beamed into Iran, Kashmir, Kurdistan, Saudi Arabia, and many other far-flung places. My work has been reviewed in, and translated into, many European languages, including Portuguese, Polish, Korean, Hebrew, Japanese, and Chinese. And I have been interviewed on every blessed continent. I also used to travel widely, funded by foreign publishers and governments. This meant that I got to meet the most fabulous feminists around the world, women who were eager, even desperate, to discuss feminism with an American counterpart.

England

I first visited England in 1961, on my way to Kabul. How I rushed to the British Museum to see the Elgin Marbles and then to Russell Square, where some members of the Bloomsbury Group (including Virginia Woolf and Vita Sackville-West) once lived. I stayed at a bed-

and-breakfast, and because I was so young, I found the greasy British breakfasts charming, not alarming.

In 1969, when I visited England again, I once more visited the British Museum, and I spent hours writing in my diary at outdoor cafes, looking up every so often just in time to see an oversize black London taxicab or red double-decker bus rumble by.

On my next visit, I spent some time in a thatched-roof cottage in Oxford and stayed in London with the late, great Polish-British documentary filmmaker Mira Hamermesh, who directed *Maids and Madams*, about black maids and their white employers in South Africa; *Caste of Birth*, about the untouchables in India; and *Loving the Dead*, about Poland's longing for its murdered Jews. She lived in St. John's Wood, and we spent hours walking and talking on Hampstead Heath. In 2004, Mira also published a Holocaust survivor memoir, *The River of Angry Dogs*.

In the late 1980s, my feminist publisher, Virago, brought me to London to participate in a public debate about surrogacy and to publicize its edition of my book *Sacred Bond: The Legacy of Baby M*. This was a different England for me. I signed books, gave interviews, visited bookstores, and sparred with some ferocious surrogacy advocates. I also met many honorable British feminists who were more invested in global issues of racism and colonialism than in issues involving violence against women.

The last time I was in London was in 2016, to attend a friend's birthday gala. She treated her guests to a suite at the Dorchester (!) and to sublime performances of Shakespeare's *The Tempest* at the Globe and *As You Like It*, and to Bellini's opera *Norma*. We took high tea almost daily at the Dorchester. Most luxury hotels and homes in all the upscale neighborhoods are now owned by Gulf state Arabs; I was assured that the major London shops would have had to shut down long ago were it not for Gulf Arabs' summer shopping sprees.

During that same trip, I met Dr. Paula Boddington, the Oxford-based philosopher. She wanted to tell me about the work she was doing for the victims in Bradford, Rotherham, Leeds, and Oxford who had been courted, gang-raped, beaten, and held hostage by gangs of South Asian men, mainly from Pakistan, who had been openly preying upon the youngest and most vulnerable infidel (non-Muslim) as well as upon Muslim girls in their own communities—girls aged nine to fourteen from impoverished and broken families, many of them living in state-run group homes. While pimps and sex trafficking are global phenomena, most sex traffickers usually do not seduce, kidnap, and trap girls or boys in their own neighborhoods and lock them into brothels near their own homes. What had been going on in the UK was rather different.

The men (and their younger male allies) plied neighborhood children with attention, took them on "dates," gave them small gifts, and made outlandish promises. As soon as the children ran away from their group or individual homes, the men gang-raped, beat, and isolated the girls and got them addicted to drugs. Then the men forced the girls to have sex with paying johns. Thousands of British children have been trafficked within the British Isles. Until recently, social workers, teachers, and law enforcement officials turned a blind eye to this crime, to avoid being charged with Islamophobia and causing community unrest.

Paula told me one hair-raising story after another: "When a child victim is actually strong enough to bring legal charges and has at least one family member who will support her, the pimps' extended family harasses the girl and attacks her home. It gets so bad that the police have to install panic rooms and alarm systems or guard the home. Then, when they go to court, swarms of pimps' relatives throw rocks, make threats, glare, and terrify the girls before they take the stand."

This too is now Shakespeare's "sceptered isle."

France

I visited Paris for the first time in 1961, on my way to Kabul. I literally raced to the Louvre for the day and then to Les Deux Magots, the coffeehouse where existentialists once took their arguments and their caffeine. I spent hours at the book stalls on the Left Bank and walked along the Seine.

I sat at a cafe on the Avenue des Champs-Elysées (named after the pagan Elysian Fields) and watched the people go by. I visited the Sorbonne, where I hoped to study the history of ideas. Before my husband and I left for Munich, we attended a show where the women danced and sang like Radio City Music Hall Rockettes, only they were bare-breasted. This left me slightly ill and slightly excited.

I was such an American in Paris.

In 1982, French feminists tried to explain their issues to me, but as hard as I tried, as much as I love the French language, I could not understand them. Postmodernism—the seductive and poisonous influence of Lacan, Foucault, Derrida, Irigary, and Cixous—has rendered French feminist writing practically incomprehensible to me. Soon the plague infected American postcolonial and postmodern feminist writings as well. Nevertheless, I enjoyed sitting at a cafe in the south of France and listening to French feminists speak. Our conference took place in Apt, in the castle once owned by the Marquis de Sade—that well-known sexual libertine, pornographer, and philosopher, who sexually tortured the most vulnerable women.

Israel

I visited Israel for the first time at the end of 1972, a few months after *Women and Madness* came out. This was not a feminist trip; it was a flight from sudden fame and a long-overdue search for roots.

Israeli *Jewish* feminists specialized in criticizing their own government—well, they did live in the only democracy in the region—and also helped rescue potential Arab honor-killing victims. An Arab peace activist confided in me: "I have a great secret." I thought she was going to tell me that she was gay. But no. "I have a boyfriend," she said, "but no one can know or I'm dead."

I returned in 1975, under the aegis of Writers and Artists for Peace in the Middle East. I brought journalists, including the feminist Ellen Willis and the socialist Jack Newfield, on their first trip to Israel, so that they might form their own impressions of the country.

I also lectured at the American embassy and drew a large crowd of Israeli women eager to hear me preach the feminist word. In Haifa, I stood with the American-born left-winger Marcia Freedman, who in 1974 had been elected to the Knesset (the Israeli parliament). We chose a site for what would become a shelter for the victims of domestic and sexual violence. It serves Jews, Christians, Druse, and Muslims, just as Israeli hospitals do. In 1983, the Haifa Feminist Center would arise nearby. I took Andrea Dworkin there to lecture with me.

The Original Women of the Wall (WOW and OWOW)

In 1988, I went to Jerusalem to attend the First International Jewish Feminist Conference on the Empowerment of Women, which was coordinated by the American Jewish Congress (AJC) and the Israel Women's Network. Letty Cottin Pogrebin and Lilly Rivlin, my Passover seder sisters, worked hard on this conference. At our first meeting as a conference, Bella Abzug ordered us to turn out the next morning to demonstrate against the Orthodox rabbinate and the State of Israel on the issue of who is a Jew. I stood up and asked in what way this issue was a *feminist* one and suggested that we should achieve an understanding of the issue more democratically before allowing ourselves to be led like sheep to the Headline.

"You!" she bellowed. "Sit down!"

But we also smiled at each other. Letty and socialist-feminist organizer Heather Booth were there to function as Bella's wing women.

Suddenly, unexpectedly, I heard that Orthodox Jewish women were meeting to plan a women's prayer service at the Western Wall

(Kotel). The room was packed, the mood both electrified and somber. Once it became clear that the AJC had already sent out a press release about this, I persuaded everyone to agree that we would not talk to the media but would say only "We have come to pray."

What we were about to do was analogous to nuns officiating at Mass at an all-female service in the Vatican.

A small group of us tightly guarded the writer Francine Klagsbrun, who had been chosen to carry the Torah. When we reached the Kotel, the women swiftly donned their prayer shawls (angels' wings, capes of sheltering glory) and prim head scarves or exotic skullcaps—and we became Jews. We stood before the wall under the morning sky and began the Thursday morning service.

Without knowing it, this is what I had longed for all through my Orthodox childhood in Borough Park, Brooklyn. This was a *tikkun*, a redemptive repair for my not being allowed to become a bat mitzvah (Orthodox), and for relegating me to lesser (intellectual) life in terms of Torah study. This moment was a dream come true—one I never knew I'd been harboring all those years. I stood there in a reverie.

"Would you do us the honor of uncovering the Torah for us?" Rivka Haut, an Orthodox feminist activist from Brooklyn whom I did not then know, asked me. It was a transformative honor. It wedded me fatefully, faithfully, to this legendary struggle. Years later I asked her, "Why me?" Her answer: "You had such an otherworldly expression on your face as you were praying."

We had stepped onto holy ground, experienced a moment in time in which we constituted a sacred congregation. We had glimpsed what might be possible if women dared to claim their religious inheritance without patriarchal approval or support.

Many hours later, I said to Rivka, "We've just crossed a psychological sound barrier. This is a major event in history."

She said simply, "Do you really think so?"

Oh, I did. I still do.

Many people, including secular feminists, underestimate or even despise the psychological importance of organized religion and of religious symbols. As a liberation psychologist, I'd been writing about female role models and about God's female face since the early 1970s. So long as we continue to psychologically envision God as a tall white man with a long white beard, the goals of gender equality can never be realized *psychologically*. Thus I believed that our religious struggle might have a profound psychological impact on the self-esteem of all women. I had theorized about this for years. Putting this theory into action in a Jewish setting had eluded me until now. And what a setting it was.

This struggle made international headlines and seized the imagination of Jews and feminists around the world.

After we left, Israeli women wanted to pray just as we had. They encountered terrifying violence. After about five months of being tear-gassed, cursed, and insulted, as well as dodging heavy chairs being thrown at them, both the Israeli women and those of us in the diaspora jointly sued the State of Israel and the rabbinate for our legal and religious rights.

That was how I accidentally became a leader in a landmark struggle for Jewish women's religious rights in Israel. We were known as Women of the Wall (and now as Original Women of the Wall). With Rivka Haut, whose idea it was, I co-edited a book about this struggle in 2002: *Women of the Wall: Claiming Sacred Ground at Judaism's Holy Site.*

What began as a grassroots struggle has now gone on for thirty years. We have won our legal rights in the Israeli Supreme Court and the Jerusalem District Court, but enforcing them remains an issue. By now, not surprisingly, inevitably, the group has also split in two. I will not burden you with the details. Suffice it to say that it was a miracle that we remained as one for nearly a quarter century.

I must provide the reader with a necessary and often missing perspective. If religious Muslim women in the Middle East had done what we had done, they probably would have been beheaded in the town square or stoned to death. At the very least, they would have been placed under permanent house arrest and not allowed to associate with each other for a very long time.

This happens even in the West. When the journalist Asra Nomani attempted to make her mosque in Morgantown, West Virginia, more woman-friendly, her good-faith efforts resulted in her having to leave the mosque her own father had founded. When the Turkish-German lesbian imam Seyran Ateş opened the first-ever gay- and woman-friendly mosque in Berlin, she received death threats and had to have round-the-clock police protection.

Italy

I first visited Italy in 1969 and stayed in a journalist's apartment near the Piazza Navona, in Rome. My traveling companion and I had the apartment to ourselves. I had the same breakfast at the same nearby cafe every day: a cheese sandwich wrapped in wax paper and a few cups of strong espresso. Whenever I was in Rome, I visited the building in which I'd first stayed, just to make sure it was still standing.

It always was.

I traveled to Capri, where I had many adventures and misadventures. Over the years, I visited Florence, Pisa, Sicily, and Milan, but I stayed in Venice and Assisi for weeks at a time. Once, a heat wave drove me out of Venice and I landed the last available hotel room on Lake Maggiore, a sublimely beautiful region near Switzerland.

My visits to Rome, Venice, and Assisi were always feminist- and publishing-related sojourns. My Italian publisher Einaudi put me up at the Hotel d'Inghilterra in Rome, near the fabled Cafe Greco, where Stendhal, Byron, and Keats once met for coffee. It was a madhouse, mobbed by tourists. Einaudi had published two of my books; Mondadori had published one.

The feminist writer Dacia Maraini (she's a novelist, playwright, and poet) wanted to interview me for *La Stampa*. Dacia was the daughter of a princess, had been married to the writer Alberto Moravia, and founded a theater company with him and the filmmaker Pier Paolo Pasolini. She also knew Maria Callas. That did it for me; I was all hers. We met for lunch a bit out of the city and lingered for a long time in the heat of the Roman afternoon. At some point I believe we were half asleep, but we still kept talking. She found me sultry (or so she wrote). I would have followed her home if only I'd had the time.

The Sicilian feminists who had driven up to meet me could not speak a word of English. My Italian was limited to opera arias. I called my friend Paolo Milano, the literary and drama critic of *L'Espresso*, and drafted him to translate. He was no feminist, so I especially appreciated (and secretly enjoyed) his having to translate my most radical feminist ideas to them and theirs back to me.

In 2009, I returned to Rome for the G8 International Conference on Violence Against Women, an initiative of the Italian presidency. Our host was the flame-haired Fiamma Nirenstein, a journalist and politician.

I stayed at the Boscolo Exedra, a luxurious hotel located on the Piazza della Repubblica, near the Baths of Diocletian and opposite Rutelli's Fountain of the Naiads. I sat in the rooftop dining room and, one by one, the Muslim women participants gravitated to my table. I was a Muslim feminist chick magnet of some kind. Women from Turkey, Yemen, Iraq, Saudi Arabia, Iran—even Afghanistan—joined me.

I sang the Afghan women an Afghan song, and they swooned in surprised delight. They had arrived a few minutes before the conference officially began and had to leave the second it officially ended. They were not allowed to linger in the Eternal City even for an hour.

I, however, did linger. I had lunch at an exquisite terraced restaurant called Ciampini. It was midafternoon, the pace was unhurried, and

Susan, my traveling companion, and I were the only diners. Ciampini had a garden, an indoor fountain filled with turtles, old-fashioned gaslights, table linen, and extraordinary views: we could see St. Peter's in the distance. This moment of paradise was blessedly quiet. No music, no cell phones, no loud or raucous conversations. Three waiters in green jackets spoke softly and served us as if we were royalty.

Sitting there was like being in Rome fifty or a hundred years ago. It was like a dream. Or a beloved movie with Joan Plowright or Maggie Smith.

It was a bit like reliving every expatriate's love affair with nineteenth- and early twentieth-century Italy. And so I became a character in a Merchant Ivory film, or in a novel by Henry James or maybe a novella by Thomas Mann, and I did not see why I should ever leave.

Arrivederci, Roma.

Austria

In Saltzburg, feminist psychiatrists from all over Austria and Germany carefully wrote down what I said. The Germans wanted me to tell them how to diagnose patients in feminist terms. I said that diagnosing is less important than understanding and helping and told them: "In America, the *Diagnostic and Statistical Manual* is mainly of use in terms of insurance reimbursement. Diagnosing a woman usually does more harm than good. She believes that something is very wrong with her forever after, and the diagnosis may be used against her in divorce, custody, and employment matters."

They wrote this down too.

After my lecture, I went out for the evening with some of the German women, who got drunk and poured their hearts out about their mothers' rapes by Russian soldiers during World War II. Sobbing bitterly, one woman said: "No one cares about us. Germany started the war, so we deserve whatever happens to us. The world has sympathy for only the Jews."

I remained quiet out of respect for her genuine suffering, but the Jews had been on my mind for a while. I had visited the fire-bombed synagogues in Paris and in Vienna and sadly noted how police officers had to protect Jewish houses of worship in those cities as well as in Rome. I still did not yet understand how deeply rooted Jew hatred is on European soil.

In Vienna, I spent time with the Christian and very Austrian president of the Freud Museum and his wife, an Egyptian-born Jew. The museum is located where Freud's office and home had once been. They allowed me to linger alone in the waiting and consulting rooms, and I heard an earful from Herr Freud himself about *his* sorrows!

The museum officials wanted me to organize a conference about Freud and women, and I quickly agreed to do so. I was thrilled that such a distinguished forum had been offered to me and that our feminist perspectives were being invited in. Many feminists had criticized Freud and psychoanalysis, while others stood on Freud's shoulders and carried his work further. I would have loved to have convened such a conference. Only a major car accident the following month made this laudable goal impossible at that time.

Japan

Kiyomi Kawano translated *Women and Madness* into Japanese. She also founded the first feminist therapy clinic in Tokyo and invited me to speak there. I arrived after about fourteen hours in the air, dazed and sleepless. Nevertheless, a delegation met me at the airport and whisked me off to dinner at Tokyo's latest sensation—its first-ever Chinese restaurant. I tried not to nod off into my soup.

I did not expect so many coffee shops in Tokyo. I'd forgotten that foreign sailors had introduced them and that the Japanese, so fond of tea, also drink coffee from Africa, the Middle East, and South America. As I walked around the city, I saw the occasional man in full Japanese formal dress, a gray kimono. I visited the timeless mist-shrouded countryside dotted with Buddhist temples.

While I was in Tokyo, feminists held their first antipornography conference. I joined them to pay my respects. They asked me to say a few words. I suggested that all seven hundred of us consider going down to the red-light district and hang out there. Some women tittered behind their hands; only a few were willing to go with me.

I ended up going there with only one Japanese woman. It was tawdry, pathetic, and heartbreaking because the photos advertising the prostitutes were billboard photos of children. Nearby I saw pornographic comic books for sale. The scenes depicted were sadistic, and some also involved children.

After my lecture, there was a party. Somehow the Japanese feminists knew that it was my birthday. They surprised me with twenty bouquets of moist, wondrous flowers and a flamenco guitarist. One woman explained: "In case you're homesick, we saw how close Spain is on the map to New York, and we wanted to cheer you up with familiar music."

They were well meaning, but certainly geographically challenged.

Sweden

Impressively tall Swedish feminists in Umea, in Lapland, proudly showed me a museum exhibit of a small black bark canoe, which indigenous Sami ancestors had once used for travel and fishing. They had prepared a moose stew. My hosts lit candles in the auditoriums in Stockholm, Uppsala, and Umea before I spoke at the universities. What a lovely pagan custom.

I was in Stockholm to participate in a government-sponsored conference, and this was where I met the most arrogant feminist philosopher on Earth: France's Luce Irigaray (*Speculum of the Other Woman*, *This Sex Which Is Not One*).

Twenty-six feminist academics from ten European countries had gathered; I was one of three American women. For the opening night's panel, four of us had two hours to present and lead a discussion.

Luce handed a closely typed paper to an interpreter. Although a translation of her paper into English had already been distributed and read by all of us, Luce spent *one hour* of the two-hour panel reading her paper in French and having it translated into English aloud. She refused to stop, then abruptly ended by saying that, had she known the conference would not be in French, she would not have come.

Rebecca Emerson Dobash (*Women, Violence, and Social Change*) briefly discussed her research on violence against women. Luce interrupted.

"But you can't believe that the state actually exists," Luce declared. "The state is only an idea. You must respond to this point."

And Rebecca did: "Anyone who thinks the police officer coming to arrest you is only an idea is living in a fantasy of her own."

When I tried to introduce myself, Luce interrupted me: "My group in Paris decided that, with the publication of *About Men*, Phyllis Chesler was no longer a feminist."

We were out of time, and all of us were dispirited.

The women there exacted a rare revenge: No one talked to Luce for the rest of the three-day conference. I doubt she even noticed, but I pitied her and asked her to take a walk with me. She was stiff, even awkward, and seemed to exist in her own world. We talked about the weather (it was gray and blustery), the food (passable), and the scenery (Scandinavian). We did not mention what had happened on the opening night or her being shunned by the other conference participants. I think she was actually happy with this outcome because each time she dined alone at a table, one of the handsome Swedish male government officials quickly joined her. I thought I saw her flirting a wee bit.

In 1990, Merle Hoffman gave me a fiftieth birthday party. I opted to have it at Kate Millett's loft on the Bowery as a symbol of our intellectual, radical, and lesbian roots.

About sixty feminist leaders were there, including Sidney Abbott, Dolores Alexander (founder of the New York City chapter of NOW and co-owner of the feminist restaurant Mother Courage), Dr. Pauline Bart (*Stopping Rape: Successful Survivor Strategies*), Z Budapest (the founder of feminist Wicca in America), Charlotte Bunch (the founding director of the Center for Women's Global Leadership at Rutgers), Roxanna Carrillo (a longtime staff member at the UN Development Fund for Women), the musician Joan Casamo, the philosopher Linda Clarke, the poet Toi Derricotte (*Natural Birth*, *The Empress of the Death House*), Andrea Dworkin, Brenda Feigen, Dr. Lilia Melani, Dr. Eleanor Pam (a CUNY administrator and now president of Veteran Feminists of America), Gloria Steinem, and many more.

Merle captured their faces and words on a video. Z flew in from California; I had never seen Andrea Dworkin smile so much; and a photo shows me kissing the artist Buffie Johnson full on the lips.

Feminists from opposite sides of every contested issue attended this wonderful party. Merle distributed surprise T-shirts emblazoned with FEMINIST GOVERNMENT IN EXILE and illustrated with the figure of an Amazon on horseback.

In 1991, I was between books and at something of a loose end. I'm rarely between books—I always know what I'll be writing next, even before I finish my current book.

Merle said: "You ought to write about this Florida serial killer case. It has all the ingredients of a great book: madness, murder, and the media."

She was right—and I found a publisher almost immediately—but first I organized a dream team of experts to testify on behalf of the so-called first female serial killer, Aileen "Lee" Carol Wuornos. I wanted to expand the battered-woman syndrome to include prostituted women, the unlucky scapegoats for violent and murderous men. Reading about serial killers—who have tortured and murdered so many prostituted women—may be the darkest reading I've ever done. That, and reading about prostitution.

I persuaded the left-wing lawyer Len Weinglass to take on Wuornos's defense as a political case. He required a modest sum for expenses. I was about to start raising this money when I became ill.

No one came forward to take my place. The public defender, Trish Jenkins, was used to handling male serial killers and rapists, not prostituted women who kill in self-defense or who suddenly snap and kill their john. Wuornos may be guilty, but in my opinion she did not get a fair trial. (The first jury saw her confess on video to the murders of all the men she was accused of killing.) The refusal to call any of what Wuornos referred to as my "testifying" witnesses became one of the grounds for the appeal to the Florida Supreme Court, which failed.

I spoke with Lee Wuornos by telephone and we wrote to each other. She wanted me to help her write her story, which I agreed to do—only she believed that I could sell the same story again and again, just as she sold her body. She was a capitalist; I was an abolitionist. When I visited her on death row, prison officials put us in a small room. I could have slammed the door shut behind me, but I left it open a crack. I was not sure who I might encounter.

The 1980s and 1990s were the plague years. First AIDS, then Lyme disease and chronic fatigue immune dysfunction syndrome (CFIDS, also known as myalgic encephalomyelitis)—another kind of immune disease, one characterized by profound fatigue and many other symptoms.

At first, I was too tired to walk from one campus building to another. Soon I couldn't walk to the corner store. Then I was unable to get off the couch. Was I dying? What would happen to my son?

I had a flu that wouldn't quit. My throat was burning, my glands were swollen, my stomach was permanently upset. I always had a fever—either a low-grade one or a killer night fever with extreme chills. I was disoriented, sometimes nauseated, and gripped by headaches. I had severe joint pain, unbearable muscle aches and weakness (I kept dropping things), heightened sensitivity to light and sound, and a serious sleep disorder. I began suffering from allergies for the first time and from repeated infections in my teeth and gums. My fatigue was overwhelming.

These physical symptoms were not as traumatic as the cognitive and neurological deficits I was also experiencing. I would forget what I was about to say. I confused left and right. I could not read more than a few pages a day. Such cognitive deficits would frighten anyone; they *terrified* me. I was used to reading the equivalent of a book a day, writing twenty to forty pages daily of manuscript and correspondence, and having at least one, often two, working meetings, in addition to lecturing.

But I was far too sick to look after myself.

I was in danger of losing my home unless I came up with money for the mortgage, so I sold my archives prematurely to a university for a proverbial song. I lived in pain for seven years, but with the help of both experimental and traditional medication, acupuncture, high-end dentistry, and luck, I survived and prevailed. Most sufferers aren't so lucky. Many never leave their beds or homes again.

A friend, the brain scientist and psychologist Naomi Weisstein, also had CFIDS. She became sicker and sicker and never left her bed. Some CFIDS victims die, others commit suicide. Insurance companies claimed this wasn't a real illness. Back then, even the best doctors agreed.

And so, without realizing it, I became a person with disabilities.

I learned some valuable lessons: Most people aren't compassionate toward the chronically disabled, and this illness was neither brief nor dramatic. Friends and colleagues did not understand the severity of my illness; few visited more than once. My friend Merle was an outstanding exception, as were Rivka Haut, Judy Kuppersmith, and Judy O'Neil.

Insurance companies fight you when you're at your weakest in order to deny you the benefits to which you're entitled. The frequent, entirely needless medical exams they require (*their* physicians always deem you healthy and a malingerer) are an ordeal calculated to either drive you away or kill you.

Being an uncoupled, chronically ill woman without close supportive family is dangerous. We usually just slip off the edge of the Earth. If you are not living with an adult partner, you'll have no one to help manage the crisis. At moments like this, women lose custody of their children—and their homes, jobs, and life savings, as well as their lifelines back to their former lives.

But I was also the luckiest woman in the world. My son's father did not want custody. I owned my own home. I had private disability insurance—although I had to fight hard to obtain at least two years' worth of coverage. I had an employer who was legally required to pay me (at least partially) while I was out sick and was obliged to take me back when I became healthy. Treating me compassionately or respectfully wasn't part of my employer's contractual obligation.

In the depths of this illness, I published a review of the pioneering book *Trauma and Recovery* by the distinguished feminist psychiatrist Dr. Judy Lewis Herman. As the title reveals, Herman addresses a full range of responses to trauma—responses that have been diagnosed as "crazy," and she documents what is required for healing and recovery, and redefines "recovery." Essential to healing is a feminist mental health professional who bears moral witness to the details of trauma. My review, published in the *New York Times Book Review*, made all the difference. Sales soared, foreign translations appeared, and Judy was asked to lecture around the world. And millions of women would be helped.

Just as Adrienne Rich had felt obliged to review *Women and Madness*, so I felt obliged to pay it forward.

Although I was sick and still symptomatic, after four or five years, I began to have some good days.

Brenda and Wanda Henson ran a 120-acre feminist educational retreat in Ovett, Mississippi. In the mid-1990s, when they put out a call for solidarity over a Memorial Day weekend, I decided to rise to the occasion. I refused to let illness stand in my way. If I could get there, I was going to be there. But I dared not travel alone; my domestic partner, Susan, and my friend Merle accompanied me. The Hensons' version of feminism was one of service. They were not "do me" feminists. They did not lead with their sexual identities and did not demand any sympathy based on their victimhood. They were not about themselves—they were about serving others, being true to their principles. Thus they set up food banks and clothes closets, counseled battered women and incest and rape victims. They were antiracists, maintained strong ties with the local African American community, and conducted Passover seders as a statement against anti-Semitism or Jew hatred.

The Hensons bought land in Ovett, a small town with sixteen churches. They had been persistently harassed: A dead female puppy wearing two sanitary napkins and shot through the stomach was draped across their mailbox; they received a stream of threatening phone calls, letters, and bomb threats; their American and rainbow flags were torn down; intruders kept appearing on their property. The house of a local lesbian supporter mysteriously burned down.

The Hensons were under the most profound and deadly siege, and the international media had been covering their situation intensely.

Volunteers drove us to the camp on back roads in pitch darkness. Our headlights were the only lights for miles around. Here we were, three unarmed city girls with overactive imaginations, driving a long distance in the dark without guns or walkie-talkies, trying not to be scared. I actually clutched copies of Sojourner Truth's 1851 speech "Ain't I a Woman" and Mattie Griffith's *Autobiography of a Female Slave*. I drew on their strength, given their far more endangered lives. I half expected the state police or the Klan to suddenly stop our car, but no one did, and we proceeded on to Camp Sister Spirit. I wrote: "Camp Sister Spirit is like Woodstock, Lesbian Nation, and the Michigan Woman's Music Festival all rolled into one. Really, it's like nothing else. It's as if Diana Rivers's tale about a tribe of psychic-military lesbian feminist warriors (*Daughters of the Great Star*) has come to life."

Diana herself was there, and she had built a little goddess shrine. I was pleased to meet her.

The Hensons were disappointed that only thirty women had come. I told them that I had waited twenty-seven years to see American feminists gathered together—not on television panels or at conferences and parties but on woman-owned land, taking a stand for what they believe in, risking violence and even death. I thought it was a pretty good showing.

A few years later, the Hensons stayed with me when they came to New York for the Gay Pride Parade. They hoped to raise some money by holding aloft Camp Sister Spirit banners. Many gay men gave them a high five and a ten- or twenty-dollar bill—no questions asked. Many lesbians interrogated them about why they *had* to be in Mississippi. Wearily, the Hensons tried to explain: "We're *from* Mississippi, it's our state, we're southerners; we don't want to be exiled from our roots."

Only a few lesbians gave them money.

Camp Sister Spirit is no more—but it represented a glorious moment in American feminist and lesbian history. Its disappearance remains a permanent indictment of sexism and homophobia in the American South.

In 1998, when I returned to teaching, I developed pneumonia for the first time in my life. The antibiotics made me feel better. My doctor tested me again for Lyme disease, and this time I tested positive. Apparently I'd been suffering from both (untreated) Lyme disease and CFIDS. My immune system had been fatefully weakened.

My second semester back, I developed bronchial pneumonia—I was dealing with sick building syndrome. (In the early 1990s, CUNY Staten Island took over the old and dreadful Willowbrook State School compound.) I begged my university to move me to any other location in any one of the five boroughs. They refused. I dared not subject my immune system to whatever it was that was making me and several other professors sick. I had no strength to contemplate a lawsuit. So I retired early with a tiny pension.

Once I've pioneered an area or cofounded an organization, I tend to move on, allowing others to take over. I never lingered at either the Association for Women in Psychology or the National Women's Health Network.

After about seventeen or eighteen years, I also retired from one of the first, and perhaps the most famous, of the feminist Passover seders, the one that has been written about, filmed, and memorialized so many times.

Remember E. M. Broner—the author of *Her Mothers* and *A Weave of Women*? When Esther (E.M.) returned from Haifa, she began to court me; there's no other word for what she did. E.M. moaned with delight at my every thought; she gravely, reverently, read my work, called me daily, made me feel superspecial.

E.M. wanted me to join her in leading a feminist Passover seder. You may recall from chapter 9 that we held the first feminist seder in my home and that E.M. and I led it together. I had invited the *Ms.* editor Letty Cottin Pogrebin, the filmmaker Lily Rivlin, and the artists Bea Kreloff and Edith Isaac-Rose. We became the core members. Over the years, a series of well-known guests—Gloria Steinem, Bella Abzug, Grace Paley—occasionally joined us. The Canadian journalist Michele Landsberg, who was married to Canada's then ambassador to the UN (and was assiduously courted by E.M.), returned again and again.

I introduced E.M. to everyone I knew. That was what she was after, but why would I withhold such introductions from someone who was so warm to me? To her everlasting credit, E.M. supported me in Oslo against my rapist and against Robin, who collaborated with him, and she did so for years afterward. She was brave on my behalf and on behalf of the truth. I was grateful to her for this and therefore put up with many things that made me increasingly uncomfortable.

The Jewish holiday of Passover teaches us that freedom is a miracle but, with God's help, this miracle takes place no matter what one's earthly historical circumstances might be. Whether a Jew has survived the ancient destruction of Jerusalem or a European or Arab pogrom, is imprisoned in an Iranian or Iraqi jail or a Nazi concentration camp, she is still commanded to celebrate her freedom from slavery.

I once participated in a Passover seder in Bedford Hills, a women's prison. It was an amazing, perhaps awesome, experience. Women behind bars were celebrating their freedom. Freedom from what and for what? A few high-profile political prisoners were present, as were former drug addicts, petty thieves, and prostituted women. Many said that they had never felt safe before; now, in prison, no father, no husband, no pimp could batter them.

Is a story this monumental, a message this universal, meant for Jews of one gender only? Isn't freedom a Jewish religious value meant for all people, all faiths? Can only religiously learned Jewish men officiate at a seder—or can any Jew, male or female, learned or not, also do so? Isn't Passover *the* holiday of women and slaves and therefore an opportunity to wrest our freedom away from patriarchal Judaism?

If you study Torah, even a little bit, you develop a perspective about a human being's rather humble place in the universe. For example, the prophet Moses, God's greatest intimate, our teacher and liberator, is never mentioned in the Haggadah, the text that is a guide to the seder. (There are complex historical and theological reasons why Moses is not mentioned.) Most feminist seders elevate the prophet Miriam, the sister of Moses. It is understandable but childlike, this hunger to see our own gendered human image writ large. I once had this hunger, and I fully satisfied it. In the beginning, after so many centuries of God the father, feminist women hungered for God the mother.

We introduced ourselves by our first names and by our mothers' first names. "I am Phyllis, daughter of Lillian." "I am Letty, daughter of Ceil." Thus the earliest women's seders were created in our own image. They were meant to be a World of Our Mothers. We were a band of (motherless) sisters in search of our female ancestors. We created a ritual of verbal matrilineage, and introducing ourselves this way was—and remains—psychologically empowering.

Once we were as silent as slaves at our family seders (or *Sedarim*); now we were as free as Jews at our own feminist seder. This was no small achievement.

We devised a parallel universe—one filled with only mothers and daughters. At the time, what we did was take the first steps out of Egypt, but they were not the steps that would ultimately bring us to the Promised Land. Comforting as it was, to continue taking only our first step, year after year, was not enough for me.

Rivlin and I conjured up the rituals for each seder. We found creative ways to bind the women together and to elevate all of us. One year, my first female domestic partner, Pat, stitched together a large diaphanous lavender sash that literally bound us physically; I called this the sacred *schmatta*. E.M. and Rivlin took it with them when they participated in an international and interfaith peace conference in Israel. The seder sisters wanted to use it every year. Finally, I suggested tossing it into the fire, telling them, "This has become a form of idol worship."

"No, not the sacred schmatta!" Letty cried. She rescued it and vowed to keep it—and keep it she does. It was a poignant moment.

E.M. worked on the themes—which she always wanted to change. Eventually the plagues God visited upon the Egyptians had nothing to do with God, Egypt, Moses, or even Miriam but with American racism, sexism, military spending, the Republican Party, and the destruction of Earth. Letty, Bea, and Edith made decisions about food and assigned different dishes to designated guests.

We invited Jewish and Christian feminists, white feminists, and feminists of color—usually well-situated academics, prominent authors, playwrights, physicians, artists, museum curators, literary and theatrical agents, television personalities, and celebrities—most of whom were non- or antireligious in orientation.

Our guests brought cameras and snapped away. Few knew the difference between a politically correct feminist event, group psychotherapy, a Jewish ritual, and career-driven performance art.

Letty and E.M. lovingly published articles, Rivlin directed a wonderful film (*Miriam's Daughters Now*). Mea culpa: I too spoke to reporters about the sedarim.

For me, something was rather confusing about E.M.'s dressing up in partly Jewish and partly pagan religious garments and presenting herself as a rabbinical or spiritual figure—mainly in order to conduct a secular feminist political event. In my opinion, we were not exactly transforming a patriarchal ritual. We were creating a minor cult of our own celebrity. All my life I had wanted a beloved community, and now I wanted one even more for my son's sake, even a facsimile of one, at least once a year—but, maddeningly, the core seder members refused to include sons, only daughters.

Each year E.M. and Letty brought their daughters, and each year I came alone. I was finally allowed to bring my son—but only once. To her everlasting credit, Rivlin opened her film *Miriam's Daughters Now* with me talking about the importance of including boys.

In hindsight, I blame myself for expecting this core group of five, three of whom had first become mothers many years earlier, to make room for me and a young child.

I now also realize that when I had initially joined forces with E.M., I was a primarily secular being; in time I became a more religiously knowledgeable person.

As the years went by, I began to demand that we invite fewer people, fewer celebrities; that we invite sons, husbands, and male friends; and that we stop focusing so much on ourselves and how important we were. As a seder host, I increasingly came to believe that we all had an obligation to be minimally learned in Judaism. But I stayed on. I dared not disconnect. These women represented *the* Jewish feminist world, at least in New York City. If I left, I feared I would have nowhere else to go.

I wanted to belong *somewhere*. Writers lead isolated lives, and I had known these women for a long time.

A year had passed since we first prayed at the Kotel. Letty arranged for Nadine Brozan of the *New York Times* and a photographer to cover our seder. E.M. was pushing for us to "act out" the fight for the wall as if it were a psychodrama. She envisioned positioning a line of women to represent the wall—and positioning an equal and opposite line of women to overpower it.

I strongly opposed this, saying, "This is not a home movie or a game. This is a serious theological struggle. You can't simply appropriate it as a prop, a gimmick, for use in our seder."

I prevailed. E.M. was grim, her jaw set, her eyes thunderously dark. The air became thick between us.

Why couldn't I simply go with the flow, allow E.M. to keep luring would-be agents and publishers, Letty to publicize, Rivlin to film—everyone to keep inviting accomplished people to join us? Why did I have to let my hunger for real, not ersatz, community and my evolving Torah knowledge stand in the way of my following the herd? Why couldn't I just look the other way, compromise, for the sake of cherished, flawed others?

Because that is not who I am. And because I was now working

with religiously knowledgeable women—I was one of the named plaintiffs in a historic lawsuit which began in 1989 on behalf of Jewish women's right to pray at the Western Wall. I had something to protect, something to which I had obligated myself.

Letty is an extremely hardworking, productive, and well-connected woman. I have always admired her ambition, persistence, and indefatigable energy.

However, I felt that Letty had been nervous about me ever since the post-Oslo tribunal that I convened in Gloria's apartment.

In the seventeenth year of our seder, I convinced everyone to hold it only for ourselves. No media, no paparazzi. The group agreed. However, E.M. had secretly written an entire book—*The Telling*—about this seder, and it was all about us. (Her portrait of me is loving, flattering, only slightly harsh.) The book had just been published, and Margo Adler of National Public Radio wanted to tape the next seder live at Letty's home.

At the last minute, E.M. called to say that if I don't change my mind and allow Margo to tape it (everyone else had agreed to this; I was the last one she was calling, she said), I'd be personally responsible for destroying her career. I took a deep breath and said: "You've nothing to worry about. My ritual for us this year will consist of my not coming to worship the golden calf."

And so I left our feminist seder.

Our murmuring queen never spoke to me again. Eventually, at Rivlin's insistence, we all agreed to sit down to work things out—all except E.M., who flatly refused to do so.

I once loved E.M., but I lost her to her unbridled ambition and Hollywood-style social climbing. I once loved E.M., but she was a dramatic fabulist and it mattered little to her if she got the details wrong. What mattered to her was her own incantatory prose, her dreams of grandeur.

Once, a lifetime ago, we were all laughing girls together, radiant with hope. I loved us all, I miss us still. One can forever miss Paradise before the Fall; one can also mourn one's exile from simpler times and from illusion itself.

16 The End of an Era and Saying Goodbye to Sister Soldiers, Brave and True, Near and Dear

After 9/11, I felt as if the Afghanistan I'd fled so long ago had followed me right into the future and into the West. That distant, dangerous country began to dominate American headlines. Muslim women started wearing burqas (head, face, and body coverings) and niqab (face masks) on the streets of New York City.

As global violence against women gained horrendous momentum, many Western feminists became increasingly afraid to criticize that violence lest they be condemned as colonialists and racists. This fear often trumped their concern for women's human rights globally.

This was not the universalist feminism I helped pioneer. We favored multicultural *diversity*; we were not multicultural relativists. We called out misogyny when we saw it and didn't exempt a rapist, a wife beater, or a pedophile because he was poor (his victims were also poor) or a man of color (his victims were often also people of color). We had little sympathy for a perpetrator because he had suffered an abused childhood (so had his victims).

Fighting for abortion and gay marriage rights in America is a legitimate undertaking, but so is standing with Muslim, ex-Muslim, Hindu, and Sikh dissidents, gays, and members of religiously persecuted minorities, all of whom are fighting for their lives.

World events have made feminist ideas far more important—yet, at the same time, Western feminism has lost some of its power. It's now a diversionary feminism that is also far more invested in blaming the West for the world's misery than in defending Western values, which have inspired countless liberation movements, including our own feminist revolution.

Celebrity endorsements or feminism or media-inspired Celebrity Moments, are not necessarily movements. If Helen Mirren, whom I love, wears a sparkly skirt in which the word "feminist" is embroidered again and again, I may like it, but I do not think it equivalent to the Emancipation Proclamation. The Balkanization of identity that passes for feminism in the twenty-first century saddens me. Such Balkanization makes it almost impossible to unite in coalition to fight for issues that may not personally affect all the protestors.

Many feminist academics and journalists now believe that speaking out against head scarves (hijab), face veils (niqab), the burqa, forced marriage, female genital mutilation, and polygamy is somehow racist. Postmodern ways of thinking have also led feminists to believe that confronting narratives on the academic page or signing petitions are as important and world shattering as rescuing living beings from captivity.

I did not foresee the extent to which feminists who, philosophically, are universalists would paradoxically become isolationists. Such timidity (presumably in the service of opposing racism) is perhaps the greatest failing of the feminist establishment.

I recant none of the visionary ideals of second wave feminism. Rather, as a feminist—not an antifeminist—I feel obliged to say that something has gone terribly wrong among our thinking classes. The multicultural canon has not led to independent, tolerant, diverse, or objective ways of thinking. On the contrary; it has led to conformity and totalitarian herd thinking.

Do I now regret founding women's studies?

No, I do not. Expanding the canon to include women of ideas, women's history, and radical and original feminist views was long overdue, as was the inclusion of works by and about people of color.

My generation's feminists forever empowered me. I'm in their debt. They share in my accomplishments.

That the "good-old bad-old times" didn't last, that illusions were shattered and people were betrayed is hardly unique. Perhaps, if the world keeps spinning on its axis, another great opening in history may come 'round, and if our best work is preserved, and preserved accurately, future generations may be able to stand on our shoulders.

May this memoir stand against the rank and swelling tide of revisionist feminist history.

By now, at least one hundred active pioneer feminists I knew or with whom I worked or whose work brightened my days have died—and with them, an entire universe is gone.

I'm here—but without so many I've cherished.

Most women cannot survive without their female friends; we tend to have a handful of best friends, not just one. I could not have stayed the warrior's course without such intimates.

Here are some of the souls with whom I served. We were soldiers, brave and true; we were friends, near and dear.

The Canadian-born **Dr. Ruby Rohrlich (1913–1999)** was an anthropologist and old enough to have been my mother. Ruby smiled whenever I entered the room, praised my work, and glistened when I praised *her* work. Thus, we loved each other.

Ruby wrote many articles and books, including *The Puerto Ricans: Culture, Change, and Language Deviance*; *Peaceable Primates and Gentle People*; *Women Cross-Culturally*; *Women in Search of Utopia*; and *Resisting the Holocaust*. Ruby penned one of the most eye-opening chapters for Vivian Gornick and B. K. Moran's excellent 1971 anthology, *Woman in Sexist Society*. She wrote about the variety of roles that women assume in non-Western cultures in both the premodern and the modern eras. While women were never quite equal to men, they nevertheless were often independent and self-reliant. However, once

European colonial powers took charge, they imposed a sharper sex-role stereotyping that often "adversely affected the role of women."

Ruby did not prove that women once ruled men in goddess-worshiping non-Western cultures—but that is what many feminists chose to believe.

When she died, Ruby was working on a biography of the Nobel laureate Rita Levi-Montalcini. I had so hoped Ruby would be able to complete it—and I wonder who has that manuscript now.

Ruby rarely spoke about her work as a propaganda analyst for the U.S. Office of War Information during World War II; eventually she directed the Office of Psychological Warfare, which was based in Casablanca.

Learning about Ruby's life taught me how privileged mine was. She was born before World War I to a traditional Jewish family in Montreal and could not go to college because she had to support her beloved but impoverished mother. And that is exactly what she did, just as my own mother did. After Ruby moved to New York City and got married, she was expected to stay home and take care of her two young sons. She did that, too—and therefore did not obtain her doctoral degree in anthropology until 1969, twenty-nine years after she had received her bachelor's degree.

Ruby faced discrimination in the university world as a woman, as an older woman, and as a Jew. Although she suffered, this never stopped her, and she always prevailed. Ruby knew the anthropologist Ruth Benedict, who had worked with Margaret Mead. Ruby had also worked with the anthropologist Eleanor "Happy" Leacock.

Ruby was a longtime member of a feminist poker game downtown. However, Ruby told me that everyone smoked—and refused to stop smoking, even when she revealed that she was suffering from emphysema and that smoke was dangerous for her. The refusal of her younger friends to refrain for her sake broke her heart and embittered her. She moved to a city where one of her sons lived. When she lived near Lincoln Center, Ruby had the most genial gatherings.

What makes me smile: Ruby was a short, round senior citizen, a woman about my mother's age. When I introduced them, Ruby told my mother: "I was married for years. Now I'm a lesbian and proud of it. What about you?"

For once my mother was silent—but I saw a smile in her eyes.

I also smile when I think of how much Ruby enjoyed the company of free women and how hospitable she was to us.

Andrea Dworkin (1946–2005) was a daring thinker and consummate intellectual. We always and only talked about ideas. This was how we played. She treated my young son as if he were an adult (Kate Millett did the same thing), and I found this rather touching—in its completely out-of-touch kind of way.

Andrea understood other people's suffering, but she was also in close touch with her own. She turned her pain into art and a struggle for justice. Such a life has a way of calling down the demons. Andrea's literary persona was that of an outlaw, but I knew her as someone who, like me, spent most of her waking hours thinking, reading, and writing—as well as plotting her own version of the French Revolution.

In 1991, I published a review of Andrea's novel *Mercy* in *On the Issues* magazine. Gravely, somberly, with enormous dignity, Andrea told me that she wished to be buried with this review. Here is part of what I wrote:

> *Andrea Dworkin is, without question, a great writer, a writer's writer: as "masterful" as Miller or Mailer; as passionate as Fanon; as gentle and as world-weary as Baldwin; as much a troubadour on the literary high road as Whitman or Ginsburg or Kerouac; raw and rough and cynical and fierce; pitiless as she challenges God on His lack of "mercy." Dworkin is bitter, shocking, like Baudelaire or Rimbaud, when they were new in*

the world; brave, heartbreakingly brave, like Leduc—except the
truth is, Dworkin really has no predecessor.
I only want to put her in her place, where she belongs.

Andrea, I hope you are now ensconced in that great library in Al-
exandria, checking out scrolls; I hope you're visiting Atlantis and
Eden or relaxing in whatever kind of heaven exists for agnostics, cyn-
ics, secularists, revolutionary feminists—and you.

May you finally rest (or play) in peace.

Beautiful, elfin **Buffie Johnson (1912–2006)** was an artist and an
author. She knew Gertrude Stein, Tennessee Williams, Gore Vidal,
Jane and Paul Bowles—and was one of the only women who was
counted among the abstract expressionist painters of the 1930s, 1940s,
and 1950s. Her work now hangs in museums everywhere.

One memory: Buffie serenely descending into a hot tub at Merle
Hoffman's country home, still wearing her pearls—our Lady of the
Hot Tub.

Another memory: We're out for dinner in SoHo and I use the
word *lesbian.*

"Oh, no, my dear," she whispers, horrified, "we do not say such
things out loud."

This was as close as I'll ever come to experiencing what life was
like for closeted bisexual bohemians, circa the late 1920s and 1930s.

In 1988, I gave Buffie a party for her book *Lady of the Beasts: Ancient Images of the Goddess and Her Sacred Animals.* She wore a black
hat with a veil (très couture) and was quite the coquette.

Buffie had husbands and a long line of male as well as female par-
amours. She retained her porcelain, fine-boned patrician beauty well
into her late eighties.

Perhaps my funniest Buffie anecdote is this: She flew out to California for an opening of her work. I called my friend Z Budapest and

asked her to take care of Buffie. Z sent her lover and right-hand woman to escort Buffie around. And then Z called me: "That crone is making a big play for my girlfriend! You sent me trouble."

"Oh, Z. She's just a big flirt, but she's also in her late eighties. How far can this go?"

Arlene Raven (1944–2006) was a cofounder of the feminist art movement. She also was a founder of the Women's Caucus for Art and a cofounder of the Woman's Building (an independent school for women in Los Angeles), the Lesbian Art Project, and both *Chrysalis* magazine and *Womanspace Journal*.

Arlene had worked in the civil rights movement and had been a member of Students for a Democratic Society—but her commitment to feminism became primary after she was kidnapped and brutally raped by two men. She writes: "I realized that as long as I had a pussy between my legs, that was the only requirement to be oppressed. I was just as vulnerable as anybody else and that fact was shocking to me."

This rape changed her life. It also enriched her work. Arlene published articles, monographs, catalogs, and books, including *Crossing Over: Feminism and the Art of Social Concern* and, with Cassandra Langer, *Feminist Art Criticism: An Anthology*. In 1985, Arlene also wrote the introduction to the catalog for an art exhibit about rape.

Arlene was always meeting with museum curators, covering art exhibits, visiting artists' studios. She was fiercely ambitious, hardworking, and a bit zany. She was Judy Chicago's greatest champion—but Arlene was also devoted to "new people, marginalized people, [those] who haven't had a voice yet. This is what I've chosen to do, as opposed to those who are more 'bankable.'"

Arlene and I spent time hanging out in Santa Monica near the cottage of filmmaker Donna Deitch (*Desert Hearts*), who had put me up for the night. Arlene and I talked hard-core feminist revolution—

as dreamers on roller skates and well-oiled bodybuilders kept drifting past.

Eventually Arlene moved in with the artist Nancy Grossman in New York City's Chinatown. They called their convertible Enna (I could never understand why) and took jaunts far and wide. Eventually they were evicted and moved to a building in Brooklyn, in Bedford-Stuyvesant, that they totally renovated. They lived there while the work was being done, and I always thought that Arlene's already weakened immune system could not withstand the poisons; she would die of cancer.

Both Arlene and I had suffered embattled relationships with supercritical mothers. We both had wrecked immune systems. Once or twice we spent the entire evening talking on the floor, too tired to get up. We both struggled economically but accepted this as the price of doing work we loved.

It was always thrilling to talk about art with Arlene. She was so imaginative and so knowledgeable that I felt privileged when she listened to my views.

We fantasized political museum-related actions: removing the sculpture of Perseus holding up Medusa's severed head at the top of the main staircase of the Metropolitan Museum; quietly hanging the name of Camille Claudel on every one of the sculptures by the great Rodin, the scoundrel who ruined and abandoned her and didn't rescue her after her family had her committed to an insane asylum for life. Claudel was a major sculptor in her own right and worked with Rodin.

Barbara Seaman (1935–2008) was the author of *The Doctors' Case Against the Pill* (1969), *Free and Female* (1972), and *Women and the Crisis in Sex Hormones* (1977).

Barbara and the Boston Women's Health Collective essentially founded the feminist health movement. Barbara lost her lucrative income as a magazine writer when the drug companies—whose ads fueled women's publications—insisted that she be blackballed. And so she was—but she saved the lives of millions of women.

Barbara cofounded the National Women's Health Network—and the network was really her baby. Under Cindy Pearson's leadership, it is still going strong. Barbara mentored newcomers and strategized and shaped the network's agenda. She was generous with her time and resources. She turned no one away and would find just the right physician for any woman who asked, no matter where she lived. Always, always, when she had to change literary agents, she would insist that I move with her. I did so only once, but it was a good fit until that agent died.

Barbara was as generous to stars as she was to woebegone waifs. With a few exceptions, she thought the best of everyone.

Barbara remained connected to me even though we probably disagreed on certain issues. I write *probably* because we were careful not to discuss these subjects. When ideological or political splits of one kind or another swirled around us, we held each other close. I have no doubt that she took some heat on my account, but she never mentioned it if she did.

Barbara was a lady. She wore dresses and low-heeled shoes and perhaps a string of pearls. I suspect that she probably once wore hats and gloves. But she was one of us, perhaps a more gracious rebel than most.

Barbara never complained about her personal woes. She shared some heartbreaking secrets with me—but never belabored the point. She told only a few of us that she was dying of lung cancer and did so only toward the end. Although she was dying, she came to my son's wedding. I have her happy, smiling face in a photo that I'll forever treasure.

———

Jill Johnston (1929–2010) wrote many articles and a host of books: *Lesbian Nation: The Feminist Solution, Gullible's Travels, Mother Bound.*

We knew each other before she became famous for her girl-on-girl kiss at Town Hall in Manhattan in 1971—a great piece of performance art, if you ask me—and an action that horrified both Norman Mailer and most of the assembled feminists.

Of course, I was there—we all were—to see Germaine Greer (*The Female Eunuch*), Jacqueline Ceballos (then president of the New York City chapter of the National Organization for Women); Diana Trilling, the distinguished literary critic; and Johnston, the irrepressible lesbian journalist, take down the ever-pugnacious and attention-hungry Mailer (*The Naked and the Dead*), who had been spoiling for a fight with feminists.

Mailer had written an antifeminist screed, "The Prisoner of Sex," for *Harper's Magazine*, in which he had been grossly unfair to Kate Millett. Germaine had a feather boa and flirted outrageously with him that night. Billed as a debate on the issues, it was, in turn, serious, ridiculous, upsetting, and funny. The women were in favor of women's liberation. Mailer was just in favor of women, so long as they knew their place.

Jill was a bohemian, a butch girl, an artiste, a gadfly, an outcast, a word dancer. Her long public kiss at Town Hall was her out-of-the-box response to an otherwise serious evening. Jill did that a lot—tried to steal the show, mess things up.

Jill kept asking me why I thought she *had* to come out as a lesbian in her 1971 *Village Voice* column under the famous headline "Lois Lane Is a Lesbian." I had no answer for her.

I saw her through a long list of lady loves until she found Jane O'Wyatt and then Ingrid Nyeboe, both of whom grounded her most nobly. Jill loved being legitimately married; she and Ingrid tied the knot in Denmark, where gay marriage was legal. At the time, I thought that marriage had laid the ladies low—but because Jill was so obsessed with being legal (her parents had never married, and she never knew her father), I understood that she was driven by psychological as well as practical motives.

Of course, we had our differences—many differences—but to her credit, our credit, we continued to wrestle with them. The subject of anti-Semitism was a live wire for us. However, Jill and I fought to remain connected to each other no matter what.

One time, in the early 1980s, we saw *Gone With the Wind* at a movie theater out in the country. We mourned the death of poor Gerald O'Hara, the loss of Tara, the doomed Melanie and Ashley, Bonnie Blue, and Scarlett, too. It was like an opera, really. We were two opera queens who happened to be female.

Jill reminds us of our youth, both aesthetically and politically; she is gone now and so is our youth—it is gone, gone with the wind.

She was an original. We will not see her like again.

I cannot believe she is dead—although it's been years now—or that she—that changeling child, that Huck Finn, that quintessential Peter Pan—actually managed to turn eighty-one years old.

Judy O'Neil (1940–2011) could always be counted upon to attend the meeting, sign the petition, balance the checkbook, join the march, staff the coffeehouse. She always had a day job as a computer scientist—but her evenings, weekends, holidays—her very soul—belonged to the movement. This is what I said, in part, at her memorial service:

> *Darling Judy: Oh, how I wish you were still here with us, not only as a cherished friend but as living proof that our generation of feminists were also noble, self-sacrificing, generous, and humble. You, and a precious number of other "unknown" feminists, sustained our movement; your dedication literally built our "Shining City on a Hill," our feminist Camelot.*

You came to serve, not to be glorified. Feminism was not a career move for you, nor was it a hobby. It was your spirit made flesh, your calling.

You were very generous to me, and when I became deathly ill, you did not disconnect. On the contrary. You drew closer.

Recently, at your request, just before your brain surgery, we went to see a children's movie, "because," you said, "they always have happy endings." We saw Chronicles of Narnia: The Voyage of the Dawn Treader. *Being together was like being with family.*

Please put in a good word for me on the Other Side. And enjoy the flight—like the angel that you now are and have always been.

Words now fail me. This loss is too keen, it cuts too deep. **Rivka Haut (1943–2014)** was a woman with whom I talked at least once, often twice, a day for nearly a quarter of a century. We also studied Torah together at least once, often twice, a week. Rivka was someone I never expected to meet—much less befriend—in my lifetime.

I had fled my Orthodox Jewish childhood in Borough Park, but the rise in anti-Semitism on the Left in the early 1970s reconnected me to my Jewish roots, as did my desire to reclaim a patriarchal religion for women. I became involved in re-creating Jewish rituals and life-cycle events in feminist terms.

This was a time when Christian, Jewish, and Buddhist women were claiming spiritual autonomy and authority. Some nuns left the Catholic Church; some women became ordained as rabbis, pastors, and monks. Pagan Wicca was recast in feminist-friendly terms. (Muslim women were not yet on the move.) I did not meet any religiously learned Jewish women who were both Orthodox *and* feminist.

And then I met Rivka.

With whom else could I be such close friends?

God Herself had introduced us. We met over an open Torah in the women's section at the Western Wall (the Kotel) on December 1, 1988.

Rivka had a degree in English from Brooklyn College. She also received a master's degree in Talmud from the Jewish Theological Seminary. She was a *modern* Orthodox woman, someone who was expected to obtain a higher education. Otherwise, Rivka led a traditional life.

She chose a great Talmudic scholar as her husband (he was also a lawyer), married young, and had two daughters. Rivka never worked for a living. She studied Torah and Talmud every single day of her life. Perhaps she embodied the kind of daughter my mother might have wanted me to be.

Although Rivka remained rooted within the Orthodox tradition, she still did radical things. She pioneered prayer groups for women, which, at the time, most Orthodox rabbis vehemently opposed—so much so that one of her daughters nearly lost her future husband because his father feared that Rivka's radicalism might ruin his son's life and those of his future grandchildren.

Rivka also taught Talmud to women in her home every Sabbath afternoon. And she pioneered the cause of *agunot*, Orthodox Jewish women who were chained or anchored to dead marriages because their husbands refused to grant them a religious divorce. Orthodox rabbis betrayed these women by not granting them religious divorces unless they handed over their babies and all their money—and maybe not even then. A chained woman could never date, remarry, or have other children.

Rivka considered these women martyrs to the faith because they refused to leave Orthodox Judaism even though their rabbis continued to condemn them to lonely, outcast lives. She would take calls from agunot both day and night. I once saw Rivka interrupt a lecture she was giving to take just such a call. She studied the religious laws on divorce, compiled dossiers on particular religious courts, counseled and accompanied woman after woman to these courts, and even organized street demonstrations outside the homes of recalcitrant husbands and at rabbinical conferences.

I know, because I sometimes accompanied her. The unleashed ferocity of religious women in pursuit of justice made many firebrand secular feminists look somewhat tame in comparison.

After we first prayed at the Kotel, on the plane home Rivka turned and asked me whether I thought our prayer service would be remembered, did I think it was important. I told her that we had broken a psychological sound barrier and that I'd help her in any way I could. Then I paused and said, "But what I want is to study Torah with you."

And that is what we did for the next twenty-four years. When we studied Torah and eventually wrote *devrai* Torah (Bible interpretations), we were in heaven on Earth. This kind of companionship is intimate and irreplaceable.

My darling Rivka turned this wild rebel child into a more refined rebel. At first Rivka was afraid of me. Was I a goddess worshipper? A heretic? Would I bring shame to our struggle? Was I a loose woman? Did I gossip?

Sternly she asked me: "With whom do you live?"

"I live with a woman."

She paused but only for a mere heartbeat, and then she ruled: "That's not against *Halacha*" (Jewish religious law).

Rivka taught me that women could lead significant and fulfilled lives within religious communities and without paid careers; that feminism has a sacred as well as a secular voice; that not all wisdom is secular; that some people, like her, who are fortified by religion, are able and willing to take on evil.

For me, this was eye-opening. It rocked my former, primarily secular worldview. The study of Torah drew me close to the most extraordinary intellectual and religious legacy—and it was mine if I wished to claim it.

"But Rivka," I would often say, "it's too late, I should have started when I was three years old. I lack the skills." And she'd say: "Let's just continue. We're doing very well."

Rivka, who was a wife, mother, and grandmother as well as a Torah scholar, prized good deeds as much as she prized Torah study. Thus she loved feeding the homeless and visiting the sick. She made it possible for me to experience the pure joy of Torah study, the Sabbath, the comforts of a faith-based community—and of family.

She was also a beautiful literary writer, the author of many articles, and coauthor or coeditor of four books: *Daughters of the King: Women and the Synagogue* (co-edited with Susan Grossman); *Women of the Wall: Claiming Sacred Ground at Judaism's Holy Site* (which I co-edited); *Shaarei Simcha: Gates of Joy* (co-edited with Adena K. Berkowitz); and *The Wed-Locked Agunot: Orthodox Jewish Women Chained to Dead Marriages* (written with Susan Aranoff).

Rivka died at home, surrounded by her loving family. I held her hand as she was dying—and, as we sang psalms and other religious melodies, Rivka kept apologizing to me. She said: "I'm sorry, I'm so sorry."

I did not understand what she meant until weeks later. Perhaps she understood that I would never, ever have a friend like her again and that I would miss her every single day.

I do.

In the past, I would always lose my place among the Aramaic words on the large Talmud page. Rivka would put her finger on the spot for me so that I could follow along. Now, uncannily, when I attend a Talmud class, I almost never lose my place. Perhaps Rivka is still helping me.

Kate Millett (1934–2017). Kate: You took your last breath on Earth in the city you loved most: Paris, the city that once welcomed the expatriates Gertrude, Alice, Pablo, Ernest, and Sir James of Dublin, and where the early morning aroma of fresh bread was reason enough for you to rise, too.

I finally understood you in historical context when I read Andrea Weiss's *Paris Was a Woman: Portraits from the Left Bank*. Then I recognized your culture, one in which sophisticated and talented lesbians took many lovers, competed with each other for sexual favors, slept with their lovers' lovers, and everyone either became lifelong friends or abandoned each other or the group entirely.

You were just another Irish rebel living in exile. Wherever you lived, you were in exile. When you were in Paris, you were not at home on the Bowery, and when you were in New York, you missed the farm. Just as you belonged to many cities, you also had many different selves. You were many different Kates.

You were Kate, the highly ceremonial hostess, offering your guests wine as if it were a libation to the gods; floating little candlelit paper boats out on the lake at the farm for the Japanese holiday of Obon every August. You were also Kate the raging Mad Queen; Kate the unbearably humble; Kate the increasingly all too silent.

You were the most cosmopolitan, the most continental, the most European identified of our feminist intellectuals (well, Andrea Dworkin was, too). You believed that ideas matter and that intellectuals must lay their bodies down for the sake of revolution.

You were always broad-minded (in both senses of the word); you would not have disapproved of my exposing you here, given how routinely you exposed yourself and everyone else in book after book, and you did so in such a fine, stream-of-consciousness prose, one that was underestimated by critics but never by me. I admired it; no, I adored it.

I was going to read you the passages about you—but then you went ahead and died. You'd been drifting for some time now, whether you were in another country, upstate at the farm, marooned in a hospital, or sitting right across the table from me; before you were really gone for good, you were no longer exactly "here."

For years now, when we would meet at the Bowery Bar, right across the street from your loft, you were already far too quiet. Sophie (Kier), Susan (Bender), sometimes Merle (Hoffman) had to join me in keeping the patter going. But you still had your wonderful laugh and your wise and twinkling eyes which signaled that you understood everything.

From time to time, you'd call and leave the most heartbreaking messages: "Hi, this is your old friend Kate Millett, remember me?" And I'd call you right back. Sometimes we were able to have a real, if only a brief, conversation, but only as long as I carried the weight for both of us. You no longer raged—at least, not at me, not on our precious phone calls, never again in person either.

On one of your visits, perhaps a few years ago, you told me you were working on a book about your relationship to de Beauvoir, to the woman and her work, perhaps a book that might encompass your relationship to the entire French Literary Enterprise.

I understood that you were no longer capable of undertaking a Big New Book, but I quietly volunteered to listen to you talk about this, tape your every word, and help you edit this if you wished. You said yes—but we never spoke about it again. Eventually, I heard that you were working on introducing something that you'd written long ago, perhaps your Tokyo diary, maybe something else altogether.

Although you attended marches, protests, press conferences, and sit-ins, you mainly read, wrote books, sculpted, painted, and tried to create a utopian community for lesbian artists.

You were also the Kate who could easily pass for a homeless person, out on the Bowery trying to sell your farm-grown Christmas trees in blustery winter weather. (Oh, how chapped your hands were, how red were your cheeks.)

You were Kate the sharecropper, who, like Gerald and Scarlett O'Hara, was adamant that owning land is everything and that land must be kept in the family at all costs. You drove a tractor, cut wood, stood on dangerously high ladders to get at a failing roof.

Do you remember the time I visited one weekend when I was on a hard-and-fast deadline and you demanded that I just put my shoulder to the wheel of your sheltered workshop and help you repair the roof (I sometimes viewed the farm in just this way, as your personal alternative to a loony bin). "C'mon, Chesler," you growled, "just get on the goddamn ladder and help me do this."

I was horrified. Terrified. Flabbergasted. But you would not let go of me until I at least planted a victory garden of flowers by your side.

But even as Kate the farmer, you still sometimes drank your morning coffee from a French ceramic bowl, always made little toasts at dinner, and were, at all times, surrounded by books and bookshelves.

Your *Sexual Politics* was perhaps the most influential or at least the most famous of the second wave feminist books—although we all stood on the shoulders of those brilliant articles and demonstrations that preceded us. That same year Shulie published her equally amazing *Dialectic of Sex*.

I loved *Flying*, in which you captured the energy of the early days of breakneck activism, as well as the unexpected cruelty of some feminists, but you also described fame as something of a human sacrifice. Ah, Katie: You were tireless, relentless, in trolling the dark side on behalf of women's freedom, and you did so doggedly, even during the dark days, the dog days, the days of despair.

In *The Basement: Meditations on a Human Sacrifice*, you more than equaled Truman Capote and Norman Mailer in your fact-based but fictionalized account of the physical and sexual torture-murder of sixteen-year-old Sylvia Likens in Indianapolis at the hands of a middle-aged woman named Gertrude Baniszewski, her teenage daughter and son, and some neighborhood children. They tortured Sylvia most horribly for weeks and then carved "I'm a prostitute and proud of it" into Sylvia's skin. The details are unbearable. How did *you* bear it? Did you?

I remember how shocked I was by your art installation on this subject. I did a double take when I realized that the Sylvia mannequin on the floor was dressed in your clothing and had a wig on that was styled exactly the way in which your hair was styled.

In *Going to Iran*, you truly grasped the misogynistic nature of an Islamic theocratic regime that would go on to murder its best and its brightest.

Do you remember our Christmas Eve parties and the presents we all exchanged? And the New Year's Eve parties, too? I often had to initiate the process; each time you went along with it and were always eventually very pleased—but always, always, a bit like Shulie, you also stood a bit apart, watching it all, too silent even among your cherished intimates. You were also Kate the straight, a married lady, who genuinely loved your husband, Fumio. Do you remember how you wept when he finally left? You called and, between tears, said that "he'd left you for another woman." I was amazed but I dared not laugh. Your grief was so raw. Finally, I asked you: "But Kate, really, how many women have you left Fumio for?" I could not reason with you, your sorrow and shame were genuine.

Katie: I want to thank you for your generosity, for always trying to include me, and for suggesting that others do so, too. You introduced me to extraordinary women. As you know, some of these women became very dear to me.

It was a privilege to be your friend. I will never forget you.

Acknowledgments

My family has blessed me with their love and support: my noble and steady partner of a quarter century, Susan L. Bender; my beloved son, Ariel David Chesler; my luscious granddaughters and their incredibly patient and resourceful mother; my dearest friends, Merle Hoffman, Joan Casamo, Linda Clarke, and Barbara Joans; and my adoptive families: Sheryl Haut, Tamara Haut-Weissman, and their spouses and children.

I acknowledge my mothers of enthusiasm: my agent, Jane Dystel, and my editor, Karen Wolny. This book was entirely their idea. I hope I have not failed their expectations.

I am grateful to my assistant, Emily Feldman, and my archivist, Evelyn Shunaman, for their superb support; my IT team, especially Matt Greenfield; and my team of health care experts and maintainers, especially Dr. Tina Dobsevage.

How alone I would have been without the early (1963–80) published work of Sidney Abbott, Diane Schulder Abrams, Margot Adler, the poet Alta, Bonnie Anderson, Louise Armstrong, Ti-Grace Atkinson, Nancy Azara, Yamila Azize Vargas, Bill Baird, Kathleen Barry, Pauline Bart, Toni Cade Bambara, Judith Bardwick, Rosalyn Baxandall, Frances Beale, Evelyn Tornton Beck, Ingrid Bengis, Jessie Bernard, Louise Bernikow, Basima Qattan Bezirgan, Carolyn Bird, Bonnie Charles Bluh, the Boston Women's Health Collective (*Our Bodies, Ourselves*), E.M. Broner, Rita Mae Brown, Susan Brownmiller,

Z Budapest, Charlotte Bunch, Barbara Burris, Sandy Butler, Paula Caplan, Barbara Chase-Riboud, Judy Chicago, Shirley Chisholm, Nancy Chodorow, Lucinda Cisler, Joanna Clark, the Combahee River Collective, Noreen Connell, Gena Corea, Nancy Cott, Mary Daly, Karen DeCrow, Carl N. Degler, Anselma Dell'Olio, Barbara Deming, Dana Densmore, Toi Derricotte, Dorothy Dinnerstein, Claudia Dreifus, Ellen Carol DuBois, Roxanne Dunbar-Ortiz, Andrea Dworkin, Barbara Ehrenreich, Zillah R. Eisenstein, Mary Ellman, Deidre English, Lin Farley, Melissa Farley, Elizabeth Warnock Fernea, Shulamith Firestone, Elizabeth Fisher, Eleanor Flexner, Ellen Frankfort, Jo Freeman, Marilyn French, Nancy Friday, Betty Friedan, Leah Fritz, Sally Gearhart, Nikki Giovanni, Sherna Gluck, Emily Jane Goodman, Linda Gordon, Vivian Gornick, Joan Goulianos, Judy Grahn, Germaine Greer, Susan Griffin, Kirsten Grimstad, Beverly Guy-Sheftall, Carol Hanisch, Joy Harjo, Bertha Harris, Michelle Harrison, Carolyn G. Heilbrun, Nancy Henley, Diana Mara Henry, Judith Lewis Herman, Shere Hite, Judith Hole, Mary Howell (who wrote as both Anna Demeter and Margaret A. Campbell), Donna Hughes, Elizabeth Janeway, Barbara Joans, Sonia Johnson, Jill Johnston, Gail Jones, Erica Jong, June Jordan, Lila Karp, Naomi Katz, Jurate Kazickas, Pamela Kearon, Flo Kennedy, Maxine Hong Kingston, Anne Koedt, Larry Lader, Myrna Lamb, Bettye Lane, Gerda Lerner, Ellen Levine, Audre Lorde, Barbara Love, Eleanor Maccoby, Midge Mackenzie, Catharine MacKinnon, Pat Mainardi, Gene Marine, Del Martin, Kathy McAfee, Andrea Medea, Barbara Mehrhof, Fatima Mernissi, Eve Merriam, Nancy Milford, Casey Miller, Jean Baker Miller, Kate Millett, Nancy Milton, Juliet Mitchell, Ellen Moers, Cherríe Moraga, Elaine Morgan, Robin Morgan, Toni Morrison, Pauli Murray, Joan Nestle, New York Radical Women, No More Fun and Games, Ann Oakley, Tillie Olsen, William L. O'Neill, Elaine Pagels, Pat Parker, Marge Piercy, Joseph Pleck, Letty Cottin Pogrebin, Arlene Raven, Janice Raymond, Bernice Johnson Reagon, Redstockings, Evelyn

Reed, Rosetta Reitz, Susan Rennie, Adrienne Rich, Ruby Rohrlich-Leavitt, Phyllis Rose, Lily Rivlin, Ruth Rosen, Frances D. Ross, Alice Rossi, Joan L. Roth, Barbara Katz Rothman, Alma Routsong (who wrote as Isabel Miller), Sheila Rowbotham, Lillian Breslow Rubin, Rosemary Radford Ruether, Florence Rush, Joanna Russ, Diana Russell, Kathie Sarachild, Barbara Seaman, Robert Seidenberg, Martha Shelley, Lynn Sherr, Ann Allen Shockley, Alix Kates Shulman, Barbara Smith, Ann Snitow Jon Snodgrass, Valeria Solanas, Dale Spender, Una Stannard, Gloria Steinem, Dorothy Sterling, Merlin Stone, Kate Swift, Judy Syfers, Sandra Tangri, Meredith Tax, Kathleen Thompson, Sharon Thompson, Alice Walker, Barbara Walker, Lenore Walker, Michelle Wallace, Paula Weideger, Naomi Weisstein, Ellen Willis, Cassandra Wilson, Monique Wittig, Myrna Wood, Laura X, Judith Zinsser.

I'm listing feminists who opposed each other on many of the burning issues of the day. I refuse to write any one of them out of feminist history.

Some women of color published feminist works between 1963 and 1980. Their names are included above: Yamila Azize-Vargas, Toni Cade Bambara, Frances Beale, Gwendolyn Brooks, Barbara Burris, Shirley Chisholm, Joanna Clark, the Combahee River Collective, Roxanne Dunbar-Ortiz, Joy Harjo, Gayl Jones, June Jordan, Flo Kennedy, Maxine Hong Kingston, Audre Lorde, Toni Morrison, Frances D. Ross, Ann Allen Shockley, Dorothy Sterling, Michelle Wallace.

African American, Hispanic American, Asian American, and Native American feminist works mainly appeared only after 1980. For example: Paula Gunn Allen (1983), Gloria Anzaldúa (1981), Patricia Bell-Scott (1982), Beth Brant (1984), Cheryl Clarke (1986), Michelle Cliff (1984), Patricia Hill Collins (1990), Lillian Comas-Diaz (1994), Olivia Espin (1999), Paula Giddings (1984), Beverly Greene (1986), Evelyn Brooks Higginbotham (1993), bell hooks (1981), Gloria T. Hull (1982), Jacqueline Jones (1985), Gloria I. Joseph (1981), Cherrie

Moraga (1981), Barbara Omolade (1986), Nell Irvin Painter (1996), Gayle Pemberton (1992), Barbara M. Posadas (1993), Vicki L. Ruiz (1987), Barbara Smith (1982), Judy Yung (1999).